Jeremy Black is one of the UK's most respected and prolific historians. He is Emeritus Professor of History at the University of Exeter and a renowned expert on the history of war. He is a Senior Fellow at the Foreign Policy Research Institute. His recent books include *Military Strategy: A Global History*, *A History of the Second World War in 100 Maps*, *Tank Warfare* and *The World of James Bond*. He appears regularly on TV and radio.

Other titles in this series

A Brief History of 1917
Roy Bainton

A Brief History of Portugal
Jeremy Black

A Brief History of the Caribbean
Jeremy Black

A Brief History of the Mediterranean
Jeremy Black

A Brief History of Britain 1851–2021
Jeremy Black

A Brief History of France
Cecil Jenkins

A Brief History of Germany
Jeremy Black

A Brief History of Italy
Jeremy Black

A Brief History of Spain
Jeremy Black

A Brief History of Medieval Warfare
Peter Reid

A Brief History of the Normans
Francois Neveux

A Brief History of Slavery
Jeremy Black

A BRIEF HISTORY OF

America

JEREMY BLACK

ROBINSON

First published in Great Britain in 2024 by Robinson

1 3 5 7 9 10 8 6 4 2

A CIP catalogue record for this book
is available from the British Library.

ISBN: 978-1-47214-738-7

Typeset in Scala by Hewer Text UK Ltd, Edinburgh
Printed and bound in Great Britain by Clays Ltd, Elcograf S.p.A.

Papers used by Robinson are from well-managed
forests and other responsible sources.

Robinson
An imprint of
Little, Brown Book Group
Carmelite House
50 Victoria Embankment
London EC4Y 0DZ

An Hachette UK Company
www.hachette.co.uk

www.littlebrown.co.uk

For Andrew O'Shaughnessy

Contents

Preface

Variously described as history wars or culture wars, the contentions of the present engross American history – that of, for the purposes of this book, the area encompassed within the modern boundaries of the United States of America – from statues to statutes. Famously 'fools rush in' and it is necessary for me to explain what I am trying to do. First, there is no book that can be definitive and all of us are contributing to a debate. That is the spirit of this book. I hope you will find it of interest, and it will be great if you disagree as I will have engaged your consideration. Second, America exemplifies many of my interests in history, notably the role of geography and place, the contingencies of circumstances, and the problems with notions of a *zeitgeist* (spirit of the age).

The challenge of writing a history of America – the greater part of a continent pretending to be a country – is increased if you have few allotted words but even more so by established assumptions about what you should cover and with what emphasis. That represents both challenge and opportunity for a foreigner who may 'get it wrong', albeit with a fresh set of outside eyes, but who, nevertheless, offers that comparative perspective. Indeed, many American problems are, and have always been, larger world problems, whether we are considering natural or human elements. There is also the need for a chronological perspective. Americans in the early 2020s talked much about the nation having never been so badly divided. They tended to forget that America itself is a product of acute political divisions, and that the Democratic and Republican parties came out of a sectional rift in which Americans ended up killing each other in numbers unmatched since.

Readers will notice, in particular, a stress on the history of Native Americans, on America's role in the world, and on the interaction of environment and human action. Successive presidential administrations are less important than underlying issues and long-term developments.

'America' is a problematic term, at once geographic and political. Here it is intended to serve as a description of the land now part of the United States of America. But as such, its history includes, and notably so in Hawai'i and Alaska, many strands that were for long different from that of the major developmental narrative of United States history. As pursued in this book, notably chapter four, it is instructive to survey what became the United States from west to east and south to north, rather than the traditional focus on the eastern seaboard and particularly the Northeast. I thereby break out of the constraints caused by a focus on the birth and extension of the American polity, which can lead to an exclusive focus on the Thirteen (British) Colonies and generate what in the West is called East Coast Bias. Instead, I weave together the many geographic strands that make up the modern United States without falling into the pitfall of determinism. Indeed, moments of counterfactualism (what if?) help explain the importance of how what actually happened really shaped the United States. Rejecting the standard narratives of Whig or Whiggish history highlights the complexity of the American experience. Rather than presenting a simplistic story of how we got to the Thirteen Colonies that became the United States, it is necessary to embrace a more complex history.

Americans and their History

'The name of American, which belongs to you in your national capacity, must always exalt the just pride of patriotism more than any appellation derived from local discriminations. With slight shades of difference, you have the same religion,

> manners, habits and political principles. You have, in a common cause, fought and triumphed together; the independence and liberty you possess are the work of joint councils and joint efforts, of common dangers, sufferings, and successes.'
>
> The Farewell Address, George Washington, 1796

This book is part of a long tradition of British visitors to America seeking to understand its culture and history, and frequently coming to answers that surprise some Americans. It has a personal, contemporary and historical context. I went to America as a child, to visit my three aunts, all of whom married Americans. Aside from many holidays there, as well as visiting professorships in Alabama, New York and Texas, and research trips, I have had the wonderful activity of repeated lecturing and conferences in 36 states from 1988 on. I would like to thank those who invited me and offered me hospitality. Their friendliness had much more of an impact than they possibly realised, and it is greatly appreciated to this day.

I would like to thank Brooke Allen, Juliane Bailey, Troy Bickham, John Broom, Pete Brown, Denver Brunsman, Duncan Campbell, Alice-Catherine Carls, Guy Chet, Andrew English, Mark Fissel, Bill Gibson, Michael Grow, Will Hay, Peter Hoffenberg, Caleb Karges, James McConnell, Peter Onuf, George Robb and Neil York for commenting on earlier drafts. They are responsible neither for the opinions nor for any factual errors in what follows but have continually provided help, stimulus and encouragement. I appreciate the effort involved. Emma Smith has proved a most helpful commissioning editor and Amanda Keats yet again a very impressive production editor. It is a great pleasure to dedicate this book to Andrew O'Shaughnessy, a good friend and fellow student of American history, who taught with me many fun vacation schools for the University of Virginia in Charlottesville, Oxford and Williamsburg.

1

The Vast Span of History

Most of the human history of what became the United States of America occurred well before the arrival of Europeans and Africans. Even when the latter groups arrived, to be followed by what were later termed Asians (as well as new groups of 'Hispanics' emigrating from parts of Latin America that were never in the United States), their direct presence in America was limited for most of the 'contact' period that began with European settlement. Indeed, many states of the modern union did not have any permanent settlement by European and African Americans until the nineteenth century. Moreover, this was the period in which the current territorial boundaries of the United States were established with the Gadsden Purchase in 1854 that created the final border of the contiguous United States; although there were subsequent transitions to full statehood.

The early settlement of what eventually became the United States, a term that meant nothing at the time and matched few natural borders of note (for rivers joined not divided) other than the oceans, has involved contention. Nevertheless, it is generally agreed that the initial settlement was over the Beringia land bridge from Siberia to Alaska encompassing what is now the Bering Strait, a settlement that it was once suggested occurred from about 23000 BCE. However, in 2022, discussion of the Hartley mammoth locality, a site on the Colorado Plateau in northern New Mexico, focused on evidence that mammoths were probably butchered 37,000 years ago. The remains of a mother mammoth and her calf that had been killed by humans were found, with the bones then shaped into disposable blades to break down the carcasses, and the animals' fat rendered over a domestic fire that was a sustained and controlled burn, and not a lightning strike or wildfire. Alongside DNA work, this leads to the suggestion of two separate human dispersals from East Asia, one much earlier than that which had hitherto focused attention. This then raises questions about the nature of the relationship between this Native American arrival and the later one. In terms of this later one, there are also human footprints from New Mexico dating from 22860 BCE to 21130 BCE before the present.

Sea levels fluctuated during the Ice Ages, and the end of the last one, about 9000 BCE, led to the breaching of the land bridge. The last Ice Age had seen the southern expansion of the ice sheets into the modern US, and much of the current physical geography in its northern parts was affected by the ice, including the scouring out of lakes and valleys by glaciers. At the same time, the soil was moved south by the ice, denuding areas such as the Upper Midwest, but making the land at and beyond the edge of the ice sheet more fertile. This land was also greatly affected by the lakes and valleys created by ice melt. In comparison with this scale and power of change, the human impact was for long much less, but it was to become important, at least at the surface level, as a result of deforestation.

Although helping to wipe out large animals, notably mammoths in about 9500 BCE, humans were of only limited importance to the environmental changes of the Ice Ages. Instead, they responded to them, benefiting in particular from the creation of a corridor southwards through the ice sheet from 10,000 years ago as the ice melted; although there were earlier settlements to the south of the ice sheet, notably the Meadowcroft rock shelter in Pennsylvania from about 15000 BCE. Settlement beyond the reach of the ice, for example in the Boston area in about 10000 BCE, focused on the forest, open woodland and grasslands, and, in particular, on freshwater sites. These attracted animals, providing opportunities for hunting. That remained a key basis for economic activity, settlement patterns and social values into the nineteenth century.

The use of large stone spear-points, known as Clovis points, able to pierce the hides of mammoths, and dissimilar from those in the New Mexico site, ensured that, from about 16000 BCE, there was effective hunting of mammoths and, by about 9000 BCE, they had been largely wiped out. This was part of a fundamental shift, one shared with other parts of the world. Indeed, 'exceptionalism', American or otherwise, is of only limited value as a concept when considering most of human history. Other animals continued to be present in America, especially bison, antelope and deer, and they provided a protein-rich diet. Hunter-gatherer sites survive from the following millennia, including Casper and Folsom in the Great Plains, Sloan in the Mississippi Valley, Flint Run and Bull Brook on the Atlantic, and Danger Cave in the Rockies. Many of these sites saw settlements over a considerable period, as with Koster in the valley of the Illinois River, which had episodes of occupation from 7500 BCE to CE 1000.

However, in America, as elsewhere, there was a perceived need to respond to rising human population, as well as to the inroads of hunting on the numbers of big game, and climate change. These encouraged a focus on the hunting of small game as well, including beaver, grouse, hare, porcupine, quail and turkey. Animal migrations required organisation by hunters. Thus, in the Boston area, fish-weirs were constructed in Back Bay about 5,300 years ago in order to capture migrating fish. This was an aspect of the use of marine resources that included clams and other shellfish on tidal flats. In addition, there was an emphasis on food from wild seeds, plant foods, and the domestication of the last. Grindstones were used from about 8000 BCE to process food, a development that required production and learning techniques, as also with sieves and winnowing trays.

Farming encouraged a greater fixity in settlements, with wooden houses, as well as techniques, such as tree-clearing, irrigation and drainage, that represented an investment in particular sites. In turn, there were innovations reflecting such a commitment, for example cemeteries, with the first known one being the Sloan burial site to the west of the River Mississippi in modern Arkansas.

In part due to continued reliance on hunting and on wild food resources, and notably so outside the Mississippi Valley, North America was relatively late, notably compared with Middle Eastern and African settlements, in the development of agriculture. However, by about 4500 BCE, there was the cultivation of maize, sumpweed and the tepary bean in the Mississippi Valley, from which it spread north into the Missouri Valley and also east of the Appalachians, while, separately, cultivation spread north from Mexico into the West. In turn, sunflowers and gourds became prominent from about 1800 BCE.

Cultivation produced the resources for larger, permanent settlements, and for the specialisation of function. Craftspeople in America were first seen with pottery in the Southeast, the earliest evidence of which dates to about 2500 BCE, which was considerably later than in Asia, North Africa, and Europe. So also with much 'technology' including the wheel and metallurgy, as well as with settlement development in the shape of cities, and social processes such as writing. Although lateness is only relative, it was a product of the lower population numbers and density of North America.

Nevertheless, agricultural villages were prominent in the Mississippi and related valleys by about 1500 BCE with mounds and earthworks suggesting ceremonial and religious aspects of village life. There was also long-distance trade in these settlements, including with Central America. Rivers were the key trading routes, and wooden canoes were used in a situation that continued into the nineteenth century.

Discussion is made more difficult by the need to rely on archaeology without there being supplementary written sources.

Whereas, by the close of our period in 1500 CE, there were empires in Central and South America, there were none in North America where population densities were low, often very low, and both settlement and authority were dispersed. There was 'public' warfare, in the form of conflict between tribes, but also 'private' warfare: raids with no particular sanction, often designed to prove manhood.

The identification of some settlement groups as 'cultures' is a reflection in part of the location and success of archaeological work, and also of a degree of subjectivity, not least as it can lead to an underplaying of the differences between Native American groups. These differences were not necessarily lessened by the authority provided by a tribal coherence. Indeed, part of this lack of consistency was posed by the extent to which 'tribalism' varied, much being subsequently created and read back by European Americans. This was a process also seen in Europe as with the Roman creation of tribal identities. In America, the lack of records is a serious issue, not least for reading back linguistic identities and relationships. In particular, there can be idealisations of prehistory by Native American groups who also attempt to claim prehistoric groups as their own, often with tenuous historical claims which, in addition, frequently do not take into account how much movement and mixing were involved.

Nevertheless, cultures are readily distinguished from about 1000 BCE, with the Adena in the middle Ohio River often the first to attract attention. As is often the case, burial sites, as in Adena, Ohio itself, left particular evidence, in this case burial chambers underneath earth mounds. Grave goods included polished stone tools, tobacco pipes, beads and bracelets. There were also signs of an ability to organise for activities other than hunting, as with the major earthworks of this culture, for example the Great Serpent Mound.

Over the following half-millennium, this culture was matched by others further south, indeed across the southeast of modern

America. Earthwork ceremonial centres and rich grave goods were found in the Mississippi Valley and further east, for example in Marksville and Mandeville.

The process by which cultures interacted and succeeded each other is unclear. The mound-building villages of Louisiana developed into what is termed the Tchefuncte culture and then the Coles Creek culture in the lower Mississippi, and there was the Depford culture in Florida, while the Adena culture further north was succeeded by the Hopewell culture by 200 CE. The presence of sufficient humans and of settled sites was clearly important, as was the nature of woodlands that were reasonably temperate and also not sufficiently dense to make movement or cultivation difficult. The Hopewell culture appears to have operated in part through trade, and the related exchanges provided opportunities for a spread in influence. Turtles, fish and shells were obtained from the Gulf Coast.

In the Southeast, the Hopewell culture appears to have declined from about 400 CE, but there was subsequent development encouraged by the use of bows and arrows in hunting as well as the arrival from Mexico of more effective, and thus productive, crops, particularly beans and new types of maize. The Mississippian cultures began accordingly in about 800, with large settlements, particularly Cahokia in the eleventh century and Moundville in the thirteenth. The peak population of Cahokia has been estimated at between 6,000 and 40,000. There were numerous sites including in the lower valleys of the Red, Arkansas and Missouri rivers. Coastal settlements included Fort Walton, Weeden Island, Safety Harbor, Madira Bickel Mound, Englewood and Key Marco in what became Florida. There have been controversies over the dating of sites and cultures, and concerning the classification of peoples, for example the relationship between Weeden Island and Mississippian cultures. A key element was adaptation to the subsistence possibilities of particular sites, in the shape of the relationship between fishing, hunter-gathering and agriculture. Ceremonials also varied. The Weeden Island culture is dated to 200–1200 CE and came to be characterised by chiefdoms. Used for ritual and/or adornment, and thus also as a form of currency, stingray spines and seashells were traded from the coast. The Mississippi cultures continued to be significant until the mid-fifteenth century when there was a major fall in population. Cahokia appears to have been hit by environmental change, including deforestation, floods and polluted waterways, with difficulties as a result in producing sufficient food.

The effort devoted to fortification indicates the extent of concern about conflict as well as organisation. The fortifications built in about 1100 CE at Cahokia contained what have been presented as projecting bastions, which gave opportunities for archers to provide flanking fire on attackers. So also with the Crow Creek site on a steep bluff near the Missouri River which was protected by a bastioned wooden palisade fronted by a ditch. In the Mississippi culture, Etowah, a 54-acre site occupied from about the 1100s to the 1600s, had a large encircling ditch protecting the town, inside which was a wooden palisade that contained rectangular bastions or towers located at regular intervals. So also with defensive structures at Ocmulgee, a settlement that thrived between 900 and 1150. The journals of Hernando de Soto in 1539–42 mentioned a number of such sites. Such fortified positions were frequently to pose problems for European forces, while Spanish expeditions to Florida in 1513 and 1528 were repelled by capable local archers.

Meanwhile, there was a separate pattern of development in the interior Southwest, with irrigation the basis for settlements in the sheltered canyons, for example along the Santa Fé River, where earlier evidence of occupation is followed by that of compact communities. The Hohokan and Mogollon cultures emerged in about 250–300 CE and were followed by the Fremont (*c.*400), Patayan (*c.*500), and Anasazi (*c.*700). These cultures lasted in most cases to 1300–1500 with drier conditions, possibly exacerbated through over-irrigation, then making cultivation more difficult and probably leading to the abandonment of most Anasazi pueblos in about 1350. Pueblos built for defensive purposes have survived from about 1050, notably at Mesa Verde and Chaco Canyon, suggesting more competition. Drought in the early fifteenth century may have been responsible for the end of settlements such as Arroyo Hondo (1300–1430). More positively, the Mogollon culture left pottery from about 800. In the Great Plains, which is not a region conforming to modern territorial boundaries, Alberta, Saskatchewan, the Dakotas, Montana and Wyoming from about 300 CE to about 1800 CE had the 'hoofprint tradition' ancient carving style.

In the Northwest, cultures have been distinguished in terms of environmental adaptation, notably with the Northwest Coast Culture Area, the Plateau Culture Area, and the Great Basin Culture Area. For example, there was a village site of the Ohlone people from about 2000 BCE at the southern entrance to San Francisco Bay. Tribes combined the benefits of the Pacific – especially shellfish, such as mussels and sea urchins, and fishing – with hunting. Maritime life was helped by the warm-water Japanese Current, and grey, humpback and killer whales were frequent visitors, as well as seal, salmon, sealion, and sea otters. While supernatural animals served as tribal ancestors, dugout canoes were used in the hunting of marine life. Meanwhile, the creative skills of the tribes included totem poles, armour and the masks for tribal dances, but the tribes had scant unity.

Farther north, on the sub-Arctic coast, there were indigenous people who took to the water, particularly the South Alaskan Inuit, who established themselves on Kodiak Island, and the Aleuts whose sites included Chaluka. These people were active fishermen, and also fed off shellfish and pursued sea mammals such as sea otter which were killed with harpoons and throwing sticks. Blood feuds and internecine tribal warfare were common.

Frequently treated as separate to the history of America, there was relevant settlement elsewhere, with the movement of Polynesians reaching the Hawai'ian Islands from the Marquesa Islands to the south in about 400 CE. This was more impressive than any movements in the Atlantic in this period. The Polynesians used double-hulled canoes for their journeys. The radiocarbon dating of the pollen layers of sediment cores in O'ahu in the Hawai'ian group reveals the early presence of the *loulu*, a tall palm with edible nuts, only for this indigenous palm (as well as other indigenous trees) to decline, possibly because of human deforestation, the transformation of forests into taro farms, and the eating of the palm nuts by the Polynesian rats that accompanied the settlers. These settlers were presumably responsible for the marked decline of creatures whose habitats were in the forests that were cleared, notably indigenous snails and flightless geese and ducks, which would also have provided a source of food.

There was no comparable link from East Asia to North America. Whatever knowledge of the latter existed in East Asia, it was not exploited. Nor, despite what is claimed by enthusiasts, notably Mormons, were there transatlantic migrations by Mediterranean peoples.

North America had perhaps six and a fifth million people by 1400, but that would only have been about 2 per cent of the world's population, compared to 14 per cent in Europe, 10 per cent in Africa, 6 per cent in South America and 6 per cent in Central America and the Caribbean. The percentage in North America was higher than would otherwise have been the case due to the savage inroads of the bubonic plague (Black Death) in Eurasia the previous century; there were not only small numbers but also nothing to compare with the developed states in Central (including Mexico) and South America. Moreover, many technologies had not developed in North America, including wheeled vehicles, the use of barrel and groyne vaulting, windmills and watermills, writing, and oceanic transport (other than in Hawai'i).

Nor were there any draught animals in use, unlike the llama in South America, let alone the buffalo, oxen, horse, mule, camel or elephant elsewhere. If North America was exceptional, in the sense of different, then this was most clearly the case in 1450.

It would be commonplace to end this chapter at the point of the arrival from Spain of Christopher Columbus in the Bahamas in 1492, and then to focus on its consequences for the New World, notably on Native American society in response to European pressure. This would have included the expedition across the Southeast of Hernando de Soto in 1539–42, and then the arrival of English, Dutch and French settlers. That approach, however, seriously misrepresents the history of what becomes America. Early European settlement was limited, as will be discussed in the next chapter. Moreover, the rapid diffusion of European 'civilisation' in the shape of firearms and horses gave greater vitality to that of Native Americans. So also did a capacity for independent action that was not determined by this diffusion or by European competition, however much they may have served to influence or enable or heighten other elements. There was no prospect of American maritime pressure on Europe, Africa or the Caribbean. Yet, the ability of the Europeans to prevail in America, even coastal America, was unclear.

2
The Sixteenth Century

Far from a rapid impact, as with the Caribbean from 1492, it is the slow burn of the initial European contact with what became the United States that is most apparent. The first with North America was perfunctory and did not even extend to what became the United States. Icelandic sagas indicate that there were four Norse/Viking expeditions to North America, two of which carried settlers. A settlement was established at L'Anse aux Meadows in northern Newfoundland in 1003, and the Norsemen sailed south to what they called Vinland as a result of the vines growing there. Vines currently grow in Nova Scotia. There were later to be claims of voyages farther south, including to Newport, Rhode Island, but, although entrenched in local lore, they are implausible.

However, affected by disease, climate change, the hostility of the local Inuit population, and remoteness, the settlements in North America and Greenland were abandoned in the early eleventh century and around 1500 respectively. Moreover, the greater cold of the medieval 'Little Ice Age' made the North Atlantic more difficult to sail. In the sixteenth and seventeenth centuries, Denmark (the kingdom that ruled Norway and Iceland) was a major naval power, but it pursued interests in Germany, West Africa, India and the West Indies, not in North America.

Spain sustained and expanded a presence in the West Indies that began in 1492 with Columbus, and extended it to the American mainland, but far less to North than to Central or South America. There was expansion north from Mexico, with expeditions by Francisco Vásquez de Coronado and Juan de Oñate in 1540 and 1595 respectively, into both New Mexico and the Great Plains, and Santa Fé was established in 1609. Nevertheless, this activity, which was on the peripheries of the more settled areas of their empire, was not developed, in part because of a lack of opportunities to seize bullion, combined with the strength of Native American opposition. Similarly, there was no follow-up to the expedition from the Spanish base of Cuba of Hernando do Soto who, between 1539 and 1542, brutally pillaged the Lower Mississippi and nearby lands. After his death, his successor pressed on in 1542–3 into eastern Texas. The diseases brought by this expedition proved devastating for the local people, which was to be a pattern for the fate of Native Americans who were hit hard by smallpox, typhus and syphilis.

On the Pacific coast, Francis Drake, an English rival of the Spaniards, landed on what is now northern California, which he claimed as New Albion: Drake's Bay is south of Cape Mendocino. Like his Spanish contemporaries, Drake apparently never saw the entrance to San Francisco Bay and sailed past it. Drake repaired his ship and sailed on with no consequences for permanent settlement. So also, in 1592, when Juan de la Fuca found what he thought to be a strait into the interior, which in reality was Puget Sound. In 1595, a Spanish Manila galleon was wrecked in Drake's Bay, again without consequence.

In contrast, readily accessible Florida was in effect part of the Caribbean. After unsuccessful expeditions by Juan Ponce de Léon, in 1513 and 1521, Spain established bases there in the 1560s, in part in competition with French Protestants who were killed in 1565, and also with the native Timucua who proved a more difficult foe. Despite a major Spanish effort at Christian proselytisation among the Native American population from a number of bases, especially St Augustine, Florida was very much a marginal colony. As such, Florida was not an effective base for power projection farther north, nor a source of profit or lobbying that provided an encouragement for such action.

There was still some Spanish activity farther north, including the short-lived base of San Miguel de Guadalupe in Georgia in

1526, plus a base from 1566 until 1587 at Santa Elena on Parris Island in South Carolina (earlier briefly French-held). From there, Spaniards travelled overland to western North Carolina in 1566–7. The Ajacán Mission of Jesuits in Virginia was established in 1570, but they were massacred by Native Americans in 1571. In 1572 and 1573, Spanish explorers visited the Chesapeake. No more colonisation was pursued by the Spaniards in Virginia, but in Georgia's coastland there were Franciscan missions from the 1580s to 1706.

Spanish colonisation practices did not fit well with the future United States and the realities there. The heart of the Spanish empire rested on the areas where there had been the most highly advanced and organised civilisations in the Americas: Mexico and Peru. Though inhabited later than North America, these areas had much more developed and specialised economies with sophisticated divisions of labour and large urban settlements, internal trade networks in market economies, and some external trade. The ready infusion of European pack animals and technical knowledge helped drive these Late Stone Age civilisations into the late Iron Age and beyond. As with the Hellenistic empires that followed the conquests of Alexander the Great, the people stayed the same, the rulers changed, and over time the values of the conquerors disseminated down to the locals. Native Americans were not replaced by Spaniards but interacted with them.

In contrast, in Florida, where the Native Americans mostly subsisted through hunting and gathering, the Spaniards largely stuck to the coast. St Augustine and other bases acted more as garrisons and lookouts to protect Spanish claims than as proper colonies. Very differently, New Mexico, with its already developed agricultural tradition, made for a more 'ready-made' colony than Florida. In the latter, the Spaniards did not know how to live as hunter-gatherers, and also suffered from a lack of local knowledge. They saw the area round St Augustine as practically a desert, with little food, but the Matanzas inlet is teeming with seafood.

In 1585, the English landed 108 colonists on Roanoke Island, North Carolina. This was far enough from Florida not to prove too easy a target for Spain. However, the colonists found it difficult to feed themselves, had tense relations with the Native American population, and were taken off the following year. Another attempt was made in 1587, but, when a relief ship arrived in 1590, it found the village deserted, the only hint the word 'Croatoan' carved on the wooden palisades. Disease, starvation or Native Americans may have wiped out the colony, the last possibly involving assimilation. The latter can be downplayed in the historical record, but many modern White Americans claim some sliver of Native American ancestry.

Defeated by the Spaniards in Florida, the French had already explored farther north. In the service of France, Giovanni de Verrazzano sailed North Carolina's Outer Banks, entered New York Bay, sailed along Long Island, and entered both Narragansett and Cape Cod Bay in 1524, but his following voyages were to Brazil and the Caribbean. Calling the new lands in North America Francesca, a reference to Francis I, did not meet the king's hope to find a sea route to the Pacific between Florida and Newfoundland and thus help France compete globally with its bitter rival Spain: America was an obstacle not an advantage, and the French did not persist.

More lastingly, England named Virginia in honour of the unmarried Elizabeth I. Moreover, the positive impression created by Thomas Hariot's *A Brief and True Report of the New Found Land of Virginia* (1588) and other reports encouraged fresh attempts to establish a colony after the failure at Roanoke.

However, the sixteenth century was one of only a very limited European presence in what was to become the United States, and this contrast emerged more clearly with reference to Central and South America. The demographic impact of the Europeans in the future United States was greater than it would otherwise have been as a result of the disease brought by Europeans, but settlement was limited, both in the case of Europeans and with reference to the African slaves they brought with them. Instead, the history of the century was still very much that of Native Americans. In 1568, Native Americans destroyed the Spanish forts established in the interior of North Carolina in 1566–7. As the Guale uprising against the Spaniards in 1587 showed, they were able to put pressure on the Europeans. Indeed, in response to that uprising, the Spaniards abandoned Santa Elena on Parris Island, South Carolina, moving the settlers to St Augustine. Santa Elena had already been burned in 1576 and attacked in 1580.

While early exploration was not as tentative as the Portuguese (and later Dutch) contacts with Australia, America was scarcely in the European ambit. However, in the so-called Columbian Exchange, the Europeans did bring Christianity, influenza, measles, smallpox, whooping cough, syphilis, and diphtheria, as well as horses, pigs, cattle, wheat, apples and citrus fruits, although many of these plants and animals did not arrive until the seventeenth century. They took back far less from North America than they did from Central or South America, in part due to the limited agriculture in North America. Most were from what became Latin America, including potatoes, tomatoes, cacao, maize, chillies and tobacco. They were of much greater value to European society initially than the colonies in the Americas.

3
The Seventeenth Century

The headlines for this century focus on English colonisation, not least because that was to be the genesis of an independent America, while the different strands of this colonisation helped explain subsequent strands in American history. We will indeed turn to that history, but it is necessary first to note that even in 1699, still more 1649 or 1619, that history seemed distinctly unlikely. In each case, the European presence appeared as much set by Spain as by England. This was so at least where Florida and New Mexico were concerned, in part because Spain's role rested on the nearby colonies of Cuba and Mexico; despite the links between Barbados and Carolina, there was no comparable assistance for the English colonies. Even at the advent of the United States in 1776, the population of Mexico City was several times that of any town in the British North American colonies.

By 1699, although the independent Dutch and Swedish presence on the east coast had been subsumed by the English, that of the Spaniards was being challenged not by England but by a French expansion from Canada, via the Mississippi Valley, to what was named Louisiana after Louis XIV. This led the Spaniards to found Pensacola in 1696. Earlier, they had no real incentive to establish posts along the northern shore. René-Robert Cavelier, Sieur de la Salle, who had founded a series of trading posts on the Illinois River, having canoed down the Mississippi to its mouth, raised the arms of France on 9 April 1682 and claimed the river basin for Louis XIV. The king criticised these discoveries as worthless; but his opinion on the latter was changed by clerics eager to extend Christianity, and because Louis, who also presented himself as a champion of the

Church, came to see an opportunity to challenge the Spanish position in the Caribbean.

La Salle, accordingly, was sent in 1684 to the Gulf of Mexico with four ships and three hundred settlers to establish a colony at the mouth of the Mississippi, but, attacked by pirates and missing the Mississippi delta, landed 400 miles to the desolate west at Matagorda Bay, where he founded Fort St Louis. This presence, however, fell foul of disease, the barrenness of the coast, recriminations, the mutiny that cost him his life in 1687, and, lastly, the hostility of the Karankawa who wiped out the surviving colonists at the close of 1688.

Nevertheless, La Salle's initiative bore fruit with the foundation of a colony named Louisiana in honour of the king. In 1698, Jérome, Count of Pontchartrain, the active Minister of the Marine, a key expansionist who supported the development of Saint-Domingue, organised the expedition to found the colony, and Fort Maurepas in Biloxi Bay was built in 1699. In his *Description de la Louisiane* (Paris, 1688), part of a longstanding tradition of Caribbean boosterism, Louis Hennepin, a missionary who had accompanied La Salle, had described Louisiana as the future breadbasket for the French empire, a fertile area able to produce wine and foodstuffs for the French West Indies; but reality in the swamped Gulf Coast proved otherwise. This exaggerated expectation was an issue for all the French islands, but particularly for Louisiana which, in practice, was initially an island-style colony in the midst of difficulty.

Discussion of the Europeans encompasses Native American opponents from New England to New Mexico, where there was a major revolt in 1680 that was only ended in 1696. This revolt owed much to the attempt to suppress native religion. Indeed, much of the history of the Native Americans was increasingly affected, even set, by this presence and rivalry. This was notably so with the diffusion of horses and guns. These were key aspects of the changing Native American experience, although neither horses nor guns spread across the entire area. This situation underlined anew the variety of that experience.

Native Americans started to compete over European goods as they became strategic resources, as in northern Nevada where the Paiute soundly defeated the Washoe and imposed a peace denying them the use of horses, limiting Washoe mobility and thus giving the Paiute a distinct military advantage that ensured that the Washoe could not become a threat.

At the same time that there were long-distance trade links, a process facilitated by the length of the river network but not restricted to it, there were also the drags caused by distance, terrain, seasonality and enmity. The latter factors also all served to limit not only the direct impact of Europeans but also their indirect effect via trade and disease. The resulting variety of developments was related to the environment, and to Native American adaptability to it, but was not limited to those factors. The coastal communities of the Northwest were different from those of the Great Plains not simply as a consequence of contrasting methods of winning food, but also as a result of differences in social organisation. Much of this diversity is poorly integrated into general accounts of American history that, in contrast, are only too ready to consider varieties within European culture. In part, this is a reflection of the extent to which the latter are more open to research, but there is also a misleading assumption that non-European societies were in some way limited and, as it were, reactionary or remnants; an assumption that owes much to the views about development and hierarchies central to both Christian and Enlightenment thought. It is the case that modern America owes most to European culture and processes, but that does not mean that other cultures were unchanging or without consequence at the time.

Current contentions about American history can be readily summarised in terms of the recently advanced 1619 project, one concerned to argue that the African-American contribution to

American history has been underplayed and that slavery and White supremacy are the heart of American history and the American founding, and thus of America today. In this interpretation, slavery and White supremacy are woven into the DNA of the society and the country.

The date 1619 was that of the arrival of the first enslaved Africans in Virginia (in Massachusetts it was 1638). In practice, the Spaniards brought some slaves with them to South Carolina in 1526, while there is considerable controversy over the status of those in 1619: 'legally' they were like indentured servants, most receiving their freedom and lands after servitude. Slavery appeared in Virginia more clearly from 1661 when larger tobacco plantations became more of a fixture. By emphasising 1619, the project, which appeared initially in *The New York Times Magazine* and has been expanded upon since, sought to make that a key moment in American history, indeed 'as our true founding,' and thus to move attention from 1607, 1620 and 1776, the dates respectively of the foundations of the colonies of Virginia and Massachusetts and of the Declaration of Independence. This initiative developed with the 1619 Project Curriculum and with related publications. In turn, it fed through the contentious politics of modern America, with President Trump in 2020 founding the 1776 Commission as a reply, one designed to focus on the Declaration of Independence and White history.

The details of the controversy are instructive, as is the extent to which events in the early seventeenth century are regarded as of direct relevance today. In part, this is because America has a constitution based on one written text, much of it from nearly a quarter-millennium ago, rather than one derived from recent events and on ready change through governmental or democratic action. There is also now a strong focus on race as a key element in American history while underplaying the degree to which the circumstances of particular groups today are different to those in the past. The 1619 project asserted a direct link to the present with essays such as 'American Capitalism Is Brutal. You Can Trace That to the Plantation' and 'What the Reactionary Politics of 2019 Owe to the Politics of Slavery,' but another was also pertinent: 'Their Ancestors Were Enslaved by Law. Now They're Lawyers.'

In practice, the colony established at Jamestown in 1607 was vulnerable: to Spanish attack, which, in the event, never came, Native American hostility, disease and food shortages. Despite heavy losses, largely due to disease, the colony expanded as a result of the continual arrival of new settlers and the willingness to put an emphasis on growing food. After much bloodshed, Native American resistance was overcome in 1622–4 and again in 1644. Tobacco helped make the colony viable and thus worthy of investment, a point that it can now be convenient to forget.

Virginia was part of a diaspora of English effort that also saw settlements in this period in Bermuda, Newfoundland and (conquered) Ireland. To treat these in isolation is unhelpful, for, far from seeing America as different and advancing an American exceptionalism, there were clear overlaps in personnel, investment, trade hopes, and attitudes between these different colonies. This was a situation also to be seen with French and Spanish colonies, and also with later English (from 1707 British) colonisation, as in the tea of Britain's East India Company being dumped into Boston harbour in 1773. From this perspective, the significance of American independence, and then of the American acquisition of French and Spanish colonies, was in part a matter of the end of this context, and thus the transformation of a set of linkages.

A very different background to that in Virginia was present in the foundation of colonies in New England, with ecclesiastical independence from the hierarchy and rulers of the Church of England as the key element, albeit one that posed a potent conformism of its own. Indeed, the reaction against the pressures of the latter was instrumental in the foundation of new colonies that broke from the authority of Massachusetts.

In 1602, Bartholomew Gosnold, who had sailed from Falmouth with 32 on board, established a settlement on an island near what he had named Cape Cod. This was rendered redundant by Gosnold's failure to develop initial trading contacts with the Native Americans, and, in the face of the latter's hostility, the settlement had to be abandoned. Gosnold went on to play a major role in founding the Virginia Company and died in Jamestown in 1607.

Commemorating the Pilgrim Fathers

'We have come to this Rock, to record here our homage for our Pilgrim Fathers; our sympathy in their sufferings; our gratitude for their labors; our admiration of their virtues; our veneration for their piety; and our attachment to those principles of civil and religious liberty, which they encountered the dangers of the ocean, the storms of heaven, the violence of savages, disease, exile, and famine, to enjoy and to establish.'

Daniel Webster, 1820

In turn, in 1620, the Pilgrim Fathers, a group of Protestant nonconformist separatists or 'saints' as well as 'strangers' who had been recruited by Thomas Weston or his agents, a group who had leased a concession from the New England Company, sailed from England on the *Mayflower*. They made a landing at Cape Cod, and then established a settlement at New Plymouth, literally building on the villages and cleared fields of the Patuxet, who had been recently wiped out by disease unintentionally spread by the French. New Plymouth began the development of a colony in New England, a term first used in 1614 by Captain John Smith when, while unsuccessfully seeking copper, gold and whales, he described the coastline north of the River Hudson, and one popularised by his *Description of New England* (1616). The settlers sought to create a godly agrarian world, and believed their righteousness made them more entitled to the land than the Native Americans, although it was not only Protestant nonconformist settlers who saw Native Americans as savages. Attitudes hardened with time, as the culture was seen as demonic or evil, while there was an apparent lack of 'order' to Native American farming techniques, and a very different separation of labour, with women doing the farming and household tasks while the men hunted and fished, which were seen by the English colonists as leisure activities.

After earlier settlements, Boston, which was to be the local metropolis as well as the capital of Massachusetts, was established in 1630.

A City on the Hill

'We shall find that the God of Israel is among us, when ten of us shall be able to resist a thousand of our enemies; when he shall make us a praise and a glory, that men shall say of succeeding plantations, "The Lord make it like that of New England." For we must consider that we shall be a city upon a hill. The eyes of all people are upon us.'

John Winthrop, Governor of the
Massachusetts Bay Company, 1630

The Native American population had been hit hard in 1616–19 by epidemics linked to contact with European fishermen and traders, but the colony was nevertheless obliged to adapt to local people, and the Massachusetts Bay Company formed an alliance with the Narragansetts. The Company's official seal showed a

Native American saying 'Come over and help us,' which was a way in which proselytisation was perceived by the settlers, including, from 1651, the creation of English-style villages for the Native Americans known as 'Praying Towns'.

In the event, alongside more peaceful interactions, conflict in 1637 in the Pequot War affected the Native American population, some of whom were enslaved and sent to the Caribbean. Yet, in another light the war was a product of rivalries between Native Americans, with the Narragansetts and Mohegans both guiding the English to fight the Pequots for their own purposes, before the Mohegans did the same against the Narragansetts. Furthermore, in 1675–6, King Philip's War hit the Native American population hard, and made them marginal in what had been their own homeland. Nevertheless, the Native Americans were not a united front. In each war, some tribes were devastated, but others, that were allies of the English, benefited. New England expanded rapidly as a result of the high birth rate among settlers and their limited exposure to hostile diseases, and the settlers established a series of largely autonomous self-governing communities in which men worked their own land, which was distributed relatively uniformly, and followed their own trades.

By 1642 there were over 15,000 English settlers in New England, most of whom had arrived since 1630, many as Protestant nonconformists seeking to establish a Christian commonwealth; and by 1650 nearly 23,000. An emphasis on spreading settlement can lead to an underrating of the role of ports, particularly Boston, and, more particularly, the importance of the beginning of the annual sailing season and the arrival of ships that brought immigrants, products, money and news: their likely arrival was the focus of continual discussion and concern.

Virginia had a more hierarchical society, one that was a closer approximation to that of England. Economic opportunity, crucially land ownership, varied greatly in Virginia, and much labour was provided by harshly treated indentured workers from Britain who bound themselves for a time to local masters in return for receiving their passage. This was not the same as being reduced like enslaved Africans to chattels. Separately, there were particular differences between Tidewater planters and their upcountry rivals. For the former, tobacco had become the major crop in both Virginia and Maryland. Its limited capital requirements and high profitability encouraged settlers and investment. Because it was an export crop, the links with England were underlined. The needs and difficulties of tobacco cultivation and trade, however, created serious problems for farmers, and this situation ensured a particular sensitivity to labour availability and cost that encouraged a shift to slavery. This shift was encouraged by population stagnation in Britain from mid-century. In 1662, the Virginia General Assembly decided that slave status was inherited.

Economic volatility contributed to political tensions, as with Bacon's Rebellion in 1676 among part of Virginia's English settlers, many of whom supported Nathaniel Bacon, a landowner who pressed for firm action against Native Americans and opposed the governor, Sir William Berkeley, a wealthy landowner representing elite interests. These were challenged when Bacon took and burned down Jamestown and began recruiting indentured servants and slaves into his army. The crisis ended when Bacon died and Charles II sent a new governor and over 1,000 troops.

The political cross-currents that were to be seen more widely a century later were also present in Maryland in 1676 with a rebellion against the authoritarian policies of the proprietor. So also in 1689, when the overthrow of James II in England led to a rising against his measures and supporters in America. This helped strengthen a community of interest and sentiment that spanned the Atlantic.

The range of English colonies had been increased by the foundation of a series of different ones, notably Maryland, Pennsylvania and Carolina, and by the conquest of non-English colonies in the shape of New York, New Jersey and Delaware (earlier a Swedish colony) from the Dutch in 1664, the combined result of which prefigured the pluralism that was to be characteristic of America. New York had been settled as New Amsterdam from 1624, and by the time it was conquered and renamed after James, Duke of York, the population was about 1,500 Europeans, 300 slaves and 75 free Blacks.

Maryland was founded by George, Lord Baltimore as a Catholic colony, and was very different to the New England colonies in having, until the Glorious Revolution of 1688–9, a proprietary owner. Maryland also saw plantation agriculture using slaves. Founded in 1681 by the entrepreneur William Penn, who sought to manoeuvre in a complex and changeable world of royal favour and political change, Pennsylvania was a Quaker colony in origin. Penn saw such a colony as advantageous, notably as attracting investment, but adapted to different political regimes in London.

Founded in 1663, Carolina was very much a slave-using plantation economy that was an extension of the similar English Caribbean colony of Barbados. In part as a consequence of coercion, slave society eventually became a Black American identity different from that of the various African peoples from whom the slaves came. Indeed, partly due to oppression, which became more rigid and brutal as the economic value of the crops produced increased, Black society was eventually to be more coherent than its White equivalent. However, this was more true for the nineteenth than earlier centuries. Early slavery featured vast and deep cultural and sociological differences among slaves, linked to area of enslavement in Africa and location of work in America. In South Carolina, high death rates required the constant importation of more slaves. This had the effect of 're-Africanising' the population, thus preserving religious and linguistic divisions among the slave population, as with the development of the Gullah creole in coastal South Carolina and Georgia derived from West African languages, and slowing the formation of a uniform African-American culture and identity.

Separately, a racial caste system defined society alongside slavery, for free Blacks also had only limited rights, as well as suffering violence, both legal and otherwise. In 1697, African Americans were excluded from churchyards in New York City, and, instead, buried in a different graveyard.

However, these colonies should not be understood as controlling the territory now covered by these states. Most of New York and Pennsylvania was under the control of Native Americans until the late eighteenth century. Similarly, much of Florida, especially the south, was outside the Spanish sphere of influence.

By 1700, the population in English North America was greater than that in its French counterpart. In part this was due to more propitious circumstances for agriculture, with the growing season in the French-ruled St Lawrence valley far shorter than that in English colonies farther south. There was also a greater willingness to emigrate in England, both within the country and abroad, and thus an establishment of norms. While a matter of social values, this willingness was paralleled by the readiness of the English government to permit the settlement of religious minorities, which contrasted with the French determination to retain a monopoly position for Catholicism. The great growth in the English colonies, especially the middle and northern colonies, however, was due principally to prosperity and multiplying, and not immigration, although about 350,000 English people migrated to America during the century. There was also an extension of English government, including the revised Navigation Act of 1696, which authorised colonial Vice-Admiralty courts and the creation in 1700 of a General Post Office that had branches in the colonies.

Salem in 1692

The witch trials in Salem, Massachusetts, which led to 20 executions, indicated the nature and extent of psychological tensions that could burst to the fore, and that victims were not restricted to Native Americans or Blacks. The instability of New England politics contributed to the crisis, as did the pressure of a rising population on the local economy. As a crucial aspect of the religious nature of the episode, the potent and disruptive conviction of a living presence of evil was also fundamental.

It is interesting to consider how far the history of America would have been different had French patterns been followed for part of its history: New York is very different from Québec. Similarly, the coherence of English North America would have been much less had New York and New Jersey remained under Dutch control, let alone passed under that of France.

The spread of European settlement had major implications for the environment. These included deforestation, the introduction of new crops, animals and vehicles, and pollution, for example in the leather and timber industries. Local ecologies were hit hard, as in the Connecticut Valley where the killing of beavers for fur, as well as the logging that was central to clearing for settlement and the timber industry, led to the drying out of wetlands and to subsequent erosion. The 'conquest' of the environment expressed control as much as did the defeat of local Native Americans, and both were highly destructive.

4

To Independence (Eventually), 1700–76

Particularly if space in the text is limited, the eighteenth century can readily be presented in terms of the move to independence, with the years before the outbreak of fighting in 1775, leading the next year to a war of independence, discussed largely in terms of causes and portents. As before, however, this is understandable in terms of the history of what initially became the American state, but less so if the area of modern America is considered. At the most marked, the eighteenth century for Hawai'i, Alaska and the Pacific coastline was also a matter of a spreading European presence, represented in part by exploration and trade, but also, notably in the Aleutian Islands and southern California, by conquest and settlement by Russia and Spain respectively. This Pacific perspective may appear tangential, if not quixotic. Yet, that is to assume that American history was inevitably to have an Atlantic configuration, or, alternatively, that there would not be a separate development and even separatism based on a Pacific alignment, or that these other areas are somehow inconsequential.

A similar point can be made about the Gulf (of Mexico) where the rivalries between Britain (as England became in 1707 as a result of parliamentary union with Scotland), France and Spain remained the key element throughout the eighteenth century. Indeed, to a degree, they helped shape the subsequent period as America took over the British and French interests, and Mexico those of Spain.

Had the Spaniards been allowed to continue their missions among the Apalachee, Florida would have started to develop over the eighteenth century along the same lines as California. However, during the War of the Spanish Succession (1702–13), the Apalachee and the missions were wiped out by the Creek, with the support of the British based in South Carolina. In turn, Creek migrated into Florida and became the Seminole. Florida's marginality owed much in the eighteenth century to its proximity to British colonies.

Precarious in the face of Native American opposition and economic difficulties, the French presence in Louisiana, in contrast to prosperous Saint-Domingue, Martinique and Guadeloupe, remained a sparsely populated colony, and hopes that it would serve as a base for trade with the Pacific or, at any rate, the Spanish positions in modern New Mexico, proved abortive, as did the search for bullion deposits. Nevertheless, the colony served as the basis for a wider-ranging trading system in the hinterland. Its beginnings were difficult, not least due to the environment. In 1710, the wood of the fortress at Fort Louis (later Mobile), which had been built in 1702, was so rotted by humidity and decay that it could not support the weight of the cannon. The garrison suffered from an absence of fresh meat, from an insufficient supply of swords, cartridge boxes, nails, guns and powder, from demoralisation and desertion, and from the lack of a hospital. The survival of Louisiana at this stage rested on its acceptance by the Native American population, with trade the key element of mutual benefit. Relocation led first to a temporary fort and then to the greater commitment of a new brick fort with a stone foundation, which was begun in 1723 and renamed Fort Condé. Founded in 1715, New Orleans was named after Philip, Duke of Orleans, regent for the infant Louis XV.

Commitment to the colony was to be given dramatic form in the financial speculation of the Mississippi Company, which became a proposal to refinance the French state, only for its greatly overinflated share value to collapse at the close of 1720. As with the South Sea Company in Britain, a company that established a position in trade to the Spanish Caribbean, the Mississippi Company reflected the bold hopes placed on the Caribbean, hopes that represented a highpoint in European interest. The hope of striking it rich was to be a key theme in American history.

Efforts to encourage immigration to Louisiana had scant success, in part due to its climate's unsuitability for either sugar cane or tobacco. In 1717, there were 700 Europeans in the colony, but the Mississippi Company led to an increase, not least by arranging the dispatch of freed prisoners and prostitutes. Voluntary settlers were promised a benign environment, but, once there, did not find it easy, and faced a high death rate. Alongside French settlers, others, including Germans, were given land, in order to provide food; but all had to be Catholic. Initial hopes that Native Americans would provide a willing labour force proved naïve and this encouraged a reliance on African slaves. The cultivation of tobacco was not a great success, but these slaves brought knowledge of rice growing which helped feed the colony, although that cultivation did not provide the necessary revenue stream. Free Black people became an important part of the population of New Orleans and offered valuable skills. They were a key element of the nuances and adaptability of a frontier society, their skills both pushed to the fore by the resulting opportunities and providing the ability to meet them.

The population of Louisiana remained small, despite the forced migration there of Acadians (Cajuns) from Nova Scotia after the British conquest as well as many French colonists from Québec. By 1763 there were only about 4,000 White people and 5,000 Black people in the colony which was associated by the French with savage Native Americans. Meanwhile, the *Code Noir* (1724) sought to define a racial hierarchy. There were also the results of relationships among groups, such as Quadroons, who were a quarter Black, and such categories became more common with time. The earliest map of New Orleans, that of 1744 by Jacques-Nicholas Bellin, showed only about 100 buildings, most of which were not to survive a series of fires that hit hard at the close-packed wooden structures. Founded in 1718, the city within its fortifications had a grid structure radiating from the riverfront *Place d'Armes,* now Jackson Square. Similarly, Philadelphia's central grid reflects its foundation and early development.

Spain on the Pacific Coast

The surveying voyage of Bruno de Hezeta, in 1775, led to the sighting of the estuary of the Columbia River, although the currents were too swift for his scurvy-weakened crew to enter the river. Earlier, seven of the crew had been killed by indigenous people when they put ashore for water. Francisco de la Bodega y Quadra, who had sailed on when Hezeta turned back, reached 58°30'N, despite scurvy affecting most of the crew. His surveying voyages led to a far better map of the coast from there to 17°N. Facing the usual problem of deciding how best to interpret and integrate new information, the viceroy of New Spain, Antonio María de Bucareli, speculated that the Columbia might be the outflow of the inland sea marked on maps, and, in 1793, Revilla Gigedo, his successor, suggested that the river might cross the continent. This led to an unsuccessful Spanish attempt to establish a settlement at the mouth of the Columbia and to penetrate up the river: it was thwarted by the difficulty of the river channel and the hostile attitude of the indigenous people.

Meanwhile, there was a major Spanish expansion into what became California, in large part in order to assuage fears of Russian activity. San Diego was founded in 1769, Monterey in 1770, San Francisco in 1776, and Los Angeles five years later. Expansion was helped by the local availability of Spanish naval power, not least in moving settlers and goods, and thus ensured a ready possibility for economic advantage. As a reminder of how much the history of what became America involved other places at a distance, San Blas, Mexico was founded as a port in order to support military activity further north, with a shipyard and a fort part of the new project. Ships built there were used for navigation into California, while the port also provided a stopping point for others. Spanish California was consolidated by missions, the monks of which helped begin California's wine industry.

However, California's coastal situation also ensured that other powers could challenge Spanish claims and establish positions, the Russians doing so at Fort Ross in 1812. Advancing overland, the Americans were to do so at the expense of Mexico, which took over Spain's position in the early 1820s.

As before, there are the Native American perspectives. This period saw the further extension of the use of horses and of guns, and, in particular, the development of far-ranging tribes on the Great Plains. Horses made the hunting of bison easier, allowing the Native Americans to follow herds of bison or deer for hundreds of miles. Moreover, the resulting improvements in diet led to a larger and healthier population. Requiring much organisation and planning, these animal drives served as preparation for human conflict. Horses also altered the human relationship with that environment, with the horses also competing for grazing with the bison. Horses gave a new speed and power which contributed to a westward intensification of the Native American presence, one that reflected the dynamic instability of the Great Plains before the advance of the Euro-American frontier of settlement.

The Western (both European and European-American) idea of civilisation developing in stages, the stadial theory, allocated Native Americans a primitive status as tribes (rather than states) heavily dependent on hunter-gathering, instead of settled agriculture and industry. A Biblical view of 'husbanding the earth and subduing it' made the Native Americans appear reprehensible to the settlers of the seventeenth century, and by the eighteenth the view had set in deeply. As tribes, moreover, they were largely seen as lying outside the law of nations, with no effective counter to European claims of the right of discovery and subsequent settlement. Numbers were smaller among Native Americans, and, partly as a result, there was more emphasis on the individual prowess of warriors. Yet, warfare also reflected and sustained social roles. In particular, aside from building up tribal cohesion, men hunted and fought, while women were responsible for agriculture. Furthermore, conflict was in some respects not unlike hunting, both because opponents, some of whom were enslaved, could be regarded as akin to animals, and because emphasis was both on the masculinity of the individual, who was pitted against other individuals and against the environment, and on the group, which was also important in hunting. Thus, the half-moon tactic, employed in hunting, was also successfully used in warfare.

The absence of large armies did not entail any lack of organised and deadly conflict. Instead, Native Americans, notably the Iroquois, had developed effective tactical formations, and a form of warfare well attuned to the forested nature of much of the eastern half of the continent, with ambushes, rushes and feints, and a combination of accurately aimed fire and an astute use of cover. These tactics were more important than the weapon which was used, whether bow and arrow or musket, although musket shot was less likely to be deflected by vegetation. Moreover, offensive warfare against fortified villages developed, notably with the growing use of indirect assault tactics rather than the more costly direct assaults.

The Europeans held no monopoly on fortifications. Eastern Native Americans had many palisaded villages and, with the introduction of firearms, European-style bastions appeared to provide the defence with the opportunity to use crossfire. Changes in Iroquois fortifications and siege warfare transformed the power ranking in the Northeast. These changes were an instance of an application of Western martial practices, but can also be seen within a wider context of more traditional Native American practices that remained viable in wars with Europeans. Nevertheless, the vulnerability of fortified villages to firepower encouraged their abandonment when hostile forces approached, especially when the latter included cannon. The Native Americans had learned that forts could be death traps.

Warfare between Native American groups was affected by the spread of muskets and horses. In about 1730, the Comanche became the first Native American group to equip an entire people with horses, building an empire that stretched over much of modern-day Texas, Oklahoma, Mexico and Kansas. In any conflict, the side that acquired muskets and horses first dominated.

More generally, tribal warfare was affected by trade and animal movements, and by competition for hunting grounds. At the beginning of the century, the Cree fought the Chippewa, and the Comanche fought the Penxaye Apache, while the Assiniboine were defeated by the Blackfoot. Raids and ambushes played major roles in conflicts, which lasted for considerable periods, as between the Navajo and the Southern Ute from the 1710s to the 1750s.

Across the century as a whole, the Europeans made major advances in North America. They were helped by their maritime and amphibious capabilities. Moreover, by the mid-eighteenth century, compared to a century earlier, the Europeans had more developed logistical networks, with shorter supply chains, especially as settlements had begun to create their own industries. In addition, Europeans now had extensive knowledge of the local conditions. Native American allies were still very helpful in this regard, but European settlers, many of whom were multi-generational, also performed an essential function as scouts. This could create the situation in which knowledgeable settlers or Americans interacted with relatively ignorant off-the-boat Europeans, which could create tensions if the latter conducted themselves with an air of superiority.

The general impression of European military superiority and territorial expansion has to be supplemented by an awareness of the setbacks that were faced and of the often complex reasons for European success, part of which depended on Native American support. These points are particularly apparent in the early years of the century, not in general a period of major European success. Thus, the British faced determined resistance in the Carolinas where the Yamasee, with Creek support, nearly destroyed the colonies in 1715.

Such conflicts, however, look different from Native American perspectives, as indeed did and does the history of America. For example, both the Creek and Carolinians sought to influence the Cherokee during this war, and, in the end, the Cherokee hoodwinked the Carolinians into the war with the Creek. As in India, European powers, and the goods and opportunities they provided, were fed into local antagonisms, helping to fuel them at the same time that the powers were affected, if not manipulated. The French vied with the British to win allies, while the French and Spaniards competed among the Alabama and Creek in the late 1710s, establishing a regional pattern that was to last, with important variations in participants, until the end of Spanish rule in Florida in 1819–21.

In the 1700s–20s, Native Americans pressed hard on the European colonies in New England, Florida, the Carolinas and Louisiana. Thereafter, however, the coastal colonies were less under pressure. Instead, as conspicuously with Pontiac's War in 1763–6, Native American pressure was against the advancing line of European settlement.

Guerrilla warfare by the Abenaki in Dummer's War (1722–7) kept British settlers out of the Vermont country. On the Mississippi, upstream from New Orleans, the Natchez initially accepted French trade and expansion, and the French were able to establish a fortified trading base at Fort Rosalie (Natchez) in 1716. However, in 1729, a French land fraud led to a Natchez attack in which Fort Rosalie was destroyed and more than 200 settlers killed. Nevertheless, the Natchez did not receive the support of other tribes, and in 1731 were crushed by the French and the Choctaw in a campaign of systematic extermination.

The French began a practice of burning prisoners alive. The conflict showed the weakness of the colony of Louisiana, as it had been necessary to call in troops from France, but also the strength of an imperial system that could do so. The war with the Natchez also led to a spread of French commitments. Having been driven back by the Natchez in an attempt to reach the Arkansas country in 1731, the French established a garrison at Arkansas Post in 1732 in order to keep an eye on the Chickasaw. Demonstrating the interweaving of Native American with European rivalries, the remnants of the Natchez had taken refuge with the Chickasaw, who were both rivals of the pro-French Choctaw and who, partly as a result, traded with the British and looked to their assistance. Chickasaw independence concerned the French, who, in 1736, launched attacks from Canada and Louisiana. Both were ambushed and defeated, and French captives were burnt to death. However, in 1739, a larger French force was sent and the intimidated Chickasaw agreed to a truce. As earlier against the Natchez, the French armed their slaves.

Further west, the Spanish expedition against the Apache in 1732 was hindered by the lack of fixed points to attack. Moreover, punitive expeditions were, at best, of limited and short-term value. These expeditions were dependent anyway on Native American support. Much activity was defensive, with the expansion of the *presidial* (fortress) system in the province of Sonora designed to protect northern Mexico from raiding both by Apache and by Hokan-speaking nomads from the desert coast of the Gulf of California. Russian exploration of Alaskan waters began in 1728, but fog, storms and scurvy were all serious problems. Nevertheless, later in the century, the Russians established fur-trading, often fur-seizing, stations in the Aleutians.

The emphasis on conflict can lead to an underplaying of often close links between European and Native American societies including intermarriage. Trade between them varied in its character and content. Some Northern tribes, such as the Anishinaabe and the Ojibwe, provided furs. Further south, it was more deer-skin that was traded. These supplies helped drive commercial links and established value.

The colonial powers were most concerned by their relations with each other. Worried about the new British colony of Georgia, where the fortifications of the main base, Savannah, were designed to resist Spanish attack, Spain improved those of its major position in neighbouring Florida, St Augustine, which successfully resisted a British siege in 1740. This siege saw British forces supported by Native American allies.

The Spanish presence on the northern borders of New Spain proved vulnerable to Native American opposition, including the rebellion of the Pima in Arizona in 1751, and the attack seven years later on the position at San Sabá, eighty miles northwest of modern Austin, Texas. About 2,000 Comanche and their allies, armed with at least 1,000 French muskets, attacked the mission, killing all but one of the missionaries, beheading the effigy of St Francis, a totemic act of religious violence and control, and obliging the soldiers to leave the nearby *presidio* (fortress).

Meanwhile, as an aspect of a wider contest for imperial mastery, Britain and France used trade and the supply of weapons in a competition for influence over Native Americans between the Appalachians and the Great Lakes. The French proved particularly active in the interior of North America, establishing forts as bases from which they hoped to increase their influence over Native American trade routes. This process and influence led them into conflict with hostile Native Americans and exacerbated rivalry with the British who sought allies among these Native Americans and constructed forts of their own. The destruction of villages and crops by the French forced the Chickasaw to terms in 1752.

In turn, in 1759–61, the British deployed regulars, colonial forces, and allied Native Americans such as the Chickasaw, to force the Cherokee to terms. This remark, however, provides no indication of the difficulty of the struggle, its destructiveness, which included the killing of hostages and the torching of villages leaving lasting damage, nor the extent to which, far from there being a total victory, this war was followed by a compromise peace. However, British strength was also revealed. It proved possible to move troops from elsewhere within an integrated military system. Once the French in Canada had been defeated in 1760, units could be moved south, both against the Cherokee and, in 1762, to help capture Havana from Spain as the result of a major deployment of strength. These operations showed the range of British campaigning in North America and the campaigning left them as the dominant power.

Like the conquest of Canada, the Cherokee War indicated the British ability to renew operations, notably with new forces, after initial setbacks. The latter were much in evidence in Pontiac's War (1763–6), a struggle that reflected Native American opposition to the advance of colonists. In the initial stages of the war, there were successful attacks on a series of British forts, while the British felt obliged to abandon others, and their field forces were also ambushed. The British proved less effective at fighting in the woodlands of the frontier zone than their Native American opponents, and the army's dependence on supply routes made it more vulnerable to ambush. The British, however, were quite adroit at degrading and destroying Native American logistics – fields, fisheries, stores and villages – thus crippling operations and helping ensure British victory in the medium and long run.

Owing to the British conquest of the French bases in Canada in 1759–60, the Native Americans had no access to firearms other than those they had captured. The Anglo-French rivalry that had given a measure of opportunity to the Native Americans, providing, for example, French arms and ammunition to the Abenaki of Vermont for use against New England, had been ended. Furthermore, in 1763–4, helped by the end of war with France and Spain, large numbers of British troops were deployed in North America. The capacity of the regulars and colonists to respond to Native American successes and to mount fresh efforts was indicative of the manpower resources they enjoyed, and, crucially, could deploy and sustain; and the situation was stabilised anew. The combination of demographic and economic factors led Adam Smith to suggest, in *The Wealth of Nations* (1776), that, although the Native Americans in North America 'may plague them [European settlers] and hurt some of the back settlements, they could never injure the body of the people'. Yet, had it overcome significant differences, greater Native American unity could have ensured that the Allegheny Mountains were a more effective barrier against White expansion westwards. Indeed, there were a number of attempts at such unity.

In an important indication of the political dimension, the stabilisation of relations with the Native Americans in 1764 entailed the British accepting limitations of the use of force. Instead, they turned back to diplomacy. Although the British authorities assured themselves that their terms were imposed, the settlement was in practice a compromise. The Native Americans returned all prisoners, but ceded no land. Indeed, Native American resistance encouraged the British government to oppose colonial settlement west of the Alleghenies, which greatly helped to increase colonial anger with British control, contributing to the developing crisis with the colonists. The difficulties posed by Native American opposition make more sense of British policy towards their colonists. In part, this was another aspect of the differences between European Americans being linked in at least some measure to the need to respond to Native American strength.

Whereas migration from Africa was completely involuntary, land hunger was a key element in migration from Europe. The establishment of independent European-American farming households and estates was crucial to migration, and notably so in frontier areas where there were apparently opportunities for smallholders. The possibilities for poor immigrants appeared best in such frontier farming, although there was a dependence on credit and markets. The small farm economies of the frontier were to be crucial in politics, especially with Jeffersonian and Jacksonian White democracy, and, in the face of environmental constraints and major economic pressures, the practice of such agriculture survived as the frontier advanced.

A major contrast was with the very different local opposition to the expansion of Spanish power in coastal California and of Russian in the Aleutians, as well as one of the most dramatic moments in American history, the killing of the British naval explorer Captain James Cook on a Hawai'ian beach in Kealakekua Bay in 1779.

There was no more inevitability about the fate of Atlantic America than that of its Pacific and Gulf counterparts. The expansion and development of the English colonies might seem a prefigurement to independence, but in fact there was a greater convergence between Britain and the colonies in the eighteenth century than there had been in the seventeenth century when links were less frequent and also slower. Moreover, far from economic links among the colonies becoming primarily closer, there was a convergence, economically, socially and politically, between individual colonies and the British metropole. As a result, wars that threatened trade links were a serious matter. War with France in 1744–8 led to privateering attacks that hit the agricultural staple trades of the Carolinas and the Chesapeake, while in 1747–8 French and Spanish privateers off the Delaware Capes brought Philadelphia's trade to a halt.

The introduction of the helm or ship's wheel soon after 1700 dramatically increased rudder control on large ships by removing the need to steer with the tiller by means of a bar fitted to the rudder post. In addition, the average annual number of trans-Atlantic British voyages doubled between 1675 and 1740, and the number of ships that extended or successfully ignored the 'optimum' shipping seasons also increased on several major routes. There had been what has been referred to as the 'shrinking' of the British Atlantic.

In the British Atlantic, and far more than its French, Portuguese and Spanish counterparts, sailings largely reflected commercial opportunity, not government permission, although the ability of the navy to ensure the peacetime safety of the seas, particularly by banishing, or at least containing, piracy, enabled ships to sail with fewer cannon and thus to need a smaller crew, a measure that greatly helped the profitability of shipping, not least by permitting a larger cargo, as opposed to supplies for the crew. A reduction in the time ships spent in harbour, and a fall in the cost of credit and insurance, as well as the costs of packaging and storing goods, were also important to greater profitability. Improved trans-Atlantic passages benefited the fisheries, trade and the navy, and, in particular, the growing complexity of trading relationships that criss-crossed the ocean. Average annual British exports to North America rose from £0.27 million in 1701–5 to £1.3 million in 1751–5; and that in a period of very low inflation. The changing nature of this trade reflected the development of the colonial economy with demand in the British colonies for consumer goods rising rapidly in the 1740s at the same time that a stagnant demand for 'producer goods' reflected the colonial success in producing domestic substitutes, as in textiles. British shipping tonnage rose greatly in part as a result of more trans-Atlantic trade.

It was this very strengthening of the trans-Atlantic link that helped explain the drive for independence, for, as in the late 1640s and late 1680s, events in Britain greatly influenced those in the colonies. In the case of the 1760s and early 1770s, it was the opposition to George III in Britain that was crucial and, in particular, the presentation of his intentions and policies as tyrannical. George survived the crisis in Britain, producing stability by the early 1770s, although domestic instability was to return in the early 1780s. However, in America, more especially New England and Virginia, as on other occasions in Scotland and Ireland, the strains of a political system with several centres helped ensure that it was less easy for London-based governments to maintain order, indeed retain control, in distant territories. More was entailed in independence, but this, and other contextual factors, were important.

There were tensions between different 'kinds of spaces', or geographical imaginations. These spaces and tensions have been presented as the oceanically oriented British Atlantic and, in contrast, the settler empire of 'the American Frontier'. The intermediate eastern seaboard is presented as providing a crucial sphere of tension, and therefore is brought to the fore. It has been suggested that, although in the seventeenth century English merchants and proprietors had begun the colonisation of New England, the Chesapeake and the Carolina low country, they had subsequently lost control over the process of settlement to the colonists. This loss has been attributed to structural geographical factors rather than to political ones. In particular, it has been claimed that the English merchants and proprietors were defeated by the enormous availability of agricultural land and the related difficulty of commanding immigrant labour, especially indentured workers from England. As a result, more autonomous economies had developed in North America than would have been the case had transoceanic trade remained as fundamental as in the West Indies. Furthermore, the spaces of the American interior provided colonial elites with a 'much greater geographic context in which to manoeuvre than existed on the islands of the British Atlantic', for example Jamaica, with such manoeuvre seen as a way to limit the power of the British state.

There are problems with such a reading, particularly that it is too easy to read from geography to an outcome in a somewhat deterministic fashion. It is necessary, in particular, to remember that 'the frontier' had a variety of meanings and locations. A key one was the Cumberland Gap through the Appalachians, which opened the way to the West. The discovery of this ancient Native American path led to the first pioneers crossing into Tennessee and Kentucky. The early frontier was to prove an area that was particularly difficult to influence, let alone control. Moreover, the economies of the interior were heavily dependent on transoceanic politics and economics in the shape of fighting for, and securing, trade routes, and, therefore, seeking supplies. Both in colonial times and subsequently, trans-Appalachia was linked to the Atlantic world by, and through, coastal America: ports on the Atlantic seaboard.

Separately, if there is to be a focus on geography and causation, then the latter can be traced to more than one process and outcome. For example, rather than a colonial economy, there were colonial economies linked more closely with London than with one another. South Carolina and Massachusetts, for example, had relatively little trade with each other, while within individual colonies there were economic, political, ethnic, religious, cultural, security, family and personal cross-currents.

Yet, it is also necessary to understand the major role of political geography, and its particular significance for imagining and defining new political entities, both as individual colonies and as communities. It may be going too far to claim that Britain's empire collapsed along structural faults from the colonial period, but nevertheless, these faults were significant, and it is pertinent to assess what meaning they had to contemporaries. Although there were also tensions in the West Indies over government policy, particularly, as in North America, strong opposition to the Stamp Act of 1765, there was no rebellion in these colonies. In part, this was due to a dependence by the colonies on the British state, arising both from the presence of large numbers of enslaved Africans and from the threat from nearby French and Spanish colonies. These elements introduce significant aspects of geopolitics and 'space', especially the extent to which the latter was demographically constructed, and also the role of strategic competition.

At the same time, a political emphasis on change in the Anglo-American relationship should not lead to a downplaying of social and economic continuities which included male-dominated societies and ones with an emphasis on reverence for age and rank. Yet, in each point, those in British America, with the key difference of slavery, were more liberal than in Europe. Women had legal limitations on property ownership, obtaining credit and controlling earnings, and were generally defined by family position, but they were able to operate with more significance, even autonomy, than in Europe.

Whereas enslaved people had no choice, the British, in large part due to the degree of religious freedom they accepted and the availability of cultivatable land, were uniquely successful in attracting settlers who did not have trans-Atlantic imperial systems, notably subjects of the German states. The expansion of the colonial imprint encouraged this process, particularly the establishment of Georgia in 1732, Savannah being founded the following year. Initially, Georgia was very different to South Carolina, where by 1740 two-thirds of the population were slaves. Instead, in accordance with the wishes of the London-based trustees, who sought to create a Protestant yeoman society, Georgia at first was not a slave colony. However, under pressure from the settlers, that situation did not last.

This migration of Whites (not the enforced one of enslaved Africans) was to be important to the British victory over France in the struggle for North America. The British outnumbered the French, not only in regular troops sent from Britain, but also in local militia, and, supported by naval dominance, the local logistical base for their operations to conquer Canada was stronger.

To a degree, the movement of people was destiny. In the Atlantic world, a key element was that much of the movement was of slaves, who were then kept in enslavement. Although there was the alternative, notably in the cities, of a freed Black population, it was not the opportunity for most enslaved people. Their prospects could be bleak indeed. The 1696 Carolina Slave Act decreed that for the second offence a male runaway was to be castrated and a woman to lose her ear, and that, if an owner refused to inflict these punishments, he could lose the slave to an informer, while the death of slaves as a result of such treatment was to be compensated, thus encouraging it. These provisions were maintained in the 1712 Act. Accordingly escapees were castrated like animals. Visiting Charleston in 1736, Charles Wesley noted in his journal, 'It was endless to recount all the shocking instances of diabolical cruelty which these men (as they call themselves) daily practice upon their fellow-creatures; and that on the most trivial of occasions.' He commented on a slave woman beaten unconscious and revived, before being beaten again, and having hot candle wax poured on her skin. Her offence was overfilling a teacup. Aside from often routine physical violence, there was considerable verbal abuse towards slaves, as well as the contempt of harsh gestures.

Meanwhile, there was, as part of a wider context of violence, tension over empire. In part of European North America, that from Georgia to Canada inclusive, the key developments were unification under British rule, which was obtained with French surrender in 1760, followed by the partition of British

North America in 1775–83. The two were linked, although there was no inherent reason why British North America, or the counterpart attempted in 1775–6 and 1812–14 with invasions of Canada, an American-ruled North America, should not have succeeded.

On the ground, in 1754–60, the shifting support and fears of Native American groups were also important. The French position was weakened when Pennsylvania authorities promised the Native Americans that they would not claim land west of the Appalachians. The consequent shift of Native American support obliged the French to give up the Ohio region.

In the event, the fiscal burdens for Britain arising from wartime success against France raced ahead of the fiscal growth in revenue and credit that was to come from Britain's leading role in transport and industrialisation. This led to a determination to raise revenues that combined with a liquidity crisis in the colonies as well as opposition to what appeared to be the expansion of governmental power and pretensions. Indeed, in part, the raising of taxes was intended to reduce the dependence of provincial administrations on colonial legislatures. Thus, there was a degree to which British policy was primarily a reform movement to centralise as well as strengthen the empire, one with its roots in the 1740s and 1750s before the Seven Years' War and its debts.

The liquidity crisis in part arose from the negative trade balance, especially in the case of New England which had nothing to match Chesapeake tobacco in exporting so as to buy British imports. Furthermore, as a key element in the economy and political geography of America, there was no bullion in the east to match the silver in Mexico and Bolivia that helped Spanish imperial rule, or the gold and silver that was to be discovered in the West in the mid-nineteenth century.

The Americans no longer felt threatened by French bases in Canada and were therefore unwilling to see British troops as saviours. The Stamp Act of 1765 led to a crisis, as Americans rejected Parliament's financial demands, and thereafter, relations with Britain were riven by a fundamental division over constitutional issues.

In the 1760s, the British government did not face the opposition nor respond with the level of force that was to be seen in Massachusetts in 1774–5. Yet, Pontiac's War and the Stamp Act Crisis indicated the extent to which mid-century conflict produced both changes and strains in the Native American and European societies in North America, strains that increased anxiety and tension over governmental policies.

Conflict with Native Americans tested both regulars and colonials, and encouraged the development of experience with what was termed small war or irregular warfare, as well as a process of brutalisation and fear through conflict in a challenging cultural context. Nevertheless, in 1765, despite the enhanced capability represented by British experience of small war, most of North America east of the Mississippi was still under the control of Native Americans, and both the Cherokee War and Pontiac's War had indicated their resilience in regions reasonably close to centres of British settlement. In the Southeast, moreover, the Creek Confederacy was a potent Native American element.

Settler pressure continued, but was resisted by the Native Americans. Thus, in 1774, 1,500 Virginia militia advanced against the Shawnee, who had attacked settlers in their territory and had ambushed a volunteer force that went to the settlers' assistance. The Shawnee were defeated at the Battle of Point Pleasant. At the same time, the Native American issue was much less prominent for the British in the early 1770s than it had been a decade earlier. In place of the extended network of forts, defended portages, and roads created by British troops then, there were, by the 1770s, few military posts in the interior. In part, this new distribution of troops reflected growing anxiety, instead, about the loyalty of the

British colonists who were concentrated in coastal areas, notably in Boston.

Rebellions by colonists were better able than opposition by Native Americans to strike the centres of imperial power in the colonies. Opposition to newly established Spanish rule, after trade outside the Spanish imperial system or in non-Spanish ships was banned, led to a rebellion in New Orleans in 1768. Mindful of its ally's determination to restore authority, France rejected this attempt to return to its rule (Louisiana had been transferred from France as part of the Peace of Paris of 1763, the peace settlement after the Seven Years' War), and Spanish forces reimposed control.

Once the significance of slave-owning is put to one side, White American society was less contained and deferential than that of Britain, and even those characteristics there should not be exaggerated. There was no hereditary nobility in the colonies and, instead, a wide ownership of property by Whites as well as an electorate that did not show deference. This situation contributed to the American Revolution, as well as being developed by it and crystallised in the more democratic state constitutions that were established.

Since the 1960s, signs of social radicalism two centuries earlier have attracted more attention. From this perspective, the British and the Loyalists can appear anachronistic and reactionary, opponents not only of the new America fought for from 1775, but also, more relevantly, of its fruition being contested from the 1960s. The War of Independence becomes the American Revolution, and, therefore, offers a different 'lesson' for today. This presentist approach underrates the complexities of the conflict. Reconsidering the War of Independence in terms of later values certainly leads to a major misunderstanding of empire. This was especially so from the 1960s when the war was compared with the Vietnam War in America by critics, a comparison, notably of British forces in 1775–83 with American forces in the later war, that was seriously misleading as well as conveniently arresting for its advocates. In particular, this approach underrated the extent to which the War of Independence was very much a civil war, especially, but not only, in the southern colonies.

Very different contexts continue to be offered when considering the War of Independence. The Tea Party movement of the 2000s and 2010s drew on a key moment that was part of the foundation account for America, the illegal seizure and destruction of 340 chests of East India Company tea in Boston on 16 December 1773: an episode that had had a distinctive resonance for a minority of modern Americans. The process of reaching and redefining a consensus that underlay and often constituted government in the colonial period had broken down. The drama of the Boston Tea Party reflected hatred of taxes as well as a drive for self-determination. Modern political movements reach back for imagery, rhetoric and symbols in an attempt to explain what their struggle is about. However, the events of 1773 scarcely describe modern America, not least given the role of colonial Boston as a slaving port. Furthermore, the treatment of Loyalists in Boston was to be extremely harsh, but so earlier was the treatment of those of different religious views. Indeed, in 1732, Thomas Sherlock, an influential English bishop, argued that it was ironic that those Puritans who had claimed religious freedom in England left for North America where they had turned persecutors of those who wanted freedom there.

Momentous events may have minor causes, or, rather, what appear in hindsight to be minor or even selfish. That was not how they seemed to contemporaries, although they may have disagreed. As a result, the War of Independence was the first of two American civil wars, as many in the War of Independence were Loyalists. That element was to be downplayed in the public account of America's past, and, indeed, most of its history, establishing a pattern also seen with political divisions (though not civil conflict) at the time of the War of 1812 and the Mexican-American War (1846–8). In part, this was a demonstration of the contested, even precarious, nature of American nationhood until after the Civil War. The extent of contestation also qualifies the notion of American exceptionalism. So too did the prevalence of slavery.

Government fiscal demands were unwelcome in Britain and the West Indies as well as America; and, again, there was nothing inevitable about the working out of the crisis. Indeed, by 1772, it might have appeared that the difficulties of the 1760s had been largely shelved, and notably so outside Massachusetts. In November 1747, in Boston while between assignments in the Caribbean, Rear-Admiral Charles Knowles had caused the largest disturbance against British imperial authority in the American colonies in the generation before the contentious Stamp Act by pressing Massachusetts seamen. Yet, the issue had not led to any irrevocable breakdown.

In contrast, in the 1760s, the ending of one meta-historical challenge, the external threat to the liberty of the colonies from France, a challenge that bound Britain and colonies together, was followed by another, domestic threat, that from the British government. To a degree, worry about George III repeated the concern seen in the late seventeenth century with opposition to James II. In the 1760s and early 1770s, a colonial commitment to a British identity that was seen as encompassing the colonies within an empire fell victim to a tone and style of imperial rule that appeared authoritarian. A mutual dynamic, in which contrasting negative images were built up, was fed enough provocative actions on both sides to ensure that the threshold to large-scale violence was crossed even though there was no wish to do so on the part of most of those involved.

In the event, the crisis over the Boston Tea Party of 1773 and, in particular, the vigorous governmental response hardened attitudes and led to what became a militarisation of the crisis. For example, warships had been used in the 1760s and early 1770s to try to 'improve' imperial governance, or at least centralise and rationalise it by a variety of means including producing accurate charts and enforcing fiscal and other regulations. The navy was an important tool of colonial governance both in North America and in the Caribbean because it was the means to regulate maritime trade and harbours, and because naval officers took the perspective of the imperial government rather than the colonists. As imperial authority collapsed in North America, however, the navy was unable to police the entire coastline, lacked sufficient small vessels, and, in pursuit of overawing opposition, was able to concentrate ships in Boston harbour and along the New England coast in 1774–5 only by abandoning the rest of the coast to virtually unregulated trade.

The search for a new political and, eventually, governmental outcome on the American part had become destabilising from a British perspective. In 1775, without any intention to launch a war, this process resulted in armed clashes at Concord and Lexington, as a result of an ill-advised attempt to seize illegal arms dumps, clashes that rapidly became war.

Liberty or Death

'. . . it is natural to man to indulge in the illusions of hope . . . I am willing to know the whole truth; to know the worst, and to provide for it . . . If we wish to be free . . . we must fight . . . The millions of people, armed in the holy cause of liberty, and in such a country as that which we possess, are invincible . . . Give me liberty, or give me death!'

Patrick Henry, Virginia Convention
to the Continental Congress, March 1775

A Former President Explains

'The revolution in the southern states was initiated by wealthy and influential political leaders along the coast, but the responsibilities for combat were shifting to those backwoodsmen, some of whom would never yield even when their plight seemed hopeless.'

Jimmy Carter, *The Hornet's Nest. A Novel of the Revolutionary War* (2003)

5

New Boundaries, 1775–1825

America in 1788

In his *New Travels in the United States of America, 1788*, Jacques-Pierre Brissot, who was to be guillotined in the Reign of Terror in France, wrote of Philadelphia's markets:

> 'Multitudes of men and women, mingling about and going in every direction, but without bumping into each other and without tumult or abuse of one another. One would think it a market of brothers, the meeting place of a nation of philosophers.'

And of New York:

> 'If there is one city on the American continent which above all others displays European luxury, it is New York . . . They are afraid to marry because it is so expensive to keep a wife.'

For Maryland and Virginia:

> '[Y]ou think you are in another world . . . Everything bears the stamp of slavery . . . you find real poverty existing alongside a false appearance of wealth.'

The possibility for new departures was clearly seen in the Hawai'ian archipelago where a state incorporating hitherto independent islands was established through conflict. This new state proved singularly durable, only collapsing as a result of the takeover by a far more powerful America in the late nineteenth century.

Replacing, or at least supplementing, spears, clubs, daggers and sling-shots, Kamehameha (*c.*1736–1819), who dominated the west coast of the island of Hawai'i, a coast frequented by European ships, and whose army increased in size to about 12,000 men, used guns and cannon to help win control of that island in 1791, and of those of Maui and O'ahu in 1795, with the key engagements, notably Nu'uanu in 1795, occurring on land. Nu'uanu, or in Hawai'ian *kaleleka'anae*, which means the leaping mullet, refers to the defended O'ahu army being driven back to a cliff edge where they were pushed over the 1,000-foot drop. In 1796 and 1803, difficult waters and disease ended Kamehameha's plans to invade the island of Kaua'i. Nevertheless, in 1810, Kaua'i submitted rather than risk invasion, although the submission was precarious for most of the decade.

Arriving in 1815, Russian traders sought to establish a mercantile and imperial presence in Hawai'i, with George Schäffer, an agent for the Russian-American Company, seeking to be the exclusive agent for Kaua'i's sandalwood trade and to lead Kaua'i's forces in a conquest of O'ahu, thus reversing Kamehameha's success. Fort Elizabeth was accordingly built on Kaua'i in 1817, with two other forts following. However, Schäffer lacked the backing of the Russian government, while the unification of the archipelago by Kamehameha put paid to his hopes, and Kamehameha's supporters gained control of the forts.

Kamehameha became the first king of the Hawai'ian Islands and unified the legal system of the islands. His successor, Kamehameha II (r. 1819–24), visited Britain, only to die there of measles. In turn, Kamehameha II's younger brother, Kamehameha III (r. 1824–54), had to confront both the impact of disease on population numbers and growing Western pressures, including over religion and independence. The future prospectus for the archipelago was unclear, and there was scant reason to see it as likely to become an American possession.

Firearms also served Western expansion, as with the Russians in the Aleutian islands in the 1760s, with cannon effective against the Aleut villages. Massacres and Western diseases were also significant. Effective resistance on the Fox Islands had started in 1761 when traders on Ilmnak were killed. However, five years later, Ivan Solovief, a merchant from Okhotsk, organised a fleet that successively overcame resistance. Moreover, mass conversions of the Kodiak Aleutians to Russian Orthodoxy began in 1794. The Tlingits in the eastern Aleutian Islands proved more formidable as a result of their greater numbers and of acquiring British and American firearms, and, in 1802, destroyed the Russian settlement of New Archangel on the island of Sitka. It was re-established in 1804 after a long bombardment of the island by Russian warships. However, the following year the Russian base at Novorossiisk was destroyed. Paralleling the situation in northeast Siberia, where resistance long continued, opposition to the increasingly unprofitable Russian presence in southern Alaska did not stop until Russian claims were sold to the United States in 1867.

Native American Slavery in Alaska

'Slaves or Kalags were taken during wartime. They have complete authority over the life of a slave. Even today they are sometimes killed during a gift ceremony or during dances or when an important leader dies. Poor, sick or weak slaves who cannot be sold or given away are killed.'

Kyrill Khlebnikov, chief clerk of the
Russian-American Company, 1817

Elsewhere in the period covered by this chapter, the role of a variety of 'European' powers in North America, including the future USA, was consolidated. This consolidation included the end of Spanish power in Louisiana, Florida and Mexico and of French power in Louisiana. In contrast, Britain strengthened its presence in Canada, not least by repelling four American offensives. The net impact was a divided Anglo North America and a United States that would have been very different had it conquered Canada. There would have been a strongly Catholic Québec within America and also states that did not have slavery. The Canadian states, with the exception of Québec, would probably have aligned with New England rather than the South, and this would have greatly affected the balance of American politics. This was not least if each former Canadian colony became a state with, in addition, the division of Ontario on the model of the American colonies that were to be divided as a consequence of westward expansion.

The Declaration of Independence, issued on 4 July 1776, was intended to encourage international backing, notably from France, by making it less likely that the conflict would end in a reconciliation within the British empire. The conflict ceased to be a rebellion and, instead, became the first instance of a trans-Atlantic European settler colony seeking independence, which was a radical step. This outcome made foreign support more worthwhile, both to foreign powers and to the American Patriots.

Conversely, it became necessary for the British to secure military results that achieved the political outcome of an end to a drive for independence. This outcome was likely to require both a negotiated settlement and acquiescence in the return to loyalty and in subsequently maintaining obedience, which would have rested on very different politics to that of the conquest of New France (Canada) during the Seven Years' War, a step secured by the governor's surrender in 1760 and the subsequent Anglo-French peace negotiations in Paris in 1762–3. The demographics were also very different. The French colonial population in North America was far smaller than that of Britain, with about 56,000 inhabitants in French Canada by 1740, compared to nearly a million people of European background in British North America. Indeed, British emigration to North America had been seen as a threat by French diplomats.

Political contexts established particular strategic issues. In the case of the War of American Independence, it was unclear to the British how to translate military outcomes into political results, and also whether the best outcomes related to defeating American Patriots or supporting Loyalists in what was also an American civil war. If the former was the policy, it was uncertain whether it was to be achieved by winning control over territory or by defeating Patriot armies. The British government did not want, and could not afford, a large occupation force. Instead, its rule depended on consent, and the solution to the rebellion was seen as political as much as military. The understanding of this may make British warmaking seem modern, involving as it did hearts and minds, but, in practice, this technique was common to counter-revolutionary warfare when the revolution, far from being restricted to marginal groups in society, included the socially prominent.

However, the availability of a linked political–military strategy did not guarantee success in North America, or elsewhere. The Continental Congress, the Patriot government, rejected negotiations, notably in 1776 and 1778, and the British found it difficult to build up the strength of the Loyalists. Indeed, John Adams, a prominent revolutionary and later second American president, suggested that the very act of revolution led to its success.

As with other revolutionary struggles, the war was a political as much as a military struggle; therefore, the revolutionaries had to convince themselves, and the British, that there was no alternative to independence, which helped encourage the denouncing of George III. Adams was certainly accurate as far as his base of New England was concerned, for it contained few active Loyalists; but the colonists were less unified elsewhere and, in particular, there was much Loyalism in Georgia, North Carolina, and in sections of the Middle Colonies, such as Long Island and the eastern shore of the Chesapeake. Indeed, divisions among the colonists meant that winning over the middle ground was significant for each side, and for both military and political reasons. Furthermore, as Canada and the British Caribbean did not join the rebellion, this helped define the America that did not happen. The French Canadians were far more suspicious of the Americans than they were of the British, in part because of their Catholicism and in part due to long-term enmity with the American colonies.

The politicisation of much of the American public, to which Adams referred, and the motivation of many of their troops were important aspects of what was conventionally seen as 'modernity' when this state was understood in terms of mass mobilisation and citizens' armies. Indeed, the conflict saw significant constitutional development. Thus, in 1780, a new constitution drawn up as the result of a constitutional convention held in 1779–80 was adopted in Massachusetts finally replacing the colonial charter of 1691. Ratified by a franchise unrestricted by property requirements, this included a Declaration of Rights and is still used now. Today, in contrast, modernity is more readily understood in terms of often only partly engaged publics and relatively small, volunteer professional armies. Ironically, this description was truer of the British in 1775–83 than of the Americans.

Such comparisons between the situation in the eighteenth century and later ideas of development and progress can be misleadingly ahistorical, which is also true of current 'history wars', politicised debates over history. However, these comparisons also demonstrate the possibly questionable nature of the tendency to ascribe probable victory to a popular fight for independence.

Until 1778, when France officially entered the war on their side, the Americans fought alone. They had no formal allies, although, seeking to harm Britain, France and Spain provided aid, especially munitions and money, for the Americans were short of both. The Americans also fought alone because Britain was not committed to any other war, ensuring that the British could devote their undivided attention to the colonies.

There was no major capability gap in the Americans' favour. Indeed, their cause was greatly handicapped by the problems of creating an effective war machine, including mobilising and directing resources and funding. The revolution's anti-authoritarian character and the presence of only weak national institutions made it hard to create a viable national military system.

The Americans failed to win the war with their offensives in 1775. Boston, the main British base, was too tough a nut to crack, while their invasion of Canada, although initially successful, led to the Americans closing the year with an intractable siege of Québec. In 1776, the British evacuated Boston, when their anchorage became exposed to American cannon fire, but also hit back: the Americans lost New York (1776) and Philadelphia (1777), after defeats at Long Island (1776) and Brandywine (1777). In 1776, they were driven from Canada.

Nevertheless, the Americans avoided decisive defeat. This was a key achievement given Britain's ability to focus on America. Moreover, at Saratoga in the Hudson valley in 1777, a British army was forced to surrender at the end of a campaign characterised by poor strategic insight, operational folly and an inability to cope with the tactical needs of the battlespace, a situation that was to be repeated at Yorktown on the Chesapeake in 1781. Furthermore, the British failed to create an effective pacification policy in the area they controlled.

Independence owed much to the war broadening out from 1778 into a general struggle for the succession to the British empire, one involving conflict from India and the Indian Ocean to the West Indies. In the event, the British retained most of the empire, in particular defeating military challenges not only to Jamaica, Gibraltar, Canada, and England itself, but also the closest comparison with the American war, that of opposition in India. Thus, there was a distinctive character to the outcome of American independence, owing to persistent foreign interventionist support, to a degree greater than France offered to eventually unsuccessful opposition in Scotland in 1745–6 and in Ireland in 1795–8.

In addition, a key (but not the sole) difference between the separatist struggles of 1775–83 and 1861–5 was that the latter did not receive foreign military backing. The latter was particularly necessary in the American War of Independence because the American colonies then very much focused, demographically, politically and economically, on coastal areas and cities. These were especially vulnerable to British amphibious operations and, conversely, aided from 1778 by French equivalents. Control over Boston, New York, Philadelphia, Charleston and Savannah proved particularly significant. In this, the Americans not only benefited from French naval and army support, notably in what became the decisive Yorktown campaign of 1781, but also from the decision to create a regular army able to take part in conventional operations and thus interoperable with the French. The commander of this force, the Continental Army, George Washington, an absolutely pivotal figure, provided a unitary, national focus very different from that of state militaries.

Washington was answerable to the Continental Congress, the peripatetic location of which reflected the difficulties of the war. Alongside the central role of the individual states, the Continental and Confederation Congresses offered a proto-national direction of the war effort, but could not deploy resources readily. There was certainly no comparison with the central direction of resources and radical mobilisation of society in the case of Revolutionary France, especially in 1793–4. In part, this reflected a political radicalisation of revolution in France that was not matched in America even when the war went badly in late 1776. Moreover, the new American government did not take over the basis of an existing state as occurred in France.

Independence was achieved in 1783, but this victory over the world's impressive leading maritime power was damaging. Much of the war was fought on American soil and with heavy casualties; many talented Americans who were Loyalists were driven into exile, banned from public life, or treated brutally; and the army was left discontented over its treatment and, notably, payment of arrears. This risked repeating the move from new republic to military rule seen in England in 1649–53, a route that was to be followed in France in 1792–9 and, in each case, with this rule culminating in a military dictatorship, those of Oliver Cromwell and Napoleon Bonaparte. The route to dictatorship was also seen in Haiti and Mexico, when European rule was overthrown in the early nineteenth century. America was highly unusual in its trajectory. In part, this was because the winning of independence, while difficult, was easier than in many other new states, notably Haiti and Venezuela. The new Spanish American nations failed to agree to any equivalent of the American 'Articles of Confederation' that could have resulted in a single, unitary Spanish American state with sufficient geopolitical power and resources to rival the United States in the Western hemisphere.

In the emerging United States (until the Constitution was ratified in 1791, the Confederation not the United States), the particular contingencies of the 1780s and 1790s were also significant. These included the compromises involved in the constitution. Territorial independence interacted with the political counterpart permitted by voting in the new state and the economic counterpart of working in a capitalist economy increasingly using cash and market mechanisms. Republicanism was the ideology, but it had many meanings and faced numerous hurdles. Indeed, anxiety was central to American republicanism, and the latter did not prevent an eventual civil war in 1861–5. The possibilities of military rebellion offered in particular in the Newburgh Conspiracy in 1782–3 and in the suspicious negotiations of Aaron Burr and General Wilkinson in the 1800s and early 1810s no more led to a breakdown than did disturbances in Massachusetts and Pennsylvania: Shays' Rebellion of 1786–7 and the Whiskey Rebellion of 1794. So also with the Alien and Sedition Acts of 1798, a contested presidential election in 1800, and New England separatist speculations in 1814–15.

Much was owed to the attempt by the revolutionary leadership to ground and maintain the new state. The constitution, which was difficult to amend and therefore favoured the status quo, served to adjust and arbitrate differences, rather than as a template for decisive state-building. In particular, Washington proved willing to transfer from military to elected leader, and then to avoid the temptation to retain his presidential post.

At the Constitutional Convention in 1787, Alexander Hamilton had put forward the idea of an 'elective monarch'. This was rejected, other than there being a presidential re-election every four years. No president, however, prior to Franklin Roosevelt (r. 1933–45), was re-elected more than once. The 'Founding Fathers' sought a mixed government, but one that, in their eyes, was free of the problems of the British constitution, which, they had argued, included an arbitrary rule that could compromise liberty. That was of course the condition of slaves. Democracy alone was seen as anarchic and, instead, there was interest in a trinity of President, Senate and House of Representatives. The checks and balances of American mixed government, which included an independent judiciary and the indirect election of the president by an Electoral College, were in part a matter of fear, Adams writing to Jefferson in 1787 about the new constitution: 'you are apprehensive of monarchy; I, of aristocracy. I would therefore have given more power to the President and less to the Senate.' This was a debate from the world of Classical republicanism, and indeed of more recent versions including both Venice and the Netherlands. This debate included fear of the authority of a president, Patrick Henry complaining:

> 'If your American chief be a man of ambition and abilities, how easy is it for him to render himself absolute. The army is in his hands, and if he be a man of address, it will be attached to him ... Away with your president! We shall have a king: the army will salute him monarch.'

Adams, who otherwise argued there was 'no special providence for Americans, and their nature is the same with that of others', was more sanguine about the presidency, but pointed out: 'It is a happy circumstance that the object of our devotion [Washington] is so well deserving of it.' Indeed, he was to be no Cromwell nor a *caudillo* on the Latin American model. In reality, combining the head of the executive with head of state created a dilemma, not least in the event of contested elections. Repeatedly, presidents were to be criticised as monarchs exceeding their power, Jackson in 1833 as King Andrew the First.

To contemporaries, a key element was the ecclesiastical settlement. This reflected both federalism and the particular Enlightenment mindset of the Founding Fathers. This was not anti-religious, but, rather, against the idea of the imposition of ecclesiastical authority. Thus, the First Amendment to the constitution banned Congress from passing any law 'respecting an establishment of religion', meaning an official church able to prevail over other churches. Some states had their own established churches, but there was none at the national level, a key element of federalism. Moreover, the last of the former, the Congregationalist Church of Massachusetts, was disestablished in 1833. As a result, religion was assumed to be a matter of individual choice.

Checks and balances were also inherent in the relationship between the federal government and the states. Thus, James

Madison's proposal at the Constitutional Convention for a congressional veto power over state laws was not implemented. Alongside identity formation in the new American nation, notably in the world of print and rhetoric, there was a reality in which there was not a consolidated national sphere or a unified economy. Instead, there was a set of localities best represented by the federalism of the political system, a situation that contributed to sectional, more than national, views. Sectionalism, in turn, was to play a major role in divisions over the incorporation of new territories, a new version of the American concern to gain control of land. Furthermore, there was a tension between an advancing frontier creating new territory to incorporate, politically, economically and psychologically, and, on the other hand, existing views of country and people, state and nation.

Pressure to build up a professional army was linked to a key division in American politics, that between proponents and opponents of a stronger state, the former the Federalists under Alexander Hamilton, and the latter the Democratic-Republicans under Thomas Jefferson. However, the implications of such an army for the American state remained latent because there were no external or internal challenges to match those that were to face France in the 1790s.

In a competitive international context, the Federalists argued for a shift of power from the states to the federal government, and from regions to the national level. This was unwelcome to many not only in specific terms but also because of the opposition to distant government already seen in the American Revolution. Key elements were the size of the military and the provision of a national bank. Rejecting the views of those who felt that the militia were more effective than regulars, the governing Federalists expanded the army in 1798, during the 'Quasi-War' with France, with Washington as commander in chief and Hamilton as senior ranking major general, although the army was not required for combat during the conflict. Hamilton sought to develop the force as a powerful permanent body able to unite America against internal subversion and foreign threat, but his intentions were suspect to many Americans and he was accused of authoritarian aspirations. Nevertheless, the Federalists built up a professional army, although it was also both politicised and greatly affected by personality-based factionalism, again pointing to American non-exceptionalism.

Hamilton's emphasis on a strong army as a defence against foreign attack and domestic subversion was to be matched by Simón Bólivar, the president from 1819 to 1830 of Gran Colombia (Venezuela, Ecuador and Colombia), a state that rapidly divided, as did that in Central America. In contrast, America survived as a united state. This reflected political skills, but also contingent events and a measure of luck, both of which ran out in 1861. The American constitution itself was not necessary, as was to be seen by the survival as united states of Argentina and Brazil. However, these saw earlier civil wars than America. Conversely, many Latin American states adopted constitutions similar to that of America, but without the consequence of avoiding dictatorship.

Benefiting from a vigour and popularity stemming from the Quasi-War, the Federalists linked foreign and domestic policies closely to military preparedness. 'Millions for defence, but not one cent for tribute' (to a foreign state) became their slogan after the 'XYZ' affair, a French attempt, when Washington's successor as president, John Adams (1797–1801), sought to settle differences, to make the Americans buy them off. The limiting consequences of federal financial weaknesses ensured, however, that the construction of ten frigates during the Quasi-War was financed by subscriptions raised in the major ports, such as Philadelphia.

The Federalist government also passed the Alien and Sedition Acts in order to strengthen it against internal opposition, a major step in the process of 'constitutionalising politics and politicising the Constitution' seen in the 1790s. This, however, proved a divisive step, for, in response, while asserting states' rights in their

Resolutions, Kentucky and Virginia denounced the Acts as violations of the American Constitution and thus, in effect, pressed the role of state governments in deciding the constitutional character of federal actions. Adams' son, the diplomat John Quincy Adams, called the Resolutions a 'tocsin of insurrection', and Jefferson, the vice-president under Adams and an opponent of Hamilton, thought rebellion in Pennsylvania a possibility. A small-scale rising, Fries' Rebellion, was played up by Hamilton in order to justify a display of federal power and to expand the army. Hamilton considered moving the army into Virginia in order to overawe opposition and prevent Virginians from preparing for resistance. In practice, opposition to the Acts was widespread and took forward the hostility seen earlier in the decade to the assumptions and policies of the Federalists, assumptions and policies that had a counter-revolutionary character in so far as they sought to contain the radical aspects and implications of the American Revolution. Separately, there was scant interest in Virginia to such radicalism as ending slavery.

Jefferson, like other Americans of his political viewpoint, was concerned that American diplomats might be corrupted by living amongst the wicked Europeans, though he had already spent some time in Europe himself and loved Paris. Jefferson discouraged the development of the American diplomatic service, which, whatever the quality of individual diplomats, retained a relatively amateurish approach until the reforms of the 1940s.

Another basis of American diplomacy was that entailed in federalism. The representation of the individual colonies was especially important as the Constitution was being negotiated and put into practice. Indeed, the Constitution was a diplomatic agreement between and among the sovereign American states. Thereafter, this representation remained a factor in American politics, with senators, in particular, serving as if diplomats, notably in negotiating on behalf of their constituencies. This issue was pushed to the fore when regional interests were especially at issue, as in the Jay-Gardoqui negotiations of 1786 when the states of New England and New York were willing to forego the right to trade on the Mississippi, thereby selling out the interests of the Southwest, in exchange for favourable trade relations with Spain.

It took time for American political practice and theory to define a workable response to the needs of diplomacy. For instance, as a result of the Longchamps affair in 1784, in which a French diplomat was attacked, the Supreme Court was given jurisdiction over international law, and the authority of the individual states was subordinated, as it also was in the case of regulating foreign and domestic (interstate) trade.

The key point as far as American diplomacy was concerned, both during the Revolution and thereafter, was that it was republican, not radical. This was shown in particular by the refusal to recognise Haiti once it won freedom from French rule. A Black state proved too much for the influential slaveholding interests, and Haiti was not recognised until 1862. Like the treatment of slavery, this was hypocritical for a nation claiming to be built on the 'self-evident truths' that 'all men are created equal and endowed with certain inalienable rights'.

Regional and other tensions led to reports of the imminent dissolution of the Union, while there was a more general localist hostility to the payment of taxes, and notably for the national government. That the latter's army provided a force that could impose taxation amplified the problem. Differences over the size and organisation of the military reflected contrasting assumptions about the nature of the newly independent American colonies as a state and about American society. A rift in the latter was discerned by foreign commentators, such as Edward Thornton, the British envoy, who contrasted 'a commanding aristocratic influence which pervades their system of government' with 'a strong principle of democracy among the common people'.

The free colonists had more equal incomes than households in England and Wales prior to the Revolution, only to be hit by a decline in real per capita terms in 1775–90. At this stage average Southern per capita White income was higher than further north, in part due to the number of poor Whites in Northern cities, but, thanks to Northern growth, the South began to lose this income lead by 1800, despite the prosperity of the late 1790s benefiting Southern staple producers, and large-scale poverty affected the southern White population thereafter. This was an important background to its politics.

There was social stratification, most clearly in societies with slavery, and less so when slavery was absent. In Santa Fé, a census of 1790 revealed strata defined by race, from Spanish-born *españoles* of pure blood, via mixed ancestry to *indio*. In newly independent America there were more free Blacks than before, but also an increase in the number of slaves in the South. At the same time, the end of slavery in Northern states did not mean the end of discrimination and segregation. What was seen as Black assertiveness could lead to harsh action, as in New York in the early 1820s when African-American actors were violently harassed.

To Jefferson, Hamilton's interest in money, notably the establishment of the first Bank of the United States, and his alliance with the growing financial interest, was part of his drive to establish an aristocratic elite of managed men, based in the national capital, and seeking to create a new centralised power. Looked at differently, Hamilton and Federalists saw federal government as a tool for economic development, an argument that was to impact later Whigs who were influential in the 1830s, such as Henry Clay, and, from them, Abraham Lincoln and the Republicans of the 1860s. Drawing on significant entrepreneurial interests, there were other aspects of integration, for example the Philadelphia–Lancaster turnpike and regular stagecoach services, including a one-day service between New York and Philadelphia.

For Jefferson, the struggle that had given rise to the Revolution was to be repeated, but with the threat based in America, although looking to Britain. Jefferson thus domesticated and politicised the

European anti-aristocratic discourse and the suspicion of finance and credit, and linked them to an account of public virtue and a narrative of American history that he indeed sought to shape, not least through arranging his papers for publication and through the use of gossip and rumour. Both of these means were related to the concern for honour and reputation that were so important to American politicians, as well as to counterparts elsewhere, for example in Colombia. The emphasis on honour made compromise more difficult as did the impassioned rhetoric of leading politicians as they additionally sought to rally support. As president (1801–9), Jefferson democratised the presidency, selling Adams' coach and six horses, abolished the formal levées of Washington and Adams, shaking hands with visitors instead of acknowledging their bows, and eliminating formal seating and service at receptions, although African Americans were present only as servants.

The racial refraction of American history ensured that Jefferson could present himself as a democrat while being the second biggest slaveholder in Albemarle County, with many slaves, extensive cash holdings, and an aristocratic consumption pattern. Jefferson had to withstand bitter criticism of slavery from Lafayette, the French posterboy of the American Revolutionary cause, when he visited Monticello in 1824 and 1825. To Jefferson, a revived America meant an America that had defeated at home its leading foe, with democracy the means and result of victory. In practice, John Adams, whom Jeffersonians attacked as an aristocrat, was a product of the highly democratic culture of New England, while Jefferson's political legacy was initially to be carried forward by Southern landowners who were slave-owning aristocrats, rather than the autonomous family farmers whom he idealised on a Classical model as well as that of eighteenth-century English Tories. A similar process can also be seen in Latin America where republicanism in practice depended on racial discrimination.

Force came close to playing a role in the bitterly contested election of 1800 in which Jefferson beat Adams, the election providing the first transfer of power from one political party to another, thus underlining the possibilities of orderly change through an electoral process as well as the significance of parties. The governors of Pennsylvania and Virginia, Thomas McKean and James Monroe, were prepared to march their militia on Washington to prevent the Federalists from, as they saw it, stealing the election. Worries that the army intended to remove the federal arms stored in Virginia led to plans to have the state secure them, and like concern about politics after the Civil War, led to pressure for a small army, which affected America's capacity for power projection. Jefferson and the Democratic-Republicans who gained power after the election rejected Hamilton's military plans. They were not interested in what they saw as an authoritarian army of imperial size, nor indeed in a European-style military, being opposed to the taxes maintaining such an army entailed and the dependency this taxation was believed to give rise to, and suspicious of the existing army, not least because most of the senior officers were Federalists and because they saw the army as a threat to liberty, both republican and individual.

Indeed, Jefferson limited the peacetime army establishment to 3,284 men, a tiny force, and sought to rely on a citizen soldiery organised in the militia and supposedly committed to a republican view of America. As president, he preferred to rely on national unity, which was an example of the comforting illusion that virtue would necessarily prevail. This view led him, in his inaugural address in 1801, to claim that America's republican form of government was the strongest in the world. Yet, subsequently, confronted by the difficulties of using the militia, Jefferson realised that he could not do without any national army, and he came both to strengthen this army and to make it, in his eyes, a more reliable part of the polity by replacing Federalist officers with Republicans and by creating the United States Military Academy at West Point (where he is memorialised) as a means to ensure both professional education and political reliability, through recruitment and training.

More generally, Jefferson, who looms largest in personality of the presidents between Washington and Lincoln, in shaping the national mindset, sought to downplay the federal government. Instead, he emphasised a national political community that took its dynamic from popular, not institutional, energy, and that was decentralised: an 'Empire of Liberty', he claimed in 1780. Independence was presented as depending on liberty, with external vigilance the price of liberty. Jefferson's concern for farming meant that land was the measure of national health as well as power, and this encouraged his lack of sympathy with the occupation of land by Native Americans, who were uncivilised in his eyes as well as failing to use the land productively. It was claimed that if the Native Americans moved from hunting to farming, as in the conventional stadial scheme of human development, they would require less land as well, freeing it for new settlers, while the Native Americans themselves became more civilised and more open to Christian proselytism. Most regarded Native Americans simply as savages and did not appreciate the character and strengths of their (varied) societies. Imperial ideas circulated, Washington declaring America in 1783 a 'rising empire'. However, that aspiration faced the reality of Native American opposition, interstate rivalry, and disagreement over the role of the federal government or indeed the state ones, the last an element that continues to the present.

The diffusion of European weaponry and horses continued to be important in North America, and, indeed, became more significant as the range of trade increased. Moreover, these arms contributed to a situation in which the Europeans were not necessarily the dominant party. For example, in 1776, there were only 1,900 troops to defend the frontier of Spanish North America. Goods and trade were used by the Spaniards to keep the peace with the Native Americans, but the idea of Comanche subjugation through external manipulation by Spanish officials in the 1780s ignores the nature of Comanche political culture. The Comanche co-operated with the Spaniards in attacks on the Apache in the late 1780s, but only to suit their own goals. Spanish attempts to direct and manipulate Comanche warmaking were repeatedly unsuccessful.

Even east of the Mississippi, the Native Americans remained formidable, notably the Creeks in the Southeast. However, an American invasion in 1779 devastated Iroquois lands in central and western New York and in the Treaty of Fort Stanwix (1784) the Iroquois lost most of their lands. There was a change in the Ohio Valley: the end of the British presence and the absence of strong government encouraged frontiersmen to seize Native American lands in the mid-1780s. In 1787, there was an attempt by the Confederation Congress to create a more orderly situation, but relations with the Native Americans were characterised by mutual distrust. Initially, the Americans found it difficult to prevail. In 1790, there was a failed invasion of Native American territory designed to end the violence stemming from Native American hostility to what were seen as extorted land cessions in treaties of 1785–9. A Native American army successfully attacked an American force at Kekionga. The Native American capacity to mount a major attack was abundantly demonstrated.

However, in 1794, the Ohio Native Americans were heavily defeated at Fallen Timbers. In part, this defeat indicated the significance of political factors, particularly the Anglo-American treaty of 1794 which led Britain to abandon its Native American allies. Linked to this, the Native Americans agreed by the Treaty of Greenville in 1795 to cede much of Ohio to the Americans. At the same time, this took time to move from being an illusion of authority over an important part of the West between the Alleghenies and the Mississippi.

In terms of control over most of North America, this campaigning was as, if not more, significant than the struggles over dominance between Europeans that had left the British in control by 1763 over the eastern seaboard and part of the hinterland, for this control to be partly lost in 1775–83 (the British retained their position in Canada and the Spaniards regained Florida). The War of Independence was important to the issue of control over the North American interior: the war disrupted relations between the British and the Native Americans, many of whom backed the British during the war. Moreover, Patriot campaigning against the Native Americans, campaigning which drew on a harsh racism, proved very damaging, notably for the Iroquois, but also for Native American societies that were not devastated, for instance the Creek. The war also affected African-American slaves, many of whom had sought to escape under its cover, while some backed the British, a pattern that was to be repeated in the War of 1812–15 with Britain.

As a result of their failure in Saint-Domingue/Haiti, Louisiana became apparently worthless to the French, and Napoleon sold it to Jefferson in order both to stop it being a target for British attack and to gain money for operations in Europe. For sixty million *louis*, or $15 million, which was arranged by the Barings bank in London, America gained over eight hundred thousand square miles, with no clear borders as the lands covered by the Louisiana Purchase were not mapped, and were to be defined by the Transcontinental Treaty with Spain in 1819. In the event, the Purchase brought America all, or much, of the future states of Montana, North and South Dakota, Minnesota, Wyoming, Colorado, Nebraska, Iowa, Kansas, Missouri, Oklahoma, Arkansas and Louisiana, while America also claimed the Oregon Country (which included the modern states of Oregon and Washington as well as part of Canada) as part of the Purchase.

In practice, the vast majority of the territory gained by this Purchase was under Native American control. Indeed, as a result of the problems in mobilising the militia, the Americans had only been able to assemble a small force at Natchez on the Mississippi in order to overcome any resistance in Louisiana that might arise on behalf of Spain. Jefferson pushed the Purchase through without Congressional approval prior to presenting it as virtually an accomplished fact. The Senate ratified the treaty on 21 October 1803, by a vote of 24 to 7, the Federalist opponents being concerned about the dangerous implications of such an expansion in terms of the balance of interests and ambitions within the country.

The different possibility that Louisiana would be the basis of a separate state was considered by Jefferson, although he was not troubled by it as he thought that common values would bind the two states (Louisiana and America) together. In particular, slaveholding continued.

Jefferson's first-term vice-president, Aaron Burr, sought, in 1804–6, British naval and financial support for his plans for an independent Louisiana, which he claimed would be followed by independence for Florida and parts of Latin America. In the event, although he gained support in New Orleans, Burr failed because he exaggerated his strength and was unable to maintain secrecy, the latter leading to his arrest. So also with the failure of the separatist plans of the self-serving American fixture Brigadier-General James Wilkinson, who had betrayed Burr in 1806, although Wilkinson was exonerated by the court martial that tried him and went on to military and then diplomatic service. Meanwhile, the varied dynamic character of the Black world, both slave and free, could be seen in the 1810s when Africans in Louisiana, both free and enslaved, met with the challenge of coexisting with an influx of slaves from the United States.

The American gain of Louisiana, including the crucial port of New Orleans, ensured that the Spanish stranglehold on the Gulf of Mexico was broken, challenging the Spanish position to east and west: in West Florida (the Panhandle of modern Florida and coastal Alabama) and Texas. Arguing that France had not complied with the conditions under which it had obtained Louisiana from Spain in 1800, the Spaniards had delivered a memorial against the Purchase, but it had no effect.

Assuming that it would take a long time to populate and develop the West, Jefferson pressed to define and claim Louisiana as hugely as possible, despite historical evidence to the contrary, and Madison followed suit. Seeking to limit British transcontinental expansion from Canada to the Pacific Jefferson despatched the Corps of Discovery in 1804. An expedition under Meriwether Lewis and William Clark that had been planned before the Louisiana Purchase, this asserted American interests across the new possessions to the Pacific. They also sought to establish an overland route there, a goal for which it was important to discover the headwaters of the Columbia and then follow it to the Pacific, which they reached at the close of 1805. The expedition was also seen by Jefferson as a way to thwart the possibility that the British would develop the potential for transcontinental routes shown by Alexander McKenzie who had crossed the continent in Canada in 1793, and it helped focus attention on the Pacific Northwest as a key area of American interest. Further south, the Red River Expedition of 1806 provided valuable knowledge, including a map of the river, that was to help subsequent American expansion.

There was a clear racist dimension to Jefferson's policies. This was seen in his treatment of the Native Americans, who were acceptable only if they discarded their culture, although they did not seek to stop the Lewis and Clark expedition. Jefferson's attitudes were also seen in his views of the Blacks, who were regarded as a 'captive nation'. The Louisiana Purchase enabled the spread of American slavery, a key expression and guarantor of wealth and status, and created the possibility for further expansion, which exacerbated New England concerns about the Southern domination of the federal government.

Slavery was also a challenge politically as the apportionment of representation in the House of Representatives and the

Electoral College by the Constitution counted each slave as three-fifths of a freeman, a provision that the Federalists at the Hartford Convention in 1814–15 were to resolve to remove. A racist agenda was also seen with the limited efforts initially made to enforce the ban on the slave trade which, in 1807, with effect from 1808, was prohibited by America.

Jefferson's attitudes were displayed by his refusal to extend diplomatic recognition to the independent Black state of Haiti, the product of the Saint-Domingue revolution once France failed there in 1803. Whereas the Adams government had responded favourably to Toussaint L'Ouverture's interest in diplomatic and trade links with America, and had sought to normalise relations with Saint-Domingue, a policy in full accord with the Quasi-War with a France that threatened both, Jefferson would have none of this. Friendly relations with France were more important to him, but there was also a racist dynamic. A Black state in Haiti proved too much for the influential slaveholding interests, for Black republicanism was perceived as a threat to the racial order in America. Jefferson's successors and fellow Virginians, James Madison (1809–17) and James Monroe (1817–25), supported the resettlement of freed slaves in Liberia and West Africa.

As a result of the Louisiana Purchase, which gave the Americans a major advantage in the competitive expansions in the West, America now had a far longer frontier with Canada, which increased the potential American challenge to the British position there. However, Jefferson and others overestimated American power after the Louisiana Purchase. He understood the potential of the West and was correct in his long-term appraisal that America would become a major power, but exaggerated America's future potential, as in November 1801 when he speculated that Americans would multiply and spread to 'cover the whole northern if not the southern continent'. More seriously, in the short term, Jefferson mistook America's marginal leverage in the threatening bipolar dynamic between Britain and France for a situation in which all three were major powers, which was not to be the case until the 1860s. Madison, who had been Jefferson's secretary of state and a long-time friend and ally, followed this reasoning reflexively when he became president in 1809.

This attitude ensured that, at a time when sensitivity to supposed British hostility in Trans-Appalachia was increased by the development, in fact separate, of anti-American pan-Native American religious revivalism, American policymakers saw little reason to compromise with Britain over the regulation of trade. Manipulated by Napoleon, Madison foolishly thought he had won concessions from France that justified his focusing American anger and the defence of national honour on Britain, whereas, in practice, French seizures of American shipping trading with Britain continued. Moreover, Madison had departed from Jefferson's principles in foreign policy. Crucial to these was an attempt to maintain neutrality in great-power confrontation, which Jefferson presented as the way to avoid dangerous entanglements. This departure was to have a serious consequence for America in that the War of 1812 did not work out as intended. However, as so often, the domestic context, with the fears of Britain and Native Americans, was crucial in leading to war. The pressures on Madison were serious and led Jeffersonians to fear for the survival of the republic, and certainly of their party.

In fact, the British need for peace ensured that even had New Orleans been taken in 1815, there were no plans to dominate the Mississippi Valley and link up with Canada as the French had sought to do from the 1680s to the 1750s. The stance of the British ministry contrasted with its far greater concern for the West Indies, as well as with both the bold interest in the Gulf shown by some of the local British agents and would-be agents, and the American conviction that Britain had continued designs on the South. The latter was always Andrew Jackson's justification for taking Florida and Native American territory, in order to ensure American security against Spain and, particularly, Britain.

To a certain extent, Jackson's view was one from the periphery, a view that the decentralised and representative nature of American politics was to make very important at different stages of his career. There were comparable views from the periphery in the British system, but they lacked political traction or governmental weight. The loss of the Floridas was certainly a sore spot for some in the empire, especially in the Caribbean, after 1783. Many of these people had lived in the Floridas, and had economic ties to the Creek. Thus, some British citizens sought to regain a Florida foothold while, in contrast, the home government (a body with relatively few bureaucrats) had no real interest.

This lack of interest in Florida was demonstrated after the War of 1812 in Josiah Francis's pitiful reception in London. Francis went to London to garner support for the continuing Creek fight in Florida, with the hope that Britain would be interested in regaining the Floridas. However, he was ignored while in London and returned to North America only to be captured and executed by the remorseless Jackson.

Moreover, major American victories over the Native Americans, especially the battles of the Thames over Tecumseh (1813) and of Horseshoe Bend over the Creek (1814), gravely weakened the latter east of the Mississippi. In addition, the divided Iroquois suffered as a result of their role in the defence of Canada. American victories also shattered the movement for inter-tribal unity based on the call for a restoration of sacred power, a nativist religiosity that can be profitably contrasted with movements in Christian America from the mid-eighteenth to the mid-nineteenth century. This was a form of federalism different to those seen in America or, differently, in the British position in Canada.

The collapse of successful British-Native American co-operation during the war, and the end of any real co-operation as a consequence of the peace settlement, were important to the changing relationship of Britain and America, each clearly empires as far as the Native Americans were concerned. In 1815, the Americans obliged tribes that had been allied to the British to agree to new treaties that accepted American dominance.

The domestic dimension was also significant as America had divided over going to war in 1812 and these divisions became more serious during its course. In the event, however, the war was too brief and limited to lead to major changes in the governmental system or to a transformation in the American military. Yet the end of the Federalists as an effective force was a key political development, one that reflected important changes in the geography and culture of American politics as well as specific events. Federalist opposition to the War of 1812, which was exacerbated by the weakness of the national defence effort in the face of British threats and the concomitant reliance on state-level expedients, had led to a New England Convention at Hartford (15 December 1814 – 5 January 1815) that proposed changes to the constitution designed to lessen the influence of the South and to insist on a two-thirds Congressional mandate for war. Despite trade between New England and the British Empire during the conflict, Federalist opposition to the war was not taken to the point of effective co-operation with Britain. However, the Convention, and extremist talk of secession by a minority in New England (and notably not the Convention), compromised the Federalists, who, in the aftermath of the war, disappeared as a national party. They were not only on the wrong side of the myth of American victory but also, from 1815, seemed redundant in an age of peace that rendered superfluous an opposition to the Jeffersonian policy of hostility to Britain and commercial sanctions. Moreover, the Federalists increasingly were presented and seen as a party contemptuous of the common man.

The War of 1812 led, on the American frontier, to squatters claiming Native American lands and, in 1815–18, as American troops were deployed to the then West, to a series of treaties that in effect curtailed Native American independence and led to the American government seeing itself as akin to a trustee. In military terms, the activity of the American government could be seen in occasional expeditions.

In already-settled territories, the war strengthened anti-Native American attitudes in America, not least because politicians who had played a prominent role in the conflict and were hostile to the Native Americans, such as Jackson, rose to power. The Native Americans were not to be part of the new United States, except on terms that destroyed their cultural integrity, a policy already seen in the attitudes of Jefferson, who had envisaged a choice between assimilation in an American agrarian order and being driven away into remote fastnesses, a choice that he believed had been made easier by the lands gained through the Louisiana Purchase. His attitudes were widely shared, for example by Benjamin Lincoln, the federal commissioner to the Shawnee in 1793. Even those who had helped the (European) Americans suffered, such as the Choctaw, who lost their land under treaties of 1816 and 1830.

The War of 1812 was followed by aggressive American operations in Florida, an inchoate world that weak Spanish authority made possible, and that Americans both exploited and sought to order. Thus, the Negro Fort on the Appalachicola River was destroyed in 1816 by an American amphibious force, with those Blacks not killed enslaved. An American base, Fort Scott, was established on the Appalachicola that year. The Florida Republic, created by a multi-national revolutionary force under the quixotic Sir Gregor MacGregor on Amelia Island off the Atlantic coast in 1817, defeated Spanish attempts to regain the island, but was overcome that year by American forces who saw the republicans as pirates.

A convention, signed in 1818 in London, recognised American fishing rights off Labrador and Newfoundland, and extended the frontier along the 49th Parallel, from the Lake of the Woods to the Rockies. This was a major agreed extension of the American frontier that entailed the abandonment of British interests with the cession of a considerable body of territory in the valley of the Red River, including much of the modern state of North Dakota, part of Minnesota, and a fraction of Montana, while the Americans ceded a tranche north of Montana. The views of those living there were not consulted by either Britain or America.

Moreover, the Oregon Country to the west (the lands between Spanish and Russian America comprising modern Oregon, Washington, Idaho and British Columbia), was, it was agreed in 1818, to be jointly administered by Britain and America for ten years without prejudicing existing claims. This agreement structured the American claim to a Pacific border, which had not been insisted upon at the time of the Louisiana Purchase, and gave the Americans a transcontinental presence as well as an opportunity to populate the region. Significantly, and in contrast to the situation for Britain and France after war ended in 1748, neither Britain nor America had used the unsettled state of the border after the War of 1812 as an excuse to attempt a wider revisionism nor, indeed, to reopen hostilities; nor were they to do so. This convention was extended indefinitely in 1827 and, in practice, until the Oregon Boundary Treaty of 1846 peacefully settled the territorial issue against a jingoistic but unrealistic background of American claims to what became British Columbia. Meanwhile, the geopolitics of North America was changing greatly, because the desire to emigrate and the possibility of migration that had been so important while America was part of the colonial world were unchanged in spite of independence, and a more populous United States was a key element in the geopolitics of expansionism.

6

Imperial and Divided, 1825–60

America was the most dynamic society in the Western world, with its population rising rapidly prior to the great territorial expansion of the 1840s, from 9.6 million in 1820 to 17.1 million in 1840, whereas Mexico's population, which had been similar to that of America in the late eighteenth century, rose from possibly five or five-and-a-half million in 1810 to seven million in 1840. If a rising population provides one element of coherence, the history of this period involved very diverse strands. It can be misleading to suggest a clear pattern, as in territorial expansion and development, and the problems generated by them that led to the Civil War, not least because that anticipated the outcome.

A sense of national destiny, indeed what in 1845 was termed manifest destiny, became more pronounced in America during these years and also seemed within grasp.

National Mission

'. . . our manifest destiny to overspread the continent allotted by Providence for the free development of our yearly multiplying millions.'

Anonymous editorial, *Democratic Review*, 1845

This sense was seen in the engagement with the American landscape as sublime and morally uplifting, a view clearly seen with the enthusiastic response to the self-consciously national

Hudson River school of painters and the novels of James Fenimore Cooper, including *The Pioneers* (1823), *The Last of the Mohicans* (1826), and *The Pathfinder* (1840). Regarded as more vigorous and unspoiled than those of Europe, the American landscape also appealed to British visitors such as Henry Addington, Richard Cobden and Charles Dickens. Addington found more grandeur and beauty in the Hudson Valley than in those of the Rhine, Elbe or Oder, sites of awe for European Romantics. Cobden was enthralled by the sight of the Hudson Valley in 1835, and Dickens by the sublimity of Niagara Falls in 1842.

Spanning the Continent

'This Republic now extends, with a vast breadth, across the whole continent. The two great seas of the world wash the one and the other shore.'

Daniel Webster, Senate speech, 1850

Similarly, transcendentalist thought, combining Romanticism and Deism and associated with writers such as Ralph Waldo Emerson and Henry David Thoreau, reflected a strong American optimism and was seen as a declaration of independence from Church control and traditionalism. Emerson presented America as a visionary poem, a country of young men, who, in 1775, had fired at Lexington on 19 April 'the shot heard round the world'. A Romanticism of national vision affected many individual Americans, and public culture as a whole, although the realities of life were less pleasant. Assassinated in 1881, James Garfield was, in Ohio in 1831, the last president to be born in a log cabin, and it was to a family in poverty.

The sense of national destiny had consequences within the country, in relations with America's neighbours, and also as far as the wider world was concerned. It was inscribed in America's future not only as rhetoric but also with the increasing number of pioneers who trekked west to Oregon and California, and with the growing sense that they represented the nation's future. Yet, expansionism also posed problems, not least because it interacted with growing sectional differences and greatly exacerbated them by threatening the regional balance between these sections. In particular, expansion helped shape the growing divide between North and South and gave it both a spatial dynamic and fresh issues of contention.

Expansionism, however, was also intended by some as a way to overcome this north-south divide by developing a contrary west-east alignment. In this, a prosperous interior was to be linked to the Atlantic littoral by new transport links, notably canals, such as the Erie Canal, opened in 1825 (and able to pay off the entire original loan by 1837), river improvements, steamships, railways and telegraphs, as well as by other measures of economic nationalism including tariffs to protect nascent industries and markets, the spread of banking, the standardisation of common law and creation of a system of universal duties focused on the good of the people, and the acceptance of paper currency. The values of the market were far from inevitable or uncontested. Instead, scarcely interest- or ideology-free, market mechanisms were a way to deal with the complexities of economic exchange in such a large and diverse economy. These values became the parameters for social and economic activity and were advocated by key figures. Henry Clay, a founder of the anti-Jacksonian Whig political party, proved a keen protagonist of this view of America's future, presenting it as a national solution to problems and a source of strength. Charles Vaughan, the British envoy, reported in 1827 that 'the Adams administration is attempting to turn a popular tide in its favour, by vaunting itself, as the avowed support of what has been lately termed "the American system"'. Transport improvements were seen as ways to boost nationalism and republicanism. Many of the labourers were recent immigrants. A new capital, Washington, and a meridian line through it, a goal approved by James Madison and in 1850 by Congress, were seen as aspects of a united new state.

Yet, as with other states, such plans were greatly affected by clashing concerns and values, local interests, and resource problems. Thus, the development of coal-based industry in Pennsylvania to a greater degree than in Virginia in part was due to the role in the latter of the traditional rural section, whereas Pennsylvania, which was more liberal in values and socially fluid, was readier to embrace industrial modernisation and provide the necessary investment. This modernisation challenged New England's industrial primacy.

Philadelphia saw dramatic evidence of its separate interests in 1842 when, responding to job competition from Blacks, Irish immigrants attacked African-American homes, while, in turn, anti-immigrant nativists attacked the Irish. After the use of artillery, the city was placed under martial law.

Separately, in the aftermath of the Panic of 1837, a serious fiscal crisis, there was more criticism of public investment in improvement which helped ensure that entrepreneurial capitalism played the dominant role, notably in transport developments. The role of government was affected as a consequence, with *laissez-faire* attitudes pushed to the fore, which was to provide a context for subsequent populist and progressive reactions. *Laissez-faire* can be in the eye of the beholder, as it often meant states' rights perspectives, according to the maintenance of slavery, rather than nationalist activity by Congress and/or the executive. These perspectives, which owed much to Jefferson, and were seen in particular in a renewed form from the 1830s to the early 1850s, did not necessarily mean inactivity. The political context was significant. Andrew Jackson, president from 1829 to 1837, presented himself as a man of the people, meaning White people, and, drawing on the Anglophobic and anti-Federalist legacy of Jefferson, was able to combine the interests, or at least paranoias, of Southern slaveholders, Western farmers and urban radicals. The idea of a national bank able to direct the economy was presented as unAmerican. Instead, the preference was for a minimal state and for local interests and government. This preference had helped defeat Alexander Hamilton and the Federalists from the 1800 election and it helped ensure that America did not see the development of a centralised state.

Early Railways

The British example was rapidly copied, notably in Western Europe and North America, a process encouraged by the diffusion of British technology and the availability of British investment capital, as seen with the Baltimore and Ohio Railroad, an American trailblazer.

With its rapid industrialisation, Massachusetts saw an early adoption of railways, such that in 1830–1, after first thinking of horse-drawn rail lines, the legislature chartered three private steam railway companies. This ensured a competition that helped provide opportunities for investment while also acting as a restraint on costs. By 1850, more than $50 million had been invested in New England railways, which made them the largest private companies in the country. As in Britain, traffic was sufficiently heavy, and capital plentiful enough, to enable investment in a far-flung system. Furthermore, the degree to which the canal system was limited not least as a means to go beyond the Appalachians was to encourage investment in railways.

Railway competition extended to that between ports that acted as outlets for the interior, and notably between Boston, New York and Baltimore. The Erie Railroad reached Lake Erie in 1851, providing New York with a link that thwarted Boston's hope of channelling trade from the Hudson River.

Railway companies were pioneers of large-scale managerial enterprise, which was to be important to American history. Early railways involved private enterprise but also, usually, the purchase of rail securities by states, counties and cities, as with Massachusetts and a line from Boston to Albany.

Railways struck Americans as providentially designed and a means to power and profit.

Population growth matched this *laissez-faire* system, with settlers moving westwards into Trans-Appalachia, the cotton-producing Southwest, Texas, and, for the first time, along the Overland trails to the Far West. Land sales were the biggest individual source of revenue for the central government until the 1840s. By the mid-1820s, Illinois was increasingly divided among White farmers. The rate of increase in these areas was much greater than further east; a process that was important to the reconceptualisation of America as a continental power as well as to the development of the political significance and voting strength of Trans-Appalachia. This significance, however, did not extend to sectionalism, and certainly not in comparison with that of North and South, let alone to separatism. The population growth both of America as a whole and of specific communities – for example Buffalo from 2,500 in 1825 to 81,000 in 1860 – was the context for the interaction of social stratification and mobility, with both affected greatly by religious and political alignments and division.

Geopolitics involves control over credit as well as territory and people. British investment played a significant role in American growth, especially in the development of railways, notably the Baltimore and Ohio. Moreover, as in Latin America, leading British exporters and banks mobilised capital to extend lengthy credits to American purchasers and borrowers. Yet, such dependence led to tension on the part of Americans, providing another example of a difficult relationship that looked back to colonial times. Separately, economic growth was also seen as a key way to resist Britain in any future war as it would lessen the economic reliance on foreign trade and the place of customs revenue in public finances, both of which were vulnerable to British naval action. Moreover, such growth would reduce the accumulated debt burden. The American army played a role in the economic development of the West, with the General Survey Act of 1824 providing a context for canal and railway surveys, which remained significant until 1838. There was no equivalent energy or growth in Mexico in part because the serious and violent divide there between centralisation and federalism acted as a barrier to good government.

American expansionism was primarily encouraged by several features already present prior to 1823. First was the weakness of the Native Americans. This weakness was particularly apparent without any countervailing support for them from Britain, and with the British government, in addition, keen to reassure its American counterpart that reports to the contrary were groundless. Second, the replacement of the powerful Spanish empire of the eighteenth century by two weaker states, Mexico and the much reduced Spanish empire, each of which themselves risked dissolution, was important in encouraging expansionist ideas. Third, the vast quantity of cheap and emptied land in frontier regions was important. Fourth, there was the extraordinarily high birth rate of American farm families, producing overpopulation and land pressures in older, previously settled communities. Fifth, generals played a major role in politics, with Jackson, William Henry Harrison, Zachary Taylor and Franklin Pierce all presidents between 1829 and 1857, and the 1852 election seeing Pierce opposed by another general, Winfield Scott. James Polk, president from 1845 to 1849, faced major problems in his relations with generals, but, a protégé of Jackson, was himself a key expansionist, only to be confronted by strong British support for Canada.

Championed by the Democrats and by advocates of states' rights, notably in Georgia and Alabama, which were in the heartland of the powerful Creek tribe, and opposed by the Whigs, the removal policy, which would now be described by most non-Americans and liberal-minded Americans in terms of expropriation and ethnic cleansing as well as expansionism, was driven by the demands of settlers for land. This policy was pursued explicitly from 1830 when the Indian Removal Act was passed. Native Americans lost their homelands in return for land west of the Mississippi which, from 1834, meant the Louisiana Purchase minus Louisiana, Arkansas and Missouri, which already had been established as states. The Chickasaw, for example, signed a removal treaty in 1832, and they and the Choctaw were moved in 1832–4. In 1834, the Topographical Bureau produced a 'Map of the Western Territory' designed to help plan the separation between the settlers and the Native Americans, a policy of separate development that provided land for American settlers and removed, to what were regarded as lands too arid for cultivation, the Native Americans who were seen as an unwelcome alternative presence. The latter was an important element, as land itself was not the sole issue: much of the cleared land indeed remained unsettled, although it was now allocated to American owners.

Force was employed against the Creek in 1836, in order to make those of the Creek who had not already moved west of the Mississippi in 1834, in accordance with the implications of the Treaty of Cusseta of 1832, do so. The fairly well-assimilated Cherokee had fruitlessly declared their independence as a nation in 1827, but in *Cherokee Nation v Georgia* in 1831, the Supreme Court declared the indigenous nations 'wards' of the American government (rather than sovereign nations), which opened the way to harsh treatment. The Cherokee were forcibly moved in 1838–9, with about 4,000 people out of the 14,000 moved dying as a result of the hardship and disease now known as the Trail of Tears. The Trail of Death of that year was that along which the Potawatomi were forced by Indiana militia. The Winnebago of Wisconsin, who had been brought under control in 1827 in a 'war' that involved no military conflict, were moved by the army to Iowa in 1840, a key part of the process by which most of Wisconsin had been cleared of Native Americans by 1848 without any large-scale resistance. West of the Mississippi, the Texans, once independent, were to try to drive the Native Americans from East Texas.

> 'One mile from here is a little village with several stores, which carry on trade with the Indians. The place is called St Peter's, and 6 miles from here is a little town, which increases every day in size and is very good for provision dealers; it is called St Paul. This place and the surroundings are settled with Indians, Frenchmen, and Yankees; in general there are a great many Indians here, and they bring us plenty of fish, prairie fowl, wild ducks, and geese.'
>
> Gustavus Otto, German immigrant in
> American garrison at Fort Snelling, Minnesota, 1848

Far from being tangential to American history, removal completed the disruption of Native American society east of the Mississippi, a process begun by commercial pressures and desires, cultural syncretism and White intimidation and violence. Removal also led to conflict between Native Americans, for example Osage versus Cherokee, as they competed in areas now under ecological pressure. Removal, moreover, was even more menacing because it was clearly intended by most Whites as a stage that was to be followed by the seizure of the land into which the Native Americans had been moved.

The removal policy was divisive within America as it enjoyed less support in New England, which had largely already completed the removal of tribes, than in frontier regions and the South. In each of the latter, there was by now far more hostility to the Native Americans and far more concern with land. This division, which looked back to differences over war with Britain in 1812–15, a war that was far less popular in New England, was also seen over policy towards the Seminole in Florida which led to three wars, and, later, in support for the Mexican-American War of 1846–8. The presence in the South of the Creek, Cherokee and Seminole helped give a frontier consciousness to Southern life, as did fear of slave rebellions. From the Native American perspective, there was no doubt of the pressure of American advance and aggression, but the Americans had a capacity to fear Native Americans, or at least to employ such fears in order to justify action.

The defeat of Black Hawk and his band of 1,000–2,000 Sauk and Fox in the Black Hawk War in Illinois and Wisconsin in 1832 reflected the vulnerability of tribes east of the Mississippi especially when they received no assistance from foreign powers, which could only have come in most cases from the British in Canada. Moreover, Black Hawk's attempt to revive the pan-Native American activity seen with Pontiac and Tecumseh fell foul of the weakness of this cause, not least due to the strength of rival tribal identities in the Upper Mississippi region. Indeed, there was considerable Native American military support for the American cause, as was frequently the case. Looking towards the Civil War (1861–5), Captain Abraham Lincoln of the Illinois militia and Lieutenant Jefferson Davis both took part in a campaign in which the Americans deployed larger numbers with relative ease. Davis, the regular army officer, reportedly swore Lincoln, an Illinois militia officer, into his office as captain. The war itself was an accidental conflict in that, in trying to remain in the Rock River Valley, Black Hawk and his followers did not seek a struggle which was falsely represented as an 'invasion'. Instead, the war began when troops attacked Sauk carrying a white flag. Subsequent attempts to surrender were ignored or misunderstood. Heavy losses to American firepower in the battle of the Bad Axe on 2 August brought the conflict to a close.

In Florida, a more intractable environment, overrun by the Americans in 1818–19 and ceded to them by Spain in 1820, the Seminole rejected the government's removal policy. The Second Seminole War (1835–42) began when a number of Seminole chiefs agreed to resist the removal to Oklahoma extorted in the Treaty of Payne's Landing of 1832. The American determination to end slave flight from Georgia to Florida was a powerful factor in causing the war as the Seminole provided refuge for escaped slaves. Over 40,000 troops (30,000 volunteer militia, and 10,000 regulars), were eventually deployed, especially after the Seminole, whose total population was only about 5,000, won several battles in the initial stages. Their guerrilla tactics caused problems to a number of American commanders, as did the racial politics of the conflict. An armistice came to an end in 1837, and Seminole resistance revived, when the Americans allowed slavers to enter Florida and to seize Seminole and African Americans. In contrast, in 1838, the racial politics of the struggle changed when African Americans who abandoned the Seminole and joined the Americans were offered their freedom, which cost the Seminole dear: they lost about 400 fighters. By 1842, the Seminole had been driven into the more inaccessible parts of the Florida Everglades, many had agreed to move west, and the government then felt able to wind the war down. There was no formal peace treaty.

As so often in the history of North America, demography proved a crucial factor in Texas, indeed one in which the Native Americans were at a serious disadvantage. The population of Texas grew rapidly in the 1820s and early 1830s as a result of immigration from the United States. People were seen as a source of strength and this immigration was initially encouraged by the

Mexican government, with 1824 and 1825 colonisation laws passed as a way to protect northern Mexico from the attacks of the powerful Comanche, as well as to foster economic growth and thus produce revenues for Mexico. In the event, this rise in population, which owed much to Southern land hunger and the potential for expanding cotton cultivation further west, made the situation volatile and led to Mexican concern about the degree of central governmental control in Texas. As a result, immigration from the United States was stopped from 1830. Moreover, the Mexican government's attempts to prevent the import of slaves into Texas aroused ire among the settlers: slavery had been abolished by Mexico in 1824 and 1829, although Texas was exempted. It would be far too simple to say that the Texan drive for independence rested on the maintenance of slavery, but it was both a factor and an aspect of the volatility of the period, one that was not only territorial but that was in part played out through territorial control.

Fighting between Mexicans and Texans began in October 1835 when troops from San Antonio sought to take back a cannon they had provided for the town of Gonzales in 1831 to help it deter attack by Native Americans. As with the American War of Independence, control over arms was a spark to initial conflict. The following month, a convention known as the Consultation of all Texans created a provisional state government which was designed to negotiate with Mexico, but the Mexican strongman, General Antonio López de Santa Anna, characteristically tried to deal with the situation by force. The abrogation in 1835 of the 1824 constitution, under which the Americans had settled in Texas, and the claim that their failure to convert to Catholicism meant that their land grants were void, were unacceptable to the Texans.

The establishment of Texas in 1836 as a result of Mexican defeat reflected a fissiparous tendency that was latent within America with its strong regional differences. As a result, Texas posed a challenge for America. It suggested that American expansion might well lead to a series of states which would both weaken America, by creating potentially strong neighbours, and, despite hopes of a federation of such states, could also provide a challenge as to how these states should co-operate with each other and with America. Texan independence posed the challenge of a model that might spread within America, in the aftermath, in particular, of the Nullification Crisis, and one that could, more plausibly, be employed in other areas not then in the United States, such as California, or as part of the result of the Oregon question. In California, a revolt in 1831 by Pio de Jesus Pico, a wealthy landowner, led not to independence but to Pico becoming governor for the Mexican government. The Nullification Crisis in South Carolina was very different in its character, but there was a common theme of regional distinction and assertiveness and the pursuit of states' rights.

Yet, if Texas was to be incorporated within America, this outcome posed the danger (and opportunity) that the balance of interests there, notably over slavery, would be greatly altered, not least if Texas entered as several states. As a result, the Texan issue threw the issues of Southern distinctiveness and the consequences of future American expansion harshly into the limelight. In May 1844, James Buchanan was certain that Martin Van Buren would not be chosen as Democratic candidate for the presidency because he had come out against the immediate annexation of Texas, which was rejected by the Senate that June by 35 to 16 in large part as a consequence of its being presented as a means to protect slavery. As Buchanan noted, the South, in contrast, was united in favour of such annexation: 'the Texas question has absorbed the Anti-Tariff feeling there'. Indeed, the economic interests and regional concerns that had been focused on opposition to the tariff regime were, instead, focused, with greater intensity and more divisive effect, on slavery. In the event, James Polk beat Van Buren to the Democratic nomination on the ninth ballot and then, with the solid support of the South, won the presidency against Henry Clay, who, like Van Buren, was against immediate annexation: although the margin in the popular vote was only 38,181.

Texas did more than accentuate American political divisions, because, as a sovereign republic, it raised the issue of America's international position in a volatile fashion. Texas was able to pursue its own policies, but also attracted the interest of other states, notably Britain and France. With a clear preference for paranoia, American politicians were soon concerned that Texas would become a protectorate for one or both, and that this would challenge American interests in the West and more generally. Slavery played a role in this issue, as in so much else, as British policy towards the recognition of Texas was affected by its reintroduction of slavery, which had been abolished by Mexico as well as Britain. In turn, pro-slavery Southerners, especially from 1843, saw Britain as having ruined its West Indian colonies by emancipation and as now intent on wrecking the competitive economies, notably the South, by making them abolish slavery. Moreover, American politicians regarded Texas as the base for the expansion of British and French interests in neighbouring areas, so that they might become active players in the future of the western part of North America. Alarmist American commentators linked Canada, Oregon and Texas as aspects of a British determination to control the future.

Texas was also very much an unfinished issue in international relations as the Mexican Senate refused to accept its independence. There were expeditions and raids by both sides, but full-scale conflict between Mexico and Texas was avoided, in part because western Texas was dominated by Native Americans, particularly Comanche. Texas was more exposed to Native American raids than other frontier areas and, in turn, sought to enforce its control over the Native Americans, leading to campaigns against them. In 1840, the Great Comanche Raid down the Guadalupe River to the Gulf of Mexico was intercepted at Plum Creek near Austin, and the Comanche thereafter did not raid settled communities east of San Antonio, but the war exhausted Texans as well as the Comanche. Further east, the Texans faced opposition from rebellious Native Americans and Mexicans near Nacogdoches in 1838, in part because the Texans sought to drive out Native American refugees from east of the Mississippi who had settled in east Texas.

The borders and future of Texas were also unclear and attempts to advance goals reflected the volatility of the situation. A fourth, far-flung empire in North America might have arisen, following America, Britain (in Canada), and Mexico; and this empire could have expanded to the Pacific. If so, it would have blocked or affected American expansion. Counterfactuals are only so useful, and Texas was greatly weakened by its lack of settlers, the factor common to all these empires in the West, but that problem would have been lessened with time. Indeed, the possibility of Texan expansion was one that worried American politicians, while the continued conflict in the area and the prospect of more large-scale warfare were also of concern. Very differently, the Mormons developed Utah and had a separatist imperial vision with the state there they termed Deseret.

Alexis de Tocqueville, a French lawyer who visited America in 1831, described in *De la Démocratie en Amerique* (1835) a new type of society and political culture that was different at this time to that of Europe. De Tocqueville saw America as a mass society organised on the basis of an equality that ignored the aristocratic ethos of honour (which did not extend to Native Americans or African Americans) and threatened to create conformism, but that also helped ensure that America would, with Russia, be one of the great powers of the future. The democratic ethos was tapped by successful politicians, notably Andrew Jackson, president from 1829 to 1837, and also influenced hostility to Freemasonry, which was seen as elitist, and to British influence.

Meanwhile, the changing nature of slavery within America was altering the geopolitics of racial control and oppression as well as affecting the political atmosphere. The development of cotton production, in part to serve rapidly growing British markets, led to a major internal slave trade, from the Chesapeake colonies to the Deep South, accentuating the already strong contrast between the racial composition of the two areas. This trade provided the slave labour that could not be obtained from 1808 when the importing of slaves from outside America became illegal, and the trade offered a parallel to the situation in Brazil, where the sugar planters of the Northeast sold slaves to the coffee planters further south, who were expanding west into the province of São Paulo, using the railway to create new links and opportunities.

Abolitionists had hoped that the end of the international slave trade, combined with the high death rate among American slaves, would lead to an extinction of slavery by natural causes, rather as the extension of settlement made Native American society less viable by reducing land for hunting, but the death rate declined in this period and the American slave population increasingly sustained its numbers and then grew rapidly. As a consequence, abolitionists became more convinced that slavery had to be ended by state action, a belief encouraged by its abolition in the British empire in 1833. This belief affected the political atmosphere in the North, contributing to the conviction that beneficial change could, and should, be introduced. Conversely, the greater centrality of slavery to the expanding cotton economy led its Southern advocates to become more vocal and to add a conviction of potent economic need to the arguments they offered for sustaining their socio-political world. That these arguments were directed against fellow American politicians was readily apparent, and racial exclusion was presented as both form and focus of Southern cultural identity.

Identity and hierarchy interacted with economic factors to ensure that slavery was not an issue of the fading past. The slave economy was transformed as a result of the major expansion of cotton cultivation, which owed much to Eli Whitney's invention in 1793 of the cotton gin, a hand-operated machine that made it possible more easily to separate the cotton seeds from the fibre. This machine, which was subsequently improved, encouraged the cultivation of 'upland' cotton, a hardy variety which could be widely cultivated across the South, but which was very difficult to deseed by hand. In contrast, the Sea Island cotton hitherto grown could be deseeded by hand, but was largely restricted to the Atlantic coastlands. As a result of the change, and the opportunities presented by demand, cotton cultivation spread westwards in the South and annual cotton output rose from 3,000 bales in 1793 to over three million in the 1850s and about five million by 1860. 'King Cotton' reigned, and America became the key source for British cotton-manufacturers, who, in turn, were a major force in the British economy, notably in Lancashire.

Meanwhile, in Louisiana, indigo, which, like tobacco, had not done well, was replaced by sugar. The first crop of sugar to be granulated in Louisiana was in 1795, and the number of slaves rose from 20,000 then to 100,000 in 1830. The steam-heated vacuum pan, introduced by Edward Howard in 1813, was an aspect of the technological developments associated with sugar. In Louisiana, this was to be followed in 1843 by Norbert Rillieux patenting the multiple-effect evaporator which lowered the boiling point of the syrup by using enclosed vats. By 1860, about 125,000 slaves worked in the Louisiana sugar plantations, which had increased greatly in scale in the 1790s, 1820s and 1840s in particular.

The 1811 Slave Rising

The largest slave revolt in the United States, that of 1811 in Louisiana, saw the rebels mostly armed only with agricultural implements. About 250–300 men rose in St John the Baptist Parish on the German Coast of the Mississippi

River, in doing so taking advantage of the disquiet among creoles about the change in control in 1803 and the impact of the new order, not least on land rights. They aimed to march on New Orleans, free the slaves there, and then take refuge in Haiti, an instance of the role of the latter in encouraging rebellion. However, their failure, with defeat at the hands of the militia and of federal troops, led to the execution at New Orleans and Destrehan of 57 prisoners, their heads placed on pikes along the river. Again drawing on Haiti, White fear in Louisiana played a role in alarm about voodoo which was based on a body of rituals drawing on West African vodun.

The profitability of the cotton economy increased the prestige of landholding in the South, lessening investment in manufacturing, and also greatly affected American internal and external trade and communications. This profitability was also a key instance of geopolitics in terms of people (rather than primarily territory) and of the geopolitical consequences of economic developments: it both encouraged the removal of Native Americans and was important to the continued appeal of slavery in the South. As tobacco became less well capitalised, and more planters in the Chesapeake shifted to less labour-intensive wheat crops, so slaves from the tobacco country were sold for work on cotton plantations. In addition, the invention of McCormick's reaper in the 1830s reduced the need for slaves in the wheat-producing region of Virginia's Shenandoah valley. Many of these slaves were also sold South. The prevalence of slave hiring in the South ensured considerable geographical mobility among slaves, which helped keep slavery responsive to the market, and thus an effective economic system. Without a trade in slaves, there would have been little room for such entrepreneurship, nor for the interaction with capital that purchase and hiring offered.

This trade underlined the contrasts that were part of slave life, both at any one moment and across time. In particular, aside from the multiple differences arising from the social structure of particular slave communities, the economic consequences of tasks, and the variable nature of slave–master relations, there were the contrasts between regions, not least those of societies with slaves, such as New York, and slave societies. The latter in turn varied not least with reference to economic trends and work needs. In the half-century from 1810, more than one million African Americans were forcibly moved from coastal areas of the South into the interior, not solely due to the move of cotton culture, but largely as a result. This changed the South, as well as the slave experience. At the same time, 'the interior' meant not only plantation work, but also in the Mountain South, Southern Appalachia, much artisanal work.

Alongside the movement of slaves from the Chesapeake, there was also, from the 1790s, an upsurge there in manumission – giving freedom to slaves. As a result, for example by 1820, about 30 per cent of the Blacks on the Eastern Shore had gained freedom, although they were usually only granted it once they had passed their most productive years and the former slaves often remained dependent on the planters. There was a mixed labour system which created opportunities for Blacks, including movement to cities. Yet families were hit as members could still be slaves, while laws and their application, including apprentice laws and vagrancy laws, hit free Blacks, who in Maryland had to have a licence to sell crops.

Although slaves became less important in the Chesapeake states, the success of the cotton economy and the ability to boost the birth rate of American slaves were such that Southern apologists did not regard the slave system as anachronistic. The earlier support of Jefferson and others for ending what he saw as the slave problem by expatriation (sending slaves abroad, essentially to West Africa), now seemed anachronistic. Indeed, the number of slaves rose considerably in the nineteenth century until the Civil War, providing an economic dimension to ideological debates about slavery. Profit, not paternalism, was the key element, and benevolence was in limited supply. That this economic dimension cannot be separated from racism was shown by the increasing marginalisation of mulattoes (people of mixed ancestry), who were more frequently treated as Black.

African-American women comprised half of the slave labour force, providing a particularly marked instance of the harsh nature of female circumstances. Slave child mortality could be very high, notably on rice plantations. Children more generally suffered from the domestic slave trade which hit family life, as did sexual exploitation and the use of arranged marriages and other means to increase slave childbearing and thus produce more revenue. Malnutrition and unhealthy living conditions contributed to high mortality. Most women, both Black and White, worked in domestic service, where wages were low. Single women, both White and free Black, were provided with more opportunities by the expansion of manufacturing, but were to be hit hard later in the century by competition from poor White male (and female) immigration and from the spread of heavy machinery. More generally, wage rates, the operation of the law, and the leadership of the churches, were but three of the many ways in which women were in a subordinate position.

Accounts from 1855: The Plight of Women, Lucy Stone

'Women working in tailor-shops are paid one-third as much as men . . . Is it a wonder that women are driven to prostitution? . . . The present condition of women causes a horrible perversion of the marriage relation . . . women must marry for a home . . . a woman who loathes you may marry you.'

The Capacity of Electricty

From *Leaves of Grass* (1855), a poetry collection by Walt Whitman (1819–92) in which he presented himself as a live wire unlocking potential:

> 'I have instant conductors all over me.
> they seize every object and lead it harmlessly
> through me.'

With other topics more prominent, the issue of slavery was in abeyance as far as most politicians were concerned during the 1810s, but the consequences of expansionism, specifically the Louisiana Purchase of 1803, threw the issue to the fore in 1819 when part of this Purchase, the Missouri Territory, applied for statehood. The proposals of James Tallmadge, a New York congressman, for the gradual ending of slavery in the Territory (by prohibiting the entry of new slaves and freeing all existing slaves born after admission to statehood once they turned twenty-five), won extensive support in the North, but was seen in the South as a threat to its identity and existence. By April 1820, Jefferson was expressing his concern at the prospect of division.

In the event, the Missouri Compromise of 1820 allowed Maine to enter the Union as a free and Missouri as a slave state in 1821, but banned slavery elsewhere above the 36° 30' N Parallel, which ran along Missouri's southern boundary. This measure, which left most of the Louisiana Purchase free from slavery, was seen as a challenge by Southerners opposed to Northern interference, notably by means of federal power over the sovereign authority of the states. As a result, the Missouri Compromise led to an increase in support for slavery, while the resulting geopolitics encouraged Southerners to press for expansion to the west and also to develop an interest in expansion into Mexico and the Caribbean.

The geopolitics expressed in the choice between free and slave labour was to become increasingly important in American politics, but it was not simply a matter of the use of labour. There was also a conviction among Southern slaveholders that territorial expansion was necessary to protect their position in both political and economic terms. Fear of soil exhaustion played a part, but so did a concern that slaves, as well as poor Whites, would become too numerous for the stability of the South unless it could gain new territories in Mexico and the West Indies. The mental space of the South thus expanded to include Texas, other parts of Mexico, Cuba and Haiti.

Organised opposition to slavery by the slaves was limited, in large part due to the coercive context in which slaves were held and the difficulties of coordinating opposition. Thanks largely to the power of planters, but also to measures such as the state-sponsored and large-scale slave patrols, control over the slaves was maintained by coercion and violence without the need for any full-scale suppression of slave activity. Nat Turner's rebellion in Virginia in 1831 was swiftly suppressed. Nine years earlier, a planned rebellion, Denmark Vesey's in Charleston, was betrayed and pre-empted. Evidence for the plans has been questioned on the grounds that they were devised to give credence to the idea of a slave revolt. From that point of view, it is instructive to note that such a rising did not occur.

Slavery was the underlying issue, though not the overt one, when South Carolina attempted to nullify a new tariff in 1832–3, on the grounds that it was unconstitutional as well as unfair, and that individual states could protect themselves from such acts by interposing their authority, and thus nullifying the federal law. This instance of states' rights as increasingly a shorthand for the support of slavery was an attitude already seen when, after the Vesey trials, South Carolina endorsed a Negro Seaman Act and enforced it in the face of the contrary provisions of federal law, and despite the Act creating problems for British diplomats who were not prepared to see Black British sailors treated like criminals and detained while their ships were in Charleston. In November 1832, the South Carolina convention passed an ordinance of nullification, and the state raised an enthusiastic army of over 25,000 men and purchased arms. The nullifiers threatened secession from the Union if the federal government sought to enforce the tariff.

The federal government did not give way, and Charleston's garrison was reinforced by General Winfield Scott, who then proved an adept manager of local sensitivities. Moreover, unsupported by the other Southern states and also facing opposition to nullification from within, South Carolina had to back down, to abandon the threat of nullification and to accept a settlement of the tariff issue which did not meet its goals. The dispute indicated the fragility of political and constitutional conventions, the clash between Southern notions of the Union as a voluntary compact among independent states, and Northern views of the indivisibility of the one American nation, and of the possibility of conflict.

These terms were thought insufficiently beneficial by Polk and the Democrats and, conversely, as leading to the gain of too much territory by the Whigs. Contributing to the 'vigour of anti-imperialist movements' in American history, the Whigs had earlier been critical of the annexation of Texas and were suspicious about the likely consequences of increasing the number of slave states. All the 25 senators who voted on 27 February 1845 against Texas becoming a state were Whig, while the 27 who voted for included all 24 Democrats and three Southern Whigs. Texas' entry as a single state, rather than, as had been feared, and indeed proposed by Senator Benton, a number of (slave) states, was significant. As in the War of 1812, the Northeast was particularly hostile to the conflict, although in the case of the Mexican War, this was primarily due to the slave issue, in the shape of opposition to more slave states.

Texas becoming a state led to war with Mexico in 1846–8. As a reminder of the extent to which expansion depended on conquest, the Mexican inhabitants in Southern California rebelled against recently won American control in 1846, while there was also an uprising in New Mexico that year. These risings, however, were defeated in early 1847 respectively. The eventual peace treaty of Guadalupe Hidalgo left the United States with what were to become California, Nevada and Utah, as well as most of Arizona, and parts of New Mexico, Colorado and Wyoming. By the 1848 treaty, the Rio Grande was recognised as the border between America and Mexico. The American government agreed to provide $15 million for the territories gained as well as to pay another $3 million as the claims of American citizens against Mexico. War and slavery were scarcely the sole matters in political dispute and, therefore, alignment. Moreover, there was a dynamic context due to migration, and thus, a moving local politics of ethnic identity and occupational interest. Into the mix came the drive for personal ascendancy of politicians. Nevertheless, the status of slavery in the newly acquired territories became a key topic of controversy. Southern politicians saw off the argument that it should be illegal and, instead, a compromise in 1850 left California, a new state, free, like the recently created states of Iowa (1846) and Wisconsin (1848), while the Oregon and Minnesota territories were also free. However, the western boundary of Texas was also settled in 1850, with New Mexico established as a territory that included land east of the Rio Grande purchased from Texas by the federal government. Some of this land also became part of the Utah Territory. As a consequence what became Texas' iconic shape was established. Alongside the slave states accepted in 1845, Florida and Texas, slavery was to be legal in the New Mexico and Utah territories, subject to popular sovereignty in the form of the settlers, as well as in the as-yet-unorganised territory that in 1907 became Oklahoma.

The Call for Abolition, 1852

'What, to the American slave, is your Fourth of July? . . . To him, your celebration is a sham; your boasted liberty, an unholy licence; your national greatness, swelling vanity; your sounds of rejoicing are empty and heartless; your denunciation of tyrants, brass-fronted impudence.'

Frederick Douglass, speech at Rochester, New York

The fate of slavery in the West remained highly contentious, with extensions to the lands opened to slavery provided by the Kansas-Nebraska Act of 1854 and the Dred Scott decision of the Supreme Court in 1857, which determined that slave-owners could take their slaves into any territory and that free African Americans did not enjoy the full rights of American citizens.

Southern advocates such as Jefferson Davis, future president of the Confederacy, saw the expansion of slavery as a way to guarantee a labour force in the West that would bring prosperity, notably by making irrigated agriculture feasible, and thus overcoming the constraints of geography and providing the security of continuous settlement. In addition, there was the impact of disease on the Native American population in the newly annexed territories, with smallpox, measles and fevers destroying much of the population from the 1790s. Native Americans were also greatly affected by the spread of settlement.

Victory over Mexico boosted the Jacksonian Democrats who pressed for expansion as a means to spread their populist vision of a Protestant, White, male, democratic and individualistic America. Yet, like the War of 1812, the Mexican War, however divisive, also strengthened the sense of America as a potent country. In the West, it was scarcely any more the case of two competing republics (America and Mexico) and a rival empire (Britain). The grip of the war on the American imagination was enhanced by the extent to which it was covered in developing media, notably photography and lithography, while the press also benefited from war reporters. The war left America with a greatly extended coastline and, combined with the California Gold Rush, which began in 1848, led to much excitement about the future.

Mid-Century Railways

The Panic of 1837 had discredited state borrowing and helped therefore ensure that transport improvement was left to the private sector, which had to spend the 1840s repairing its credit. Subsequently, the pro-big business stance of Republican administrations after the Civil War (1861–5) served the needs of railway companies, not least in ensuring that early anti-trust pressure was not driven home.

The railway was crucial in creating and improving links between coastal and hinterland America, and also in creating and developing those within the latter.

Railways helped open up resources. For example, in Piedmont (western) South Carolina, the major expansion of textile mills from the 1880s to the 1910s was linked to access to railways.

In Arkansas, railway companies were chartered from 1853 and the first line opened in 1858, but most construction did not take place until after the Civil War, when subsidies and land grants helped, leading to 822 miles of track by 1880 and 3,167 by 1900, construction peaking in the early 1930s. Short-line railways were used to tie in local needs to trunk lines. The expansion of the railways made possible a major growth in logging, while the completion of the Little Rock and Fort Smith Railroad in 1883 opened the deposits in Johnson County to northern markets. Railways also made farm specialisation and cash crops easier.

In 1850, Congress decided that the National Observatory should be the official prime meridian for the United States. Moreover, in 1853, an American squadron entered Tokyo Bay, and the Crystal Palace was constructed in New York for the Second World Fair on the design of London's one built for the Great Exhibition of 1851. The decision to hold the fair reflected Americans' confidence in their own economic development, status and future, as well as the self-mythologising referred to at the beginning of the chapter. The 1860 census was to reveal a population of 31.5 million, with a third of the population supported directly or indirectly by manufacturing industry. American confidence seems well-judged in hindsight. The solution of the Oregon Dispute and, more successfully and dramatically, victory over Mexico, meant that America became a 'new kind of country', with a coastline on both the Atlantic and the Pacific, a position that was to be of major value both economically and in power politics. Yet the 1850s were to reveal that, whatever the potential, there were still serious challenges, both domestic and international, challenges that were to become far more acute in the 1860s.

Attempts to keep the peace were not an adequate response to the pace of American migration and the nature of American activity. In particular, depredations on the bison that many Native Americans relied upon for survival were a real threat to their livelihood as the Native Americans had no alternative. The resulting conflicts were wide-ranging and encompassed the Plains and both the Northwest and Southwest, for example warfare with the Cheyenne, Comanche and Kiowa in West Texas. It also proved difficult to bring hostilities to a close. For example, the Comanche were defeated in 1859, but conflict continued.

Such a situation encouraged brutality. In response both to more difficult opponents and to a sense that Manifest Destiny required that the Native Americans be driven from the land, far more violence was used against women and children after 1848 than in earlier warfare, and there was also a greater willingness to massacre Native

Americans. Certain operations were particularly brutal. The Plains Indian Wars were touched off by American aggression in the Grattan Massacre in Fort Laramie in 1854, in which Conquering Bear, the Sioux leader, was killed. General William Harney refused to take male Brulé Sioux as prisoners in 1855 and permitted the killing of their women and children at Ash Hollow. Harney killed Chief Little Thunder at the battle of Blue Water Creek that year, and the Sioux submitted the following spring.

The fame of opponents, especially the Apache, Cheyenne, Comanche and Sioux, ensures that some wars were well known. Others, such as the Rogue River uprising in southwestern Oregon in 1855–6 and the Spokane War on the Upper Columbia Plateau in 1858, are far less familiar. These conflicts were touched off by the pressures of American settlement, the policy of forcing tribes into reservations in Oregon and Washington, and the failure of the authorities to protect the Native Americans, if not their aggressive desire to expropriate, even eliminate, them. As elsewhere, the Native Americans in this region benefited from their skill in fighting from cover and from their knowledge of the terrain, but they were disunited. Converging columns of regulars and expeditions of volunteers led to the Native American surrender that ended the Rogue River uprising, while, in 1858, the tactical skill of Colonel George Wright and the superior capabilities of the new 1855 Springfield .58 calibre rifled muskets, which outranged the Native American weapons, brought victory in the Battles of Four Lakes and Spokane Plains. The slaughter of horses and the hanging of prisoners helped terrify the Native Americans and lead them to terms. Moreover, Native American hopes of British assistance were ended when the Hudson's Bay Company and James Douglas, the governor of Vancouver Island, sent arms and ammunition to the Americans. Thanks to these campaigns, American control of the Northwest was established.

Further south, the Native American population of California was brutally reduced in the 1850s by conflict as well as disease.

The federal army did not control the situation there: instead, as in the Northwest, local volunteer forces inflicted great damage, for example slaughtering the Yahi and Yana, men, women and children alike. They were in a position to do so there as, due to large-scale immigration, the American population in California rose greatly in the 1850s (the state population rising from 15,000 in 1840 to 380,000 in 1860), while the Native Americans lacked unity or a strong military tradition. In Florida, the small number of remaining Seminole waged the Third Seminole War, a guerrilla struggle, in 1855–8, before agreeing to move to Indian Territory.

Whether by conflict or pressure, land was cleared in a process marked by treaties such as that of 1854 by which the Miami lost nearly 80 per cent of their reservation in Kansas. This cession was a result of the pressure on Native American land in Kansas from land speculators, settlers and railway companies after it became a territory under the Kansas-Nebraska Act of 1854, pressure that was facilitated by the weakness of the federal government and by the willingness of some Native Americans to co-operate for their own benefit in gaining property from the allocation of tribal land, which had been held in common. When Kansas became a state in 1861, taxation was used to take land from the Shawnee. Under pressure in Kansas, many Native Americans moved south to the Indian Territory which, in 1907, became the state of Oklahoma.

As in previous eras, the Native Americans suffered from a lack of unity. Those who lived on the Plains were not tribes, but bands, although various groups could be fitted under a general designation, such as Sioux or Comanche, which was linguistic rather than organisational. From mid-century, the Native Americans in the United States also suffered from the impact on their divisions of the replacement of the weak nature of Mexican control (and the deliberately accommodating views of the British in the Oregon Country), by the more insistent territorial demands and military activity of the burgeoning American state. Rather than simply lack of unity, there was also active and longstanding rivalry between Native Americans. On the northern and central plains, the Lakota Sioux, allied to the Cheyenne and Arapaho, used the mobility given by their embracing of a nomadic horse culture to dominate and, at times, brutalise, sedentary, agricultural tribes such as the Pawnee and Arikara, who had the horse but had not become nomadic. The Sioux, an alliance of linguistically similar tribes, fought to obtain territory for hunting bison to feed their growing population, which reached about 32,000 by 1870. With weaponry and military means similar to those of their opponents – firearms and horses – the Sioux benefited, from the 1780s on, from smallpox epidemics which weakened tribes such as the Crow, Pawnee and Shoshone that had blocked their westward move from Minnesota. The large farming villages of these tribes made them particularly vulnerable to smallpox, and Whites' diseases struck particular tribes at different times. The Sioux had been exposed and partially immunised earlier than other tribes. The Sioux also benefited from their combination of constant small raiding parties and occasional large war parties, which destroyed entire villages. The ability of the Sioux alliance to hold their own different tribes together was also important to their success.

Sioux domination encouraged many of the other Native American tribes to look to the Americans. Their willingness to do so emphasises the degree to which any discussion of relations in terms of conflict alone would be incomplete. Instead, military, political, economic, cultural and religious ties crossed American/Native American divides, turning them into zones of interaction in which symbiosis, synergy and exchange occurred alongside, and, often, instead of, conflict and war. Moreover, much of the violence also involved an important measure of collaboration between Americans and Native Americans. In the Plains Indians' Wars which began in 1854, Crow and Pawnee co-operated with the Americans against the Lakota Sioux. The Ute, Crow and Pawnee provided the army with scouts.

The process of conflict was less significant to American expansion in the West, however, than systemic factors including, as so often with this book, the key element of population. The demographic weight of the Americans, or rather the European Americans, was crucial in combination with their willingness to migrate and force their way into regions already settled by Native Americans. Rapid and continuous American population growth, across the country, encouraged significant levels of migration within America, as new cohorts sought opportunities. The linked processes of economic growth and improved infrastructure were also significant. The interior had been transformed by a series of changes including the introduction of steel ploughs, which permitted the working of the tough soils of the Midwest and were displayed at the Great Exhibition of 1851 in London, as well as railways, grain elevators and flour mills. As a result, commercial agriculture made the vast spaces of the interior a source of profit rather than a problem of distance. Technology was not the sole issue: political economy and political culture, alongside resources, helped explain why Northern industrial development was far more extensive than that in the South, not least why, of the coal-rich states, Pennsylvania did better than Virginia.

Yet, economic change had serious political, social and environmental consequences. Concerns about immigration, which was encouraged by economic expansion, led in the mid-1850s to the development of the Know-Nothings as a political force, all reflecting the uncertain position of existing Protestant workers. Resentment against Irish immigration was an important element of nativism.

There were also very different directions in political and social activism. Held in New York state in 1848, the Seneca Falls Convention was the first women's rights convention in the United States and launched the struggle of women for a broad array of civil rights, including abolitionism, temperance and woman's suffrage. It would be seven decades, however, before American women would be able to cast their first vote. Temperance reflected a drive to curb men's drunkenness, which was the cause of much domestic violence. Women were therefore taking a public stance on men's behaviour rather than being limited to a private womanly sphere.

The railway played a major role in the Western expansion, not only in speeding American troops, but also in developing economic links between coastal and hinterland America, and thus integrating the frontiers of settlement with the exigencies of the world economy. Such communication improvements were particularly significant for the spread of mining and of ranching, with the cattle being driven to railheads. Linked to railways at river and coastal ports, steamships also aided integration. These were important on the great rivers, in the Gulf of Mexico, and, especially, on the Pacific coast. The settlers' ability to derive production and profit from the land made the Native American way of life appear increasingly anachronistic, and, indeed, a threat to American strength. In the stadial view of human progress, hunting, if the major activity, was seen as a primitive form of economic activity reflecting a limited society. As elsewhere with expansion by Western powers, American advances were in part expressed through the building of forts.

In the Kansas Territory in the 1850s, disagreements over extending slavery escaped government control and became bloody. In the context of the idea of popular sovereignty (settlers not Congress determining slavery in the Territories), protagonists for the two sides sought to terrorise their opponents in order to ensure a majority for their view, which was the consequence of the Kansas-Nebraska Act of 1854, the basis for the establishment of Kansas as a territory in 1854. This Act allowed the people in the territory to decide on slavery, rather than settling the question at the federal level. In the event, rival governments were established in Kansas in 1855 and, in May 1856, conflict broke out, only to be constrained by the arrival of the army. The conflict helped radicalise attitudes, leading to a Kansan constitution in 1859 that gave African Americans the right to vote in school elections.

The admission of California, the population of which grew rapidly as a result of a gold rush, as a free state in 1850 gave the free states a majority in the Senate. The minority status of the South in the Union was a key feature of the sectional controversy of the 1850s, a feature that created problems for the South. Minnesota and Oregon followed as free states in 1858 and 1859 respectively. It is important to note that 'free states' were not free of racism. Indeed, with energy and justification provided by racism, there was active discrimination against African Americans, including from new immigrants, the overwhelming majority of whom were White. This was very much the case with Irish immigrants who took jobs from the free Blacks, not least using unionisation and violence to that end.

A sense of being under challenge ensured that Southern secession was frequently threatened in the 1850s, before it finally triumphed in 1860–1. The alternative to secession was to seek to make the Union safe for the South and slavery, in part by re-educating Northerners about the constitution, or by acquiring more slave states, or by somehow addressing the vulnerabilities of the slave system in the South. The Southerners' failure to do so was compounded by the difficulties posed by the slaves' desire for freedom.

The 1860 election gave victory to Abraham Lincoln of the Republicans, who wished to prevent the extension of slavery into the federal Territories. This was understood by Lincoln and others as a step that threatened Southern interests and identity. The election of Lincoln, who, on the pattern of Jackson, was described by one contemporary as 'a man almost unknown, a rough

Western, of the lowest origin and little education', reflected the refashioning of politics by the slavery issue, which had led, first, to pressure on the Whigs, as with the rise of Libertyites and the Free Soil Party, subsequently, to the disintegration of the Whigs in the aftermath of the Kansas-Nebraska Act of 1854 and the related rise of the Republicans as a Northern sectional party focused on the restriction of slavery, and, then, to the division of the Democratic Party, the only remaining bond between North and South, between Northern and Southern Whigs.

1856 saw the first Republican run for the presidency, a course determined by opposition to the potential for new slaveholding opened up by the 1854 Kansas-Nebraska Act. Free control of the land was a key issue, as the party also sought 'free soil' – free land to farmers in the West. Freedom was a moral position, which was embraced in the Republican party by pietist Protestants seeking public morality, whether against slavery, Mormon polygamy or drink.

In 1856, James Buchanan, the Democratic candidate, had won the South but also Pennsylvania, Illinois and Indiana, showing a winning national appeal; but, in 1860, Stephen Douglas, the Northern Democrat, competed with John Breckinridge, the Southern Democrat. This competition allowed Lincoln, the Republican, who carried the Northern states but none of the Southern ones, to win on fewer than 40 per cent of the votes cast. With moderation lacking powerful exponents, national politics was no longer being contested by effective national parties, and, partly as a result, American mass democracy could not generate a consensus. Compromise was on offer, but no longer seemed sufficiently acceptable in North and South to gather impetus. Lincoln rejected the proposal by Senator John Crittenden of Kentucky that the 36–30' line of the 1820 Missouri compromise accepting slavery for the Arkansas Territory be run towards the Pacific, a line which would include the New Mexico Territory in the world of slavery.

New York in the 1850s

Discrimination, 1854

'I told him [the conductor] not to lay his hands on me. He took hold of me and I took hold of the window sash and held on. He pulled me until he broke my grasp. They then both seized hold of me by the arms and pulled and dragged me flat down on the bottom of the platform, so that my feet hung one way and my head the other nearly on the ground . . . When the officer without listening to anything I was saying, thrust me out and then pushed, and then pushed, and tauntingly told me to get redress if I could . . . After dragging me off the car, he drove me away like a dog, saying not to be talking there and raising a mob or fight.'

Elizabeth Jennings, a Black schoolteacher, being dragged off a New York streetcar. The next year she won damages and the company was ordered to desegregate.

Central Park

Before the 1800s, common land separated upper Manhattan from the nearby town of Harlem. After the Revolution, the city authorities surveyed and sold off plots. In the 1850s, however, the idea that the city needed a great park to provide 'urban lungs' for all gained hold. It reshaped not only the topography of Manhattan but also the city's social landscape: those who had lived on the rocky, swampy site were evicted and what became the affluent Upper East Side district began to take shape. The design competition for the park was won by the naturalistic 'Greensward Plan' of Frederick Law Olmsted and Calvert Vaux, both of whom aspired to a democratic space where the city's classes could mix freely. Begun in 1858, by the mid-1860s the 843-acre (340-hectare) park was largely complete, with its pathways and promenades, woodland and lakes, bridges, architectural structures and rustic features, from rocks to individual trees, as well as a reservoir.

7

Secession and Civil War, 1860–5

Lincoln's election led to the secession of the South, beginning with South Carolina on 20 December 1860, and the formation of the Confederate States of America. The bellicosity of the Southern elites in resorting to force in a longstanding sectional political rift was to prove misplaced. Honour and duty were deployed and conflated with, and in, a series of moves to and in war. Northern tyranny was too readily used in the South as an excuse from serious thought. Yet, as a reminder of the significance of geographical factors and also at the same time of their uncertainty, and thus of the volatility of geopolitics, the Confederacy did not equate with the slave states, the variety of which was significant. Only the Lower South seceded at first and Montgomery, Alabama, was the initial capital of the Confederacy. Moreover, much of the Upper South, including Virginia, Tennessee and Kentucky, had voted for John Bell of Tennessee, the candidate of the new Constitutional Union party pledged to back 'the Union, the Constitution and the Laws'.

Looking Back to 1861

'These slaves constituted a peculiar and powerful interest. All knew that the interest was somehow the cause of the war. To strengthen, perpetuate, and extend this interest was the object for which the insurgents would rend the Union even by war, while the Government claimed no right to do more than to restrict the territorial enlargement of it. Neither party expected for the war the magnitude or the duration which it had already attained. Each looked for an easier triumph, and a result less fundamental and astounding. Both read the same Bible and pray to the same God.'

Lincoln, second Inauguration speech, 1865

Although Lincoln, seeking to build as broad a base as possible in order to isolate the most radical elements in the South, was willing to back a constitutional amendment prohibiting the federal government from interfering with slavery, secession was unacceptable to him. The Republicans argued both that the maintenance of the Union was essential to the purpose of America as well as to its strength, and that it was necessary to understand that the superiority of the federal government over the states was critical to the idea of the American nation. This superiority was demonstrated when Lincoln refused to yield to demands for the surrender of the federal position of Fort Sumter in Charleston harbour: the reality of national power in the face of a forge of Southern consciousness and separatism. On 12 April 1861, Confederate forces opened fire, and the beleaguered fort surrendered the following day after over 3,000 shells and shots had been fired, setting fire to the wooden buildings in the fort.

Far from intimidating him into yielding, as Southern leaders had hoped, this clash led Lincoln to determine to act against what he termed 'combinations' in the South. He went to war to maintain the Union, and not for the emancipation of the slaves. Lincoln's call for 75,000 volunteers, and his clear intention to resist secession with force, by invading the Lower South, played the major role in leading Arkansas, North Carolina, Tennessee and Virginia to join the Confederacy as they did not intend to provide troops to put down what Lincoln termed an insurrection. As so often, the turn to force helped to widen the range of conflict, although it is not clear that there were viable alternatives.

This subsequent secession of the Upper South greatly altered the demographic and military context of the war: political events reshaped the geography, and thus the geopolitics and strategies of the war. Arkansas was not able to contribute much to the Confederacy, but Virginia, Tennessee and North Carolina were each very important in economic and demographic terms. In order, they were the leading states in White population in the Confederacy; while, together, they were to field close to 40 per cent of the Confederacy's forces, including key generals such as Robert E. Lee, and provide half of its crops and more than half of its manufacturing capacity. South Carolina's ability to win over Virginia was important to the geopolitical definition of the South, and contrasted with the situation in the Nullification Controversy of 1832. This ability also looked to the subsequent memorialisation of the Civil War, the legacy of which came to define the South.

In military terms, the location of productive capacity in frontier areas was a problem for the Confederacy, as they were vulnerable, and thus the situation rewarded Union attack, while compromising the idea of a defence in depth. However, while the gain of the four states ensured that there was more territory to defend, it transformed the military potential of the Confederacy. The Union no longer had a common frontier with every seceding state bar Florida, and thus the Lower South became less vulnerable. It also became easier to think of the Confederacy as a bloc of territory that could be defended in a coherent fashion, and that therefore required a coherent strategy in order to bring it down. In particular, the secession of Virginia and North Carolina greatly altered the location of the likely field of operations in the east as, militarily, the front line of the secession was no longer on the northern border of South Carolina. Had that been the case, Columbia and Charleston would have been readily vulnerable to Union attack, just as Atlanta in Georgia would have been from Chattanooga in Tennessee.

Conversely, the Union was able to gain control of an important bloc of slave states: Delaware, Maryland, Kentucky, Missouri, and those parts of Virginia that, in 1863, became the state of West Virginia. Had these states joined the Confederacy, as Missouri and Kentucky sympathisers did, leading indeed to their being seated in the Confederate Congress, then the situation would also have been very different. Instead, the Union consolidated its superiority in resources, blocked invasion routes into the North, and exposed the South to attack. As, despite disaffection in Baltimore, Maryland stayed in the Union, the central battleground of the war lay between Washington, which remained the capital of the Union, and Richmond, Virginia, which became the capital of the Confederacy in May 1861.

Their proximity helped give a geographical focus to the conflict, one that reflected the political importance of the two capitals, and also cut across the potential expansiveness of the conflict arising from the extent of the area in rebellion. Indeed, this proximity offered the prospect of the rapid end to the war that Northerners sought. Moreover, these states in Union hands affected the offensive capability of the Confederacy. Given Robert E. Lee's willingness to march north across the Potomac in 1862 and 1863, advances ending in the battles of Antietam and Gettysburg respectively, it is instructive to consider what the military impact of having the frontier on the northern border of Maryland would have been. There was also a key demographic dimension in terms of the manpower available to both sides. The Union benefited from the heroism of African-American units. Native American soldiers were used by both sides, especially west of the Mississippi where the issue of slavery was highly divisive.

The Civil War, furthermore, was a civil conflict within the states that seceded. In the latter, the prevalence of slavery varied greatly, with, for example, few slaves in Appalachia. Conversely, fears of an abolitionist plot in Texas in late 1860, a major instance of the sequence of panics following John Brown's attempt on Harper's Ferry, helped lead to vigilante action and encouraged backing for secession. The variation in the prevalence of slavery was linked to the degree of support for the war, though it was not the sole factor involved: 104,000 White Southerners fought in the Union forces, a major addition to the latter and cause of Confederate weakness, and the degree of opposition to secession underlined the degree to which chance factors played a considerable role in ensuring that it occurred.

Yet, alongside a commitment to slavery, many who fought for the South did not own slaves and, alongside racism, were motivated by a sense of the need to defend communities, culture and the states' rights that were believed to protect both. These states' rights, however, were defined in part in terms of the defence of slavery. Although a minority, there were many Northern 'dough faces' willing to accept slavery, including Franklin Pierce, president from 1853 to 1857, who had opposed abolitionism and signed the Kansas-Nebraska Act. So also with 'Copperheads', pro-Southern sympathisers in the North. However, they did not provide a military support for the South equivalent to that of Southerners who fought against separation. Among the Native Americans, there were slave-owning tribes, and some tribes were divided over the issue.

Charles Dickens on the Causes of the War, March 1862

'I take the facts of the American quarrel to stand thus. Slavery has in reality nothing on earth to do with it, in any kind of association with any generous or chivalrous sentiment on the part of the North. But the North having gradually got to itself the making of the laws and the settlement of the Tariffs, and having taxed the South most abominably for its own advantage, began to see, as the country grew, that unless it advocated the laying down of a geographical line beyond which slavery should not extend, the South would necessarily recover its old political power, and be able to help itself a little in the adjustment of commercial affairs. Every reasonable creature may know, if willing, that the North hates the Negro, and that until it was convenient to make a pretence that sympathy with him was the cause of the War, it hated the abolitionists and derided them up hill and down dale. For the rest, there is not a pin to choose between the two parties. They will both rant and lie and fight until they come to a compromise; and the slave may be thrown into that compromise or thrown out of it, just as happens.'

Dickens accepted the basic
premise of the South's arguments

The number of different beliefs in the South serves as a reminder of the complexity of the issues at stake, and thus of the geopolitics and strategy of the war. Initially unprepared for the difficulty, length and bloodiness of the struggle, both militarily and politically, Union forces had to try to shift the political balance within the South in order to lead to its surrender, and that indeed occurred in 1865. The military alternative of the conquest of the entire South was not viable given the size of the Confederacy. The political options appeared clearer for the Confederacy. There was the hope that success in the conflict would lead the Union to change policy by abandoning the war and, second, that success would bring the British and French into the war, and thus ensure that the Union had to change policy. There was considerable weight in both ideas, and if the playing out of the war revealed that neither was viable, that was not readily apparent to contemporaries in America and abroad until well into the conflict.

Although the Confederacy contained about 30 per cent of the country's wealth, the Union's advantages were formidable, not only in wealth but also in the ease with which it could be employed. It had a 4:1 edge in manpower, which was significant in tactical, operational and strategic terms. The Union also had a formidable advantage in manufacturing plant, railway track and bullion resources, the gold and silver of the West being particularly important. The Union was able as well as willing to stage costly campaigns. The North had six times as many factories as the Confederacy and ten times its productive capacity, producing 97 per cent of America's firearms, 94 per cent of its pig iron and 90 per cent of its boots and shoes. The disparity was accentuated by the economic and financial dislocation of the Confederacy stemming from the Union blockade.

The Union also had a marked advantage in agricultural production, even though the South was more agricultural in character. The North had 800,000 draught animals to the South's 300,000, and the North's agricultural strength also rested on an ability to respond to new possibilities, specifically agricultural machinery. As a consequence, wheat crops rose in 1862 and 1863, and wheat, corn, beef and pork exports rose, even though about a third of the agricultural workforce served in the army and indeed had to be fed there. Supply problems in the Confederacy were far more serious and encouraged Lee, commander of the Army of Northern Virginia, 1862–5, to march into the North in 1862 and 1863: he hoped to gain food, shoes and other supplies.

Helped by a wartime prosperity that impressed foreign observers, the North also had a far greater capacity to raise both tax revenues and loans, and thus to finance what was, for America, a conflict of unprecedented expense. War bonds provided about two-thirds of the cost of the conflict, and the financial strength and stability of the North permitted the issue of close to $457 million of Treasury notes, which held their value well. Income tax and paper currency were introduced, although the latter had to be supported by government action. Union resources made it easier to equip the large numbers of troops that were raised. For example, nearly 1.5 million Springfield rifles were manufactured, a total that reflected the capacity of contemporary industry, and one that could not be matched in the Confederacy. In April 1865, in his Farewell Address to his soldiers, part of what was to become a Southern mythology, Lee argued that they had been 'compelled to yield to overwhelming power'.

Yet, resources alone do not explain conflict, first because a host of factors affect their use and effectiveness and, second, because more than resources is involved in war. Thus, Lee's defeat owed much to the effectiveness of his opponents, especially from 1863, as well as to Southern mistakes.

War goals and military methods changed in response to the difficulty of the conflict, changes that again underline the limitations of a geopolitical account, but that indicated the extent to which a difficult conflict could help radicalise the situation. Whereas Major-General George McClellan, the commanding general of the United States Army, 1861–2, opposed attacks on private property, Grant pressed it from the spring of 1862 in order to hit Confederate supplies and, thus, warmaking ability. Similarly, Major-General John Pope, commander of the Union's Army of Virginia in 1862, agreed with the Republicans, not McClellan, and claimed that it was legitimate to confiscate rebel property and move civilians who refused to take the oath of allegiance. Union forces responded harshly to opposition by becoming more destructive, and especially by living off the land. Pope's army destroyed a large amount of property and thus made its presence unwelcome. There were significant pressures on the Union home front, where frustration with the intractability of the struggle led to an abandonment of conciliation towards Southerners in late 1862.

This change was an instance of political parameters being affected by military factors. McClellan had pursued a quick victory by means of a victorious advance in Virginia alongside a conciliatory strategy to undermine Southern support for the rebellion, but this plan failed. McClellan, who had advocated modest war goals as part of a general conciliatory Union approach, a policy that reflected his political engagement as a Democrat, was unable to deliver victory and was replaced after Antietam. Instead, as hopes of a quick war faded, the emphasis came to be on how best to win a long conflict, an emphasis that led to a greater concern on securing control of the Mississippi Valley, while conciliation ceased to be the political goal, and the conduct of the war became more brutal, although not in comparison with the contemporary conflict in Mexico or with the hostilities involving Native Americans. Moreover, the Union's insistence that Southerners were still American citizens affected their treatment.

Initially, the Union had made no attempt to abolish slavery, both because Lincoln feared the impact of emancipation on sections of Northern opinion, especially in loyal border states such as his native Kentucky, and because, like many others, he hoped that avoiding a pledge to support emancipation would weaken Southern backing for secession. After Antietam, in contrast, a battle close to the 1862 midterms, which suggests a different causation, Lincoln heeded radical Republicans, many of whom were linked to the Congressional Joint Committee on the Conduct of the War, and the Union became committed to the emancipation of the slaves in those parts of the South still in rebellion. This was seen as a way to weaken the Southern economy, and thus war effort, as well as providing a clear purpose to maintain Northern morale and a means to assuage the sin that was leading a wrathful God to punish America. Lincoln's strong moral commitment led to the Emancipation Proclamation issued on 1 January 1863.

Commemorating Victory

On 19 November 1863, the day of Lincoln's famous speech commemorating the recent victory at Gettysburg, which ended the last major Confederate invasion, Edward Everett, Professor of Greek Literature at Harvard, who spoke for much longer, compared the site with that of Marathon in 490 BCE. In doing so, Everett provided an echo of the glorious defence of liberty by the Greeks against the invading Persians, and an account that cast Greek civilisation as the progenitor of modern America. This was a comparison that the listeners could be expected to understand. It annexed the Classical past for the Union cause and sought to deny it to the Confederacy, whose commentators had made much of the role of slavery in the Classical world.

Emancipation, like conscription, another radical step, was linked to the need for troops. In the second half of the Civil War, the recruitment of Blacks for the Union army was a symbol to and for the Confederacy of what was a total war. Moreover, the recruitment of all-Black regiments for the army, numbering more than 120,000 men, was also a major operational help to the Union. Black troops were frequently employed as labour, but were also given combat jobs, the action at Fort Wagner in July 1863 proving a key watershed, and sometimes made up the bulk of a force. The symbolic power of Black troops was shown in February 1865 when the forces that occupied Charleston, the site of the outbreak of the war, included Black troops recruited from former Carolina slaves.

Yet, leaving aside the murderous treatment of Black Union soldiers by the Confederates, as at Fort Pillow in 1864, which was an aspect of the way in which the war became more brutal, prejudice continued in the Union forces. Black soldiers were paid less while, faced with the pressure of creating large armies willing to fight, discipline became harsher during the Civil War, and the Union army staged many public executions. There was a racist dimension, as more Black soldiers were executed, and usually by hanging, while Whites were shot by firing squad, which was seen as more dignified. Nevertheless, Congress maintained the concept of all-Black regiments after the war, with Congress establishing specific cavalry and infantry regiments in 1866.

During the war, claims of necessity – claims furthered by the religious convictions important to the war effort – were employed to justify the extension of state power, a process eased by the absence of Southern representatives in Congress and the weak position of the Northern Democrats. Moreover, radical Republicans claimed that, by their secession, the Southerners had forfeited their constitutional rights. The power of the federal government was enhanced at the expense of the states, and a host of measures including conscription and the establishment of a national banking system were important in themselves and for what they signified. To Democrats, the Lincoln administration seemed tyrannical, as with the suspension of *habeas corpus* in Maryland, and action against critical newspapers, while, in the Congressional elections of 1862, the Democrats won the Indiana state legislature, only to find the Republicans refuse to attend the session and the governor, Oliver Morton, govern without it. Conscription, which was agreed by the Senate in 1863, greatly increased federal power and led to anger, evasion and riots. The Democratic presidential platform agreed in 1864 declared that 'under the pretence of a military necessity, or war power higher than the Constitution, the Constitution itself has been disregarded in every part'.

So also in the Confederacy. The difference between Democrats and Republicans, which contrasted greatly with the left–right alignment of today, led to predictions of change if Lincoln fell, predictions made by foreign commentators, as well as domestic counterparts. In the 1864 election, McClellan, the Democratic candidate, wanted reunion as the price of peace, but his running mate, George Pendleton, was a Peace Democrat, and the platform pressed for an armistice.

The election saw Lincoln, who drew on Republican Party organisation and patronage, win by 212 to 21 electoral votes, but the popular vote was far less unfavourable to McClellan than this figure suggests. The Republicans also won a substantial majority in Congress. Lincoln was helped by the backing of the War Democrats and by the army's support: 78 per cent of the Union soldiers who voted in the presidential election did so for him. This backing reflected the strong sense of religious mission that helped empower the Union soldiers and encourage them to prefer war for victory to negotiations. Having denied God's support by supporting sectional interests, America was to be made new, an affirmation of faith that reflected broad chords in American thought. McClellan, the former general, did not attract this emotional commitment. However, about 20 per cent of soldiers did not vote while some who voted for Lincoln did so in spite of Emancipation, and soldiers who were Democrats disproportionately resigned, deserted, failed to re-enlist, and were silenced in the ranks.

Lincoln's victory encourages a benign view of the continuance of the political process during the war, but, again, in part, this view is an instance of the broad-brush approach of hindsight. At the time, the politics of the war, at both the national and the state level, and between and within the parties, had proved highly disruptive. Moreover, this divisiveness had absorbed much political effort, posing problems for the direction of the war. Diplomats seeking signs of opposition were able to find them in plenty.

Lincoln's re-election, however, ended the political options for counterfactual speculation as far as the North was concerned. Northern morale affirmed Lincoln's position, just as his leadership helped ensure the resilience of this morale. The re-election provided the background for the pursuit of a strategy designed to stop Southern support for the war by crippling morale and destroying infrastructure, a goal shared by his troops. Although Sherman's devastation of the Confederate hinterland increased the resolve of some Southern soldiers, the ability to spread devastation unhindered across the Southern hinterland exacerbated the already serious tendency to desertion, helped destroy civilian faith in the war, and made the penalty for and limitation of guerrilla warfare apparent. Sherman had learned this when fighting the Seminole. The slave basis of Southern society collapsed as Union forces advanced, with thousands of slaves using the opportunities of Sherman's advance to escape their masters, although clogging US lines with 'contraband' as they were known.

While making territory his objective, Sherman moved beyond the unproductive nature that that goal and method frequently entailed. Instead, he used the occupation of territory to fulfil his goal of focusing on the psychological mastery of Southern society. This mastery was a goal that proved more productive than that of seeking the chimera of victory in battle, and one that matched the desire (on both sides) to achieve such mastery through humiliation and vengeance. Conversely, those who ceased resistance were better treated.

Sherman's advance also threatened Lee's rear in Virginia, and was to be praised as an instance of the indirect approach, contributing to the situation in which Lee was defeated without his army being destroyed. The home front was literally collapsing, and this collapse was closely linked to the failure of the Confederate armies.

In their different ways, Sherman and Grant, who focused on grinding down Lee's army, ensured that the uncertainty of war undermined the Confederacy, for they managed risk and uncertainty while their opponents came, in 1864, to experience it.

The tempo of Union operations exploited the uncertainty of conflict and directed it against the Confederacy's military as well as its socio-political underpinning. Sherman's advance was also the culmination of the long series of Union triumphs in the Western theatre. In 1862 and 1863, these had not prevented Lee from advancing in, and from, Virginia and, to a considerable extent, it had been possible to trade space in the West for time with which to attack in the East. This potentially war-winning Southern formula had failed, in the East, not across the Appalachians, but it was only after that the Union forces were able to exploit their success in the West in order to attack what could otherwise have been a defence in depth in the East. This exploitation of Northern success was in part a matter of a psychological shift. Grant brought a conviction that victory could be won, a confidence that reflected the repeated Union successes in the West.

The end of the war settled the issues of slavery and secession, but did not resolve the racial question, transform the economy or end the process of westward expansion that had been so important since colonial days and so significant for American nation-building.

The end of fighting left to commentators the question of why the war had occurred, a conflict that was to be refought endlessly, from bars to seminars. It became a political and racial issue, redolent with questions of and for American identity and Southern culture, and also (and not always separately) a matter of discussion for military specialists. The very sites of the war served to highlight disputes. Thus, in 2000, in response to discussion of the Interior Appropriations Bill, the National Park Service submitted to Congress a report assessing the educational information at Civil War sites and recommending that much be updated, not least to illustrate the 'breadth of human experience during the period, and establish the relevance of the war to people today'. Representative Jesse Jackson Jr. and other members of Congress had complained that many sites lacked appropriate contextualisation and, specifically, that there was often 'missing vital information about the role that the institution of slavery played in causing the American Civil War'. Subsequent disputes over statues demonstrated modern resonances of a Southern identity in the form of a symbolic Confederacy. It was only in 1998 that the 'Spirit of Freedom', the African American Civil War Memorial, was unveiled in Washington.

8
A New Power, 1865–98

A bold confidence was to the fore in paintings from the period, such as William Chase's *Boy Smoking (The Apprentice)* of 1875 which showed an unabashed, indeed brash, young man facing life. The war left the Union with a massive and well-honed military, just over a million men strong at the start of 1865, and with the second largest navy in the world: 671 warships, including seventy-one ironclads, in commission, as well as the prospect of further growth in the number of ships. This force appeared to offer options for expansion, or at least activity, notably against Canada and Mexico. Concerns about the former led Britain to press ahead with plans for Canadian unity through confederation, but the possibility of conflict focused on Mexico. After the war, American pressure for the departure of the French troops increased, and America's non-recognition of Maximilian's government became more significant.

As president, Grant favoured pressure, as he saw Napoleon III, Maximilian, Mexican conservatives and Southern exiles as the key elements in a far-ranging geopolitical and ideological combination directed against liberal progress in Mexico, and, therefore, against American interests. With the more cautious Seward opposed to full-scale military intervention, war, however, was avoided and fears of American filibustering, for example by disbanded troops against Mexico or Canada, proved groundless, although a small number of former Union troops formed Fenian parties and raided Canada in 1866 and 1870–1. The key development was a rapid dismantling of the Union military machine.

The American acquisition of Alaska and the Aleutian Islands from Russia in 1867 was scarcely the product of American pressure. The Americans were in no position to exert such pressure and, instead, for $7,200,000, bought the territory, which the Russians were keen to sell, not least because the Russian-American Company, the finances of which had long been precarious, was close to bankruptcy, while Russia could not protect Alaska from the Royal Navy in the event of another war with Britain. Critics condemned both the idea and the expense, referring to the episode as 'Seward's Folly', although only a small minority of the American press used this term or even criticised William Seward, the secretary of state from 1861 to 1869, for making the purchase, which was generally supported as another large expansion of territory.

Lincoln's vice-president and successor, Andrew Johnson, president from 1865 to 1869, a Democrat who had been a slave-owner and senator from Tennessee, sought conciliation, a rapid return to normality, at least in the shape of Southern self-government and re-entry into the Union, but the Republican majority in Congress disagreed and pushed through the Reconstruction Acts of 1867. The following year, the House of Representatives impeached Johnson, who had done his utmost to thwart Black rights and Republican policies, although he was acquitted by the Senate. A guide to Johnson's attitudes and his view on the conditional nature of Whites and Blacks sharing space was provided by his reply to the National Theological Institute for Coloured Ministers in which he declared that 'the free negro must work or seek a dime where he can live apart from the white man'.

Potentially, military control and activity was a departure not only for the South but for America as a whole, and one that would have added an entirely novel dimension to its geopolitics, one of an occupation zone sustaining a new political order. This order was ethnic as well as territorial, reflecting the overthrow of the previous system of exclusion, subordination and oppression. In 1865, the Thirteenth Amendment to the Constitution led to the freeing of about four million slaves. Slavery was ended in the loyal as well as the Confederate states. In 1866, over Johnson's veto, Congress passed the Civil Rights Act giving full citizenship to all born or naturalised in the United States, and voting rights to all male citizens. African Americans thus gained legal equality. The provisions of this legislation became the Fourteenth Amendment, which was ratified in 1868. It was followed in 1870 by the Fifteenth which prohibited denial of the vote because of 'race, color, or previous condition of servitude'. These amendments reflected the extent to which the radicalising nature of the war, and the issues to which it had given rise, made it possible to envisage improvements on the provisions decreed by the Founding Fathers.

Moreover, the Reconstruction Acts of 1867 dissolved the Southern state governments, which, in 1865, had passed racist 'Black codes' designed to limit the effect of slave emancipation; and, instead, reintroduced federal control, which gave the army the potential task of preserving this control against local opposition. The difficulty of this task was exacerbated by the unpopular nature of the new state governments that were created on behalf of the 'carpetbaggers': Northern adventurers unpopular at least as far as the bulk of the White population was concerned. Southern supporters of the 'carpetbag' state governments were derisively termed 'scalawags' in the South. In the face of this opposition, the army was expected to support the new governors and the new order, which entailed protecting government buildings, polling places, and Blacks as a population.

The South, bar Tennessee which had ratified the Fourteenth Amendment, was divided into five military districts, each under the command of a general, a technique employed in England under Oliver Cromwell in 1655–7 but abandoned because of its unpopularity. The army was not simply a latent presence in the South; it was responsible for a range of functions, mostly civil, but including the military tasks of disarming local militia and preserving order. The latter was particularly necessary in some areas, notably Appalachia, where the guerrilla warfare had left a legacy of vendettas and feuds, for example the Hatfield versus McCoy feud in West Virginia. The troops were also a restraint on any attempt to mount organised resistance or to resort to low-level seditious behaviour.

The army was confronted by the strength of White Southern belief in White superiority, a key element of a continuing Confederate nationalism. Indeed, the military burden of Reconstruction acted as a restraining factor on American behaviour elsewhere, for example in relations with Canada. The foundation of the Ku Klux Klan, a Confederate veterans' movement, in 1866, was followed by several thousand lynchings, although not all were by the Klan. In 1866, the army intervened to prevent a pogrom, if not massacre, of the Black population of New Orleans, while White militias that had been created after the Civil War were disbanded by the government in 1867. However, Whites clashed with the militias recruited by Radical Republican state governments, militias that included Blacks, as bodies such as the White Brotherhood and the White League challenged Reconstruction. Thus, in Tennessee, the role of the army was complemented by the State Guard, which included some Black soldiers and provided crucial protection against the Klan and gangs of former Confederates.

There was a danger that, fulfilling wartime warnings, for example by the French envoy, the army would become a long-term occupation force, with a task focused on controlling civilians and, possibly, even low-level counter-insurgency work. The commanding general in each district had the authority, if his actions were approved by the US attorney for that district, to arrest any civilian in state government, the governor included. The creation of the districts, in 1867, prompted the creation of the 'invisible empire' of the Klan, with the latter restructured for political combat: states as realms in the Klan empire, and congressional districts as dens.

Military support for the new political programme was modest, amounting to only about 20,000 troops in the South from 1867. As a consequence, even had it been willing, the army was not in a position to support Reconstruction once it was challenged by widespread violence against Blacks. As with the potential for foreign expansionism, this situation was a critical product both of post-war demobilisation by the heavily indebted federal government and of related and subsequent political decisions. The two should not be separated, although there was a different logic to, and context for, each. When President Johnson considered using the army against Congress in early 1868, the military proved unwilling to accept his plan for creating a sizeable new unit based near Washington. The army was then cut to 28,000 men, compared to 16,000 at the start of 1861, at which strength it remained until the Spanish-American War of 1898. The army might be small, and certainly was compared to its European counterparts, but it was no longer required to hold the country together, and it was not necessary to employ force in order to ensure that America would be dominated by Northern capital and industry.

The Klan was outlawed that year; it was abundantly clear by 1871 that Reconstruction would not be sustained by a large military presence. For example, the previous year, troops were moved from supporting Reconstruction in Florida to the Montana Territory where they acted against hostile Native Americans.

In New Orleans, in the 1873 Colfax Massacre, about 150 Black people were killed. In 1874, in 'the battle of Liberty Place', the White League, in an attempt to wrest control of the state from Vermont-born William Pitt Kellogg, the Republican governor from 1873 to 1877, occupied several key city-centre sites, only for the revolt to be quashed by federal troops.

By 1877, the Republican governments in the South had been overthrown, in part by the threat of mob violence, in every state bar Florida, Louisiana and South Carolina. It was only in these states that the troops sent to support Reconstruction remained, and these were now very few.

This situation was resolved as a result of political developments at the national level. The 1876 presidential election led to disputed returns, and, in the centennial year of the United States, amidst fears of new civil war, the army indeed made contingency plans to keep the peace. The disputed returns from Florida, Louisiana and South Carolina were crucial, and, as a result of complex political manoeuvres, a compromise awarded the presidency to the Republican candidate, Rutherford B. Hayes, a volunteer who had risen to be a major general in the Union army, but only in return for withdrawing the troops from the three states, which occurred in 1877. This withdrawal, which was welcomed by those concerned with civil/military relations and the federal system of government, led to the fall of the three Republican state governments. The new, more limited role for the army was underlined by the Posse Comitatus Act of 1878 which banned the use of the military in law enforcement, a major restriction on federal power. That was an aspect of the move back towards the state sovereignty lost, in both North and South, during the Civil War and under Reconstruction, a move back that was to be defended by the Supreme Court until the New Deal in the 1930s.

After Kellogg in 1873–7, there was no Republican governor of Louisiana until 1980 and, by then, the Republican party had changed completely, instead accommodating Southern White values. In the meanwhile, the South was a one-party state under the Democrats, while, in the late nineteenth century, there was a danger of the country as a whole becoming a one-party state under the Republicans.

The most booming city in the Caribbean world was New Orleans, which benefited greatly from the development of its Mississippi River hinterland, a development speeded by the potential of steamships, by the opportunities offered by rail, not least in linkages to steamship river ports, by population growth in the hinterland, and by the opportunities of an expanding world economy with a strong demand for cotton. There was extensive immigration to the city, which had a foreign-born population of about 40 per cent, many Germans or Irish. The population rose from about 116,000 in 1850 to nearly 170,000 in 1860, by which time America was producing about 80 per cent of the cotton traded in the world. Later in the century, there was to be a significant Italian immigration, with many finding work in the docks, but also leading to ethnic tension, as in 1890 when the murder of the superintendent of police, David Hennessy, was attributed to the Mafia and led to riots in which arrested Italian dock workers were killed. At the same time, this was a tension born of the opportunities presented by economic growth. The Italian government threatened to send a battleship.

Politics in New Orleans by then was very much a competition between two factions of White Democrats: the Ring, which was based on immigrants and organised labour and led by the corrupt machine boss John Fitzpatrick, versus reforming businessmen. Reform in New Orleans took on a particular form. In 1897, Edward Story, a ward representative, ordered a district on the low-lying and undesirable edge of the city set aside for legal prostitution in an effort to clean up New Orleans's image and restrict the prostitutes from plying their trade in the more fashionable areas. The move backfired, and 'Storyville' became a famous haunt for vice, prostitution and gambling, but also the birthplace of jazz.

As a reminder that multiple narratives are possible for the same site, New Orleans was hit hard by yellow fever in 1878. This was an aspect of the *ancien régime* of the city, but the last major outbreak there was in 1905. Public health education and measures helped wipe the disease out in the city.

In 1898, White Democrats took firm control of the Louisiana legislature and introduced a new constitution that segregated public schools and imposed poll taxes and literary tests as qualifications for voting. In the aftermath, as in 1868–80, many Black people left Louisiana, where limited opportunities were accompanied by a marked recalibration of control and oppression.

Hayes was one of four Union generals (along with Grant, Garfield and Harrison) and one major (McKinley) who became president, ensuring that veterans held the post from 1869 to 1881, 1889 to 1893, and 1897 to 1901. All were Republicans, as the party used their role in the war to justify their claim to guide the nation. The Democrats, in contrast, drew on the support of Southern Whites and Northern and Western workers. Thus, the memorialisation of the war was politically loaded, at the same time as it was a common experience for a large number. In Connecticut, for example, a state where there was no fighting, close to 50 per cent of White men and close to 80 per cent of Black men aged 15 to 50 served in the Union military. Union victory was marked in the erection of monuments, so that Washington became full of equestrian statues of generals, as well as in the celebration of anniversaries, especially Memorial Day, when graves were decorated and speeches listened to. Yet, this civic memorialisation did not lead to militarism. Very differently, African-American emancipation celebrations in the shape of Freedom Day anniversaries proved important to the creation of a particular civic identity and history.

The end of the occupation suggested a degree of return to normality, but the spatial order of America had been transformed since 1861. Aside from the devastation of much of the South, the war had brought economic growth to the North as resources had been unlocked and the vast military machine had been mobilised; thereafter, the contrast in economic and demographic development continued, although the consequences of the Civil War for the American economy have been a source of debate among economists.

Spanning the Continent

The transcontinental railway had been advocated with energy from the early 1850s, but was delayed by the sectionalism that led to the Civil War. The rebellion by the Confederacy encouraged the Union to press ahead, in part as a geostrategic measure to anchor the West. Founded in 1862, under the Pacific Railroad Act, the company began laying rails in Omaha in 1865 and joined the Central Pacific, constructed eastwards from Sacramento, California, at Promontory Summit, Utah in 1869. This was the first transcontinental railroad. The *Sacramento Daily Union* of 18 June 1866 noted: 'Almost the entire work of digging is done by Chinamen.'

In his allegorical painting of 1872 about American expansion, John Gast had, following the wagons, two trains steaming across the prairies. Areas that lacked access to river trade were opened up. Grain elevators were a dramatic demonstration of the importance of rail, and ones that recentred towns.

Criticism was widened by the extent to which railway companies were associated with fraud and/or with the use of rate structures to gain profit at the expense of communities and farmers, leading for example to populist criticism across the West, criticism seen in novels such as Frank Norris's *The Octopus* (1901). Railways, notably but not only in America, became notorious for what were known as robber barons, and many individuals, companies and communities were harmed by the ruthless competition of these proprietors, which extended to include railway construction in other countries, as with the Vanderbilt interest in Costa Rica.

On the pattern already seen with wagon road grants from the 1820s, land in the public domain was given to railway companies from the Illinois Central in 1850. These grants were much greater in the West, such as the Northern Pacific Railroad in 1864: these were larger in the federal Territories than in the area already allocated to states. There was a major element of speculation involved. Thus, in 1873, the Jay Cooke bank, which had invested in the building of the Northern Pacific, only to underestimate the cost, failed, leading to The Panic, a major fiscal crisis. Other railways also gained much land, for example the Oregon Central in 1870 which gained valuable forest land. In 1884, the map publisher Rand McNally produced a map for the Democratic Party showing the wide tranches that had been granted to railway corporations, with a printed accompanying text, including the statement, 'We believe that the public lands ought . . . to be kept as homesteads for actual settlement.'

Settlements owed their origins or development to the train. Founded by a trapper in 1846, Ogden in Utah became a major passenger and freight railway junction, not least as it was where major east–west and north–south routes crossed. Westbound passengers changed from Union Pacific to Southern Pacific services here. The city was known for brothels and bars. Las Vegas was established in 1905 by the San Pedro, Los Angeles and Salt Lake Railroad as a division point to house train crew.

America saw many improvements in railway methods, not least the patenting by George Westinghouse in 1873 of the pneumatic brake, a system employing compressed air that allowed the braking of all carriages simultaneously. The South was not an area of rail investment comparable to the Northeast and the Midwest. However, railways were important to its post-Civil War economic role of providing raw materials for Northern industries. Looked at less positively, a major one was cotton and the rail system thus served to maintain the socio-political order in the South with African

Americans no longer slaves but restricted after the failure of Reconstruction by disenfranchisement and share-cropping.

The steam railway (ie not street railways) mileage per land area was headed by New Jersey, but with Massachusetts close behind. Then, in order, came Connecticut, Rhode Island, Ohio, Pennsylvania, Illinois, Indiana, New York and Iowa, which showed the dominance, first, of New England and, then, of the Midwest.

In 1850–70, America tripled the production of iron, having already done the same in 1830–50. The availability of Western bullion and of demand from the American industrial belt helped underwrite the financing of new railways.

Immigration focused on the North. Economic growth was intended to encompass the South, although there were limits to the pro-business liberalism of Republican policies. Measures against Chinese immigration, notably the Chinese Exclusion Act of 1882, hit the provision of inexpensive labour, as well as limiting the Republican commitment to racial equality. Separately, Hispanics in Texas lost much of their land, in part due to the use of the legal system by Anglo-Texans but also due to drought and liquidity issues.

However, the political, economic and social disruption brought to the South by defeat, occupation and emancipation had a potent psychological impact, not least in leaving a backward-looking bitterness that contributed to a failure to engage with the possibilities of development within a strong America orientated on national grounds. This failure to engage also arose from the practice of many of the remaining Southern elite to maintain a smaller and poorer agricultural society with oppressive labour relations in which they remained at the top of the socio-economic pyramid, rather than joining the newer industrial order whose urbanisation and mechanisation would threaten their superiority in the

South. This course owed much to inertia. The elite did what they knew, and did not know how to do things like they did in the North. There was a similar problem for the ex-slaves; they only knew servitude, while during Reconstruction the federal government did little to help them transition to acting as free people.

These attitudes and policies led to both absolute and relative underdevelopment for the South in agriculture, as well as industry; other areas responded to the economic opportunities created by large-scale population growth, improved communications and industrialisation, the terms of which provided key elements for national politics and identity in a capitalist democracy. Looked at differently, national grounds and criteria were now understood very much in terms of the values of the North, and, in particular, scant investment was devoted to the South, both from within America and also internationally; it remained very short of capital and credit. An important electoral aspect of the post-1876 order were measures to restrict voting by African Americans, as with the poll-tax amendment to the state constitution adopted, for example in Arkansas in 1892, as well as the use by the Democratic party of White primaries as another way to disfranchise African-American voters. In 1883, civil rights cases in the Supreme Court challenged Reconstruction, as did the *Plessy v Ferguson* case in 1896. More generally, relatively few Black tenants became farm-owners. Reconstruction had only very limited success in distributing land to former slaves. Instead, essentially, the settler colonisation of the South entered a new form with a restricted labour system.

Intimidation was part of the process, as in the arrest of would-be Black voters in the 1874 Alabama election and in the defeat of the Union Labor candidate in the Arkansas gubernatorial election of 1888. Aside from Black disfranchisement, and its economic equivalent in share-cropping (landowners taking a share of the crop but trapping tenants in poverty and debt), there was segregation, and a system and ethos enforced with brutal violence through lynchings, street fights and riots, as well as insistent intimidation and imprisonment. Whatever the paternalistic vision of White supremacy, it had clearly crystallised into a vicious reality. White supremacy, which was represented in a monopoly of power by the Democratic party, destroyed the ideal of the Declaration of Independence. Textbooks and public and private memorialisation framed this experience. Another aspect of the racial use of force was that of convict labour, which became common, notably in Georgia, with a large number of African Americans sent to prison and then leased out to employers who had scant interest in their well-being. This convict-lease system ensured that African-American males were frequently visibly treated as if slaves. In Alabama, similarly, prisoners, almost always Black, were leased to coalmines where they were harshly treated, wearing leg chains and subject to whippings. In 1900, life expectancy for Whites was 48, but for Blacks 33.

The North's victory, paradoxically, was to be confirmed, in a fashion, by the theme of 'reconciliation' that became stronger from the 1890s. This theme entailed the idea of drawing some sort of moral equivalence between the combatants, and, doing so meant underplaying slavery and ignoring Blacks' role in Union victory. Reconciliation, therefore, made many, and excessive, allowances for Southern views, but it also rested on a willingness by much of a North, triumphant in its dominance of present and future, not to be overly troubled about the past, an outcome that proved beyond many Southerners who preferred the identity of collective grievance.

Washington Reborn

Victory in the Civil War moved Washington from a defended city near the front line to a capital in need of revitalisation. There was the wealth and organisation to do and a willingness to propose, plan, enact and implement that was more generally the case of America in this period. Dirt-track roads and open sewers were no longer acceptable. Instead, in the 1870s, the District of Columbia embarked on a massive programme of infrastructure improvement through its Board of Works under Alexander Robey 'Boss' Shepherd. The Board filled in the canal, built hundreds of miles of paved roads and pavements, sewers, water and gas mains, planted trees, installed street lighting, and set up transport systems. The Army Corps of Engineers reclaimed the tidal wetland known as the Potomac Flats from 1882, which helped prevent flooding.

If occupation of the South was restrained in comparison to what could have occurred, and to how it would be remembered by Southern Democrats, no such restraint was to be shown in the West. Indeed the number of troops in the South had been considerably reduced in the 1870s, prior to 1876, as securing the West became the central issue for the army. Already, as with the War of Independence, conflict with the Native Americans continued during the Civil War, although, initially, the gathering crisis led to a decline in hostilities. Thus, plans for a winter campaign against the Navajo in 1860–1 were abandoned. However, the customary tensions over settlement and control remained, and, as American activity remained incessant, so the Native American response was frequently hostile. Moreover, the Civil War encouraged a response on the part of the government to force by lessening peacetime restraints. Attacks may have been inspired by rumours of Native American support for the Confederacy. There was, indeed, some support, and a number of treaties were signed, although loyalists also rallied to the Union and fought for it.

As a result, there was conflict across much of the West, conflict that interacted, often indirectly, with the Civil War there. In some areas, the Americans were under pressure, notably in Texas, where, despite some success, the Confederates were unable to protect their western settlements, and an outnumbered Ranger force was routed by Kickapoo at Dove Creek in 1865.

More commonly, it was the Native Americans who were defeated. In Minnesota and Colorado, the extent of American settlement was the key provocation. This was certainly an issue in the Minnesota rising of 1862, which also affected the Dakota Territory. Eastern Sioux attacked American settlements in Minnesota, although they failed to capture the forts, while other Sioux attacked Americans, en route to gold workings in Montana, crossing their lands on the Bozeman Trail. The army responded by driving the Eastern Sioux back from Minnesota, and, then, during the summers of 1863, 1864 and 1865, launched columns under Brigadier Generals Henry Sibley and Alfred Sully against the Sioux in Dakota and Montana. Sully defeated Sitting Bull at Killdeer Mountain, North Dakota, in 1864.

In Colorado, violence between settlers and the Arapaho and Cheyenne led to an increasingly tense situation. In June 1864, the Governor of the Colorado Territory, John Evans, instructed 'friendly Indians' to present themselves at army posts, but also presented a military response. Evans was given governmental permission to raise the Third Colorado Cavalry, a regiment of volunteers to be commanded by Colonel John Chivington, the head of the Army military district in Colorado. Native American chiefs sought to negotiate a settlement and thought they had done so with Evans and Chivington at Camp Weld in September. As a consequence, Arapaho and Cheyenne moved to Fort Lyon. However, Evans was preparing to destroy the tribes. At dawn on 29 November, Chivington's men attacked the Native American encampment, killing many both there and a mile further on where the fleeing Native Americans adopted a defensive position, only to be bombarded by twelve-pounder mountain howitzer guns. In the Sand Creek Massacre, at least 150 and maybe about 200 Native Americans, mainly women, children and the elderly, were slaughtered. Ten soldiers were killed. Chivington's men were applauded in Denver, but the massacre, which helped to touch off a major bout of fighting across the Plains, was swiftly condemned in Washington.

There was also conflict further west, with California troops defeating Shoshone in Idaho and Ute in Utah in 1863. That year, treaties were negotiated with Native American tribes in California and Oregon. Further south, federal columns forced the Navajo to agree to move to reservations in 1864, a bland description of the use of scorched-earth policies and of the subsequent forced march of the Navajo and their confinement in the bleak reservation of Bosque Redondo. The Comanche, meanwhile, were hit hard by smallpox and by drought, the latter greatly affecting bison numbers.

The pace of expansion at the expense of Native Americans resumed after the Civil War, with the Powder River Expedition launched into Wyoming in 1865 against the Sioux, Cheyenne and Arapaho, but much of the preparatory work had been done during it, and, indeed, there was continuity in the case of that expedition which was a reprisal for raids earlier that year. The notion that it was Civil War veterans, notably Sherman (commander of the Division of the Missouri from 1865) and Philip Sheridan (commander of the Department of the Missouri from 1867), who inaugurated a harsher, exterminatory, approach to Plains warfare requires qualification as, aside from assuming a misleading consensus in frontier warfare, Harney before the war and Carleton during the war both advocated wiping out their Native American enemies and practised it to the best of their ability. Moreover, during the Civil War, the useful tactic of winter campaigning got its start.

Nevertheless, there were serious problems for the army. Many commanders from the 1850s were dead or had lost their commissions by serving the Confederacy; and their replacements, trained in, and from, the Civil War, with its emphasis on commanding and fighting large numbers of regulars, were not adept at dealing with the very mobile Native Americans. Moreover, the sharp reduction of the army in the aftermath of the Civil War ensured that there were few troops available for frontier warfare. When, in 1867, Sheridan took command of the Department of the Missouri, which covered much of the frontier, he had only 6,000 troops.

Aside from the problem that the show of force helped provoke further resistance, as General Winfield Scott Hancock's expedition of 1867 demonstrated with the response of the Cheyenne, in operational and tactical terms it proved difficult to force the mobile Native Americans to battle, not least because they knew the terrain and were adept at surprise. The Sioux showed this in 1866–8 in their successful campaigning against the army in Montana and Wyoming in the Bozeman Trail War, also known as Red Cloud's War. The Sioux surrounded and besieged American forts, forcing their abandonment.

As a consequence, the army developed techniques that focused on winter campaigning. Native American settlements were particularly vulnerable in the winter, as those who escaped risked starvation and death by exposure. In 1868, at the battle of the Washita, Lieutenant-Colonel George Armstrong Custer annihilated a southern Cheyenne village led by Black Kettle, killing women and children as well. The destruction of crops and villages and the confiscation of pony herds, none of which were new tactics, also brought misery, and the British envoy deplored such methods as 'unnecessary' and 'wholesale slaughter'. The coordination of independently operating columns advancing from different directions was also important to American success.

There was an important shift in government policy after Ulysses S. Grant became president in 1869. Believing in 'conquest by kindness' in which Native Americans moved to reservations where Christian education and agriculture were to make them good neighbours, where they were civilised and Christianised, Grant followed what has been seen as a peace policy. As a result of the shift in policy, the pace of hostilities declined at the close of the 1860s, although the situation deteriorated in the early 1870s, with the peace policy discredited in 1871. That autumn, Sherman sent troops against the Comanche who were seen as putting Texas under excessive pressure. The inexorable nature of this adversary placed the Comanche in unprecedented difficulties.

Whatever the pace of conflict, Native American resistance was largely broken, and a successful military methodology to that end had been evolved. Its focus on wrecking civil society, or, rather, on the notion that there was no civil sphere separate to the military, had been seen in the conflict between North and South in the latter stages of the Civil War. In the West, this system was made especially effective against Native Americans thanks to the mobility of the regulars and their ability, through a good logistical system, to stage winter campaigns. This success indicated the army's potential to adapt its military style and methods, and its mobility was an important legacy to subsequent American military culture and doctrine.

Industrial capacity underlay this mobility as the railway was used to move troops against opponents. The railway also provided greater profit for ranching as cattle were introduced to arid, marginal lands over which control had been established, and then moved east by rail. Mass-produced beef became a key part of the American diet, with consequences for nutrition, health and physique, not least in terms of differences to most Europeans including migrants to America. In turn, the Great Plains switched from bison and nomad Native Americans to cattle and American ranchers. The equivalent of cattle ranching in the West was the import into Alaska from Siberia in the 1890s of reindeer, but this failed in what was a harsher environment.

Other factors played a role in American success in the West, not least obtaining local support because of Native American rivalries. In the Sioux Wars (1854–77), most of the other Plains tribes joined the Americans against the Sioux, as they saw the latter as a far more immediate threat to their safety than the more distant Americans. The American army used Pawnee and Crow scouts in the major battles of the 1860s and 1870s, as well as Shoshone warriors as auxiliaries. The Sioux, in turn, viewed the Americans as merely one more tribal enemy for much of the time, and alternated attacks on American units and forts with raids against Crow and Shoshone. The same was true of the Comanche.

The Sioux suffered from the army's adoption in 1867 of breech-loaders able to fire twelve shots a minute, which provided a crucial firepower advantage. The Native American attempt to counter this by acquiring the same weaponry could be deadly, as at Little Big Horn in 1876, but suffered from their lack of access to ammunition supplies. Moreover, there were major limits to the changes in Native American war-making, notably away from the style of individual fighting that stressed bravery and yet also the avoidance of casualties. In particular, the Sioux did not attempt to institute anything like military discipline or coercive leadership, and the seasonal nature of their warfare could not be altered.

Red Cloud and his warriors came to the bargaining table for peace shortly after his fighting power had been greatly reduced by the American use of breech-loaders. By 1867 on the southern plains (Treaty of Medicine Lodge) and by 1868 on the northern plains (Treaty of Fort Laramie), most tribes had been sent to a reservation. Those who left without permission were deemed hostile. Although the Fort Laramie treaty created a large Lakota Sioux reservation, centred on the Black Hills and without military supervision, this was a new geography of power and control. Much of the landscape was given English names, notably the land not kept by reservations. Moreover, in 1877, the Black Hills, now known to be rich in gold, were taken from the Sioux. In the remaining Indian Territory that eventually became Oklahoma, tribal governance was undermined by extension of federal judicial power.

This was a geography in which the army positioned the West into America not solely by enforcing the reservation policy and maintaining security but also by playing a major role in supporting economic integration, notably by building roads and encouraging the building of railways. Sherman was particularly involved in this process. These policies were part of a wider programme by which the railway fostered public policies that encouraged the stabilisation of civil society, including public relief and law enforcement, while the reservations were intended to clear threatening Native Americans from the rail routes, particularly from those along the Platte and Kansas valleys, the routes for the Union Pacific and Kansas Pacific lines. In addition, military expenditure was important in bringing a measure of prosperity. Meanwhile, the Native Americans were subsumed into an American identity as the Wild West was presented as exemplary entertainment, for example by Bill Cody's Buffalo Bill shows and subsequently in films. They also came to be a subject for anthropology.

A basis for American political culture was offered in 1893 when Frederick Jackson Turner delivered an address, 'The Significance of the Frontier in American History', to the American Historical Association. Turner argued that the availability of 'free land' ensured that Americans developed distinctive character traits and institutions, with individualism and democracy based on economic opportunity. The frontier was presented as a 'crucible' that explained American development. The Census Bureau had itself declared the frontier closed in 1890, ending the defining period of American history. Turner thus redefined American history from a focus on European links and the East Coast to an emphasis on the West and on the American nation. Indeed, Turner's account was very much one based on the idea of agency by 'European' Americans. Accepting the nineteenth-century idea of a hierarchy of races and civilisations, Turner did not see the Native Americans as playing a significant role in the contact zone other than as resisting the advance of civilisation.

Because of the Pacific and the lure of East Asia, notably the China trade, America was not comparable geopolitically to China, in that the turn from the ocean (the Atlantic for the USA) was not simply a turn into the interior, as it was for China. However, that element was strongly present for American commentators. Turner's approach was scarcely apolitical, and it was unsurprising that Turner praised Senator Thomas Hart Benton of Missouri. A prominent expansionist of the 1830s and 1840s, Benton argued for America's westward destiny and pressed hard for America to occupy the Oregon country, pre-empting Britain.

That the Civil War represented a triumph for the urban and industrial society of the North over the agrarian-based Southern counterpart had implications for foreign policy. Seward proclaimed that 'the nation that draws the most materials and provisions from the earth, fabricates the most, and sells the most of productions and fabrics to foreign nations, must be, and will be, the great power of the earth'.

This definition of the future growth of American power excluded both the original Jeffersonian concept of an agrarian state whose farmers constituted the basis of economic and political power and the Southern manifestation of that concept in which land investors from Washington to Jackson on sought an uninterrupted march westwards. Seward's vision, indeed, required the subjugation of the agrarian alternative society of the South.

San Francisco

Annexation by America and, more particularly, the California Gold Rush that began in 1848, saw the population of San Francisco, a settlement of fewer than 100 buildings, rise from 1,000 to 25,000 by the close of 1849 and about 70,000 by 1859.

Brick and stone buildings were hastily built to provide facilities and housing, while wharfs and piers served shipping and more prosperity brought grander buildings, such as the enormous Palace Hotel with its 755 guest rooms, built in 1875, in which king Kalākaua of Hawai'i died in 1891. Hit very hard by the 1906 earthquake and subsequent fire, the city was rebuilt with more thoroughfares, broader streets, Beaux-Arts style buildings, and a new civic complex. The new city was celebrated by the Panama Pacific International Exposition of 1915 which was held to mark the opening of the canal.

The opportunities offered by California drew in large numbers of Asian immigrant labourers, but, after initial encouragement, not least in order to build the railways, discriminatory laws were passed from the 1870s in order to push them out. Chinatowns were depicted as dens of depravity, criminality and insanitary conditions as in the map of San Francisco's Chinatown produced by the Board of Supervisors in 1885. This map used colour coding to denote uses, including for gambling, prostitution and opium, and resembled those used to identify epidemic hotspots.

Once the North accomplished that end in a civil war started by the South in pursuance of its requirements for social and political development, there was the mistaken hope that the new economic and political order in the South would share Northern values. In practice, defeat, as well as the lessened profitability of cotton linked to emancipation, helped ensure a fall in the per capita income in the South as a percentage of national income to 50 in 1880, where it remained until 1930, with limited inward investment, migration, or the adoption of ideas. Politically, the expansion of statehood took place in the context of Northern control. The wartime states (West Virginia 1863; Nevada 1864) were followed by Nebraska (1867), Colorado (1876), North Dakota (1889), South Dakota (1889), Minnesota (1889), Washington (1889), Wyoming (1890) and Utah (1896).

The geopolitical policies of America, meanwhile, reflected Seward's vision. Rather like Britain's longstanding policy in Latin America, the priority became access to markets and the securing of routes to those markets, rather than the conquest of land. Most obviously, the United States no longer sought to annex Mexican territory, but, instead, gained access to the Mexican market. The Americans eventually controlled all the major extractive industries there, and foreigners, led by Americans, owned slightly less than a quarter of Mexico's land. The turn away from territorial expansion was demonstrated by the substantial public relations campaign Seward undertook to persuade Congress to fund his purchase of Alaska. The geopolitical struggle for North America had evolved into a geoeconomic struggle for markets, one that the Americans were increasingly to conduct not only in Latin America and East Asia but on a world scale.

America also became more active in the Pacific, in 1867 claiming Midway Atoll as a coaling station. In part as a response, Kalākaua of Hawai'i (r. 1874–91) commissioned and fitted out a sometime guano trader as a warship, the *Ka'imiloa*. Intended as a training vessel for the fledgling Hawai'ian navy, this was equipped with four brass cannon and two Gatling guns. The captain was British and the standing regulations for the British navy were adopted for its Hawai'ian counterpart, which was designed to give effect to the plan for a Pacific confederation of Hawai'i, Samoa, Tonga and the Cook Islands, intended to prevent Western annexations. To that end, the ship was sent to Samoa in 1887, but, faced by serious indiscipline among the crew, the Hawai'ian vessel was recalled and mothballed. In 1893, the monarchy was overthrown and, in 1898, Hawai'i became an American colony, which ensured that economic dominance by the 'Big Five' sugar-cane processing companies was strengthened. Local self-governance began in 1900.

Albeit against a weak empire, America demonstrated its power in a war with Spain in 1898 that reflected wide-ranging geopolitical interests and capabilities. The conquest of Cuba and Puerto

Rico and the arrival of American troops in the Philippines followed rapid and decisive naval victories. Cuba was not annexed after Spain was defeated there. Instead, the Americans retained control of the naval anchorage at Guantanamo and the power to control sea lanes that came with such a base. In 1912, the Americans sent Marines into Cuba in order to protect American property in the face of a large-scale, mostly Black, peasant uprising motivated by the strains of economic change, social pressure and political discrimination. Annexation was no longer an option, but the disruptive consequences of American activity remained acute.

In contrast, the peace treaty left Puerto Rico, Guam and the Philippines to America, but, in the last, control was enforced only after nationalist opposition was suppressed in a bitter counter-insurgency war. These difficulties underlined the value of not having had to face a guerrilla war in the South from 1865, for, in the Philippines, the Americans found it hard to fix their opponents for combat, and, while they were ultimately successful, their methods were often brutal.

Rather than being a case of strong or weak governance, simply defined, a key element in America in 1865 was the ability, once wartime exigencies had been put aside, to return to a large margin of self-government by the states; while Germany, in contrast, once unified through war, notably in 1866, came to symbolise the linkage of a bureaucratic, powerful state to a strong army.

Germany and America both saw significant economic growth, but there were distinctive features to the American economy, which became more self-sufficient, with much less of a dependence on supply-and-demand factors focused on Europe. As a result, an independent dynamic developed in the American economy, a dynamic that encouraged specialisation, investment and growth. The economic forces of the period included technological advances, such as horse-drawn harvesters and threshing machines, that led to a massive growth in commercial agriculture and a market economy, as well as the development of heavy capital-goods and consumer-goods industries. These developments galvanised widespread political support for the policies of the Republican Party that occupied the presidency until a split allowed the Democrat Woodrow Wilson to win election in 1912.

By the start of the twentieth century, American economic output was equivalent to that of the whole of Europe, and, by 1918, with America both a major creditor state and benefiting from large-scale wartime growth, it had the capital to match. The American economy benefited from substantial natural resources, including coal, iron, copper, silver and timber, a large domestic market, extensive immigration, an openness to foreign investment, a legal code that protected property, a governmental system that supported economic growth, and a political practice at the national level that avoided extremism. Innovation and the shock of the new were expressed in terms of the skyscrapers made possible by elevator/lift technology and investment.

Dramatic new industrial sites, and indeed cities, such as Gary, Indiana which became a centre for US Steel in 1906, affirmed rising economic power, which was presented as an opportunity to mould a technologically powered bright future. This was a potent form of Progressivism.

America's innovatory ethos derived in part from the shortages of skilled labour throughout the nineteenth century. This encouraged both large-scale immigration and also female entry into the labour force, while the position of women was also affected by mandatory public education, changes in the grounds for divorce and the passage of married women's property laws.

There was large-scale environmental damage as a result of growth. In part, this was a matter of the natural environment, such as deforestation, but there were also many problems affecting that for humans. For example, the poor quality of meat, especially pork, notably from the meat-packing plants of Swift and Armour in Chicago, was exposed in Upton Sinclair's novel *The Jungle* (1905), leading to the introduction of federal meat inspectors. The feeding of large and expanding urban markets was met by big business organisation that included branding. The period gave America Kellogg's Corn Flakes and Quaker Oats.

Regionalism was not simply a matter of North and South, but, as throughout American history, there were many other variations and cross-currents. Key ones included urban and rural, or those over finance, monopolies and in particular the nature of money. Whereas fiscal conservatives and creditors backed the gold standard, farming groups, industrial workers, and those who claimed to represent both the people and the West, notably William Jennings Bryan, criticised the gold standard. It was presented as deflationary, and as squeezing rural society for the rich, and thus challenging social mobility and democracy.

Appealing to the West, 1896

'. . . the hardy pioneers who have braved all the dangers of the wilderness, who have made the desert to bloom as the rose – the pioneers away out there [pointing westwards] who rear their children near to nature's heart, where they can mingle their voices with the voices of the birds – out there where they have erected schoolhouses for the education of their young, churches where they praise their Creator, and cemeteries where rest the ashes of their dead – these people, we say, are as deserving of the consideration of our party as any people in this country . . . we will answer their demand for a gold standard by saying to them: You shall not press down upon the brow of labor this crown of thorns, you shall not crucify mankind upon a cross of gold.'

William Jennings Bryan speaking at the Democratic Convention. He won the nomination (as he also did in 1900 and 1908), but was beaten in the election by William McKinley.

In the same period, one of environmental change due to settler farming, with the cutting down of forests, draining of wetlands, and ploughing up of grasslands, the American West was becoming a motif for the nation. This was particularly so with the foundation in 1892 of the Sierra Club and the paintings of the period, such as Thomas Moran's *Nearing Camp . . . Wyoming* (1882), taking forward the interest in a natural national identity earlier developed for New England. The establishment of national parks became part of the process. Tourists could go by train and the new motor cars. These ended dependence on less reliable alternatives: earlier, between 1819 and 1895, over 400 steamboats had sunk on the Missouri alone. Drought in 2022 has revealed wrecks such as the *North Alabama*, which was sunk in 1870 by a submerged log piercing its hull.

Change was far from universally welcomed. The sense of big business as hostile was seen across much of the country with anger directed in particular at the control of railway companies, mine-owners and banks. Jeffersonian, Jacksonian and later ideas of wealth distribution appeared to have been wrecked by the existence and practices of big business, which also undermined property rights and the idea of the just reward of labour. This was seen as a new serfdom akin to slavery, an attack on the people and on the teachings of religion. The result was a populism that led to disorder in some areas, for example the silver-mining region of Idaho in the 1890s.

More generally, there was a criticism of the 'Gilded Age' of wealth that, alongside Protestant commitment, encouraged the development of Progressivist activism. In part, this emphasis on reform and the common man, one that was to be important to the New Deal, drew on a sense of established business and government as corrupt. There was also the feeling of a need for a new politics that could revive the hope of the republic and overcome the current divisiveness, notably the compromising of the public interest and of popular control by sectarianism and ethnic activism, whether pro- or anti-immigration. Social resentments were important to the political cross-currents of the period, which included rural and small-town concern about the big cities.

There was, moreover, a lack of confidence in the legal system and therefore a confidence in violence, as opposed to civil government. This reached its atypical height in the assassinations of presidents, with James Garfield in 1881 and William McKinley in 1901 following Lincoln in 1865.

The need for a new politics encompassed movements for political reform, notably female suffrage, and others for a new society including the temperance movement which was designed to socialise in an approved pattern of moral rectitude. This was a new version of a supposedly chosen nation. It also looked towards the multi-faceted characteristic of a Progressivism that came to the fore in the 1890s but with the call for reform looking in different directions. Elizabeth Cady Stanton had asked in 1892: 'Inasmuch, then, as woman shares equally the joys and sorrows of time and eternity, is it not the height of presumption in man to propose to represent her at the ballot box?' Progressives also favoured the direct democracy of primaries, as well as antitrust laws and more business regulation. Government power was seen as a key adjunct to democratic progress, with the emphasis different to that of the Democrat Progressives, notably William Jennings Bryan.

Railways and New Cities

'In this young world the cities have come first,' commented the visiting Antony Trollope of the Midwest in 1861. This owed much to rail. Thus, Kansas City was founded as a port at the confluence of the two rivers, and incorporated there in 1850. There was competition with Chicago for dominance of Midwest meat packing. The stockyards were established in 1871 along the railway tracks of the Kansas Pacific and

Missouri Pacific (the descendant of the Pacific Railway), expanding greatly in 1878 when loading docks were added on both railways. The Kansas City and Cameron Railroad, a subsidiary of the Hannibal and St Joseph Railroad, built Hannibal Bridge in Kansas City; opened in 1869, it was the first bridge across the Missouri River. This was important to the development of the city, ensuring that it was the key node. In 1886, a tornado hit hard and the bridge had to be rebuilt. A centralised rail terminal was provided by the Union Depot which opened in 1878, designed in Gothic Revival style but prone to flooding. Expansion continued, the Kansas City Suburban Belt Railway beginning operation in 1890, and eventually becoming the Kansas City Southern Railway.

Further south, Fort Worth, Texas, which had a railway by 1876 and stockyards by 1887, became a key centre for the Armour and Swift meat-packing companies from 1902, with the companies owning the relevant linked railway. Railways delivered both live cattle and refrigerated carcasses, with the Swift Refrigerator Line established in 1880 owning 7,000 ice-cold rail cars by 1920. Hell's Half Acre, the red light district of Fort Worth, developed between the railway station and the central business district.

The people who lived in railway towns were shorter than those in non-railway towns, because the railways brought new people and therefore new germs, which had a marked impact on public health. Looked at differently, railway towns were generally more industrial and such work posed serious health problems. Both the industry and the railways depended greatly on steam power, and there was no real effort to remove particulates from the smoke before it was pumped into the atmosphere. As a result, railway towns that were not exposed to persistent wind often sat in a pall of smoke, with both air quality and visibility greatly affected.

Yet, the railway also brought activity, jobs and a measure of prosperity. All the major cities in the Midwest were railway cities. In the 1890s there were 38 distinct lines into Chicago, the population of which had grown from 360 in 1833 to 1.7 million by 1900.

Los Angeles

As with many American cities, for example San Antonio, this was older but grew greatly towards the close of the century, the population increasing from 11,000 in 1880 to over 100,000 by 1900. The growth, and the city's sprawl, depended on infrastructure, such as bridges and roads, to connect the city with outlying agricultural communities. The first permanent bridge was built in 1870, linking Los Angeles with the east bank, across the Los Angeles River, and helping the first two suburbs, known now as Lincoln Heights and Boyle Heights, to take root. A covered, New England-style bridge, it was replaced in 1904 by a structure felt to be more modern. The first car in Los Angeles appeared in 1897.

9

On the Rise, 1898–1933

By 1914, America was a major power in the Pacific, with Alaska, purchased in 1867, Hawai'i, Midway, Johnston, Palmyra, Tutula and Wake islands, as well as Guam and the Philippines. America was also increasingly assertive in Mexico, Central America and the Caribbean. This power was dramatised in the new geopolitics of the Panama Canal, which provided a link for warships and merchantmen between the eastern and western seaboards of America. A project originally and unsuccessfully begun with French capital had ended in 1914 as a triumph for American engineering and influence. In 1903, Panama became an independent state carved out from Colombia under American protection. Under the Hays-Bunau-Varilla Treaty with Panama, America gained control over the land zone, providing a parallel to British control over the Suez Canal. The construction of the canal, finished in 1914, owed much to the American army, which played a major role in its planning and organisation, as well as in providing protection for the workers from disease. The last territories in the contiguous USA were turned into states: Oklahoma (1907), Arizona (1912) and New Mexico (1912).

Territorial expansion and military strength were not add-ons to the Progressive Era that stretched from the 1890s, notably the late 1890s, to American entry into World War I in 1917. Instead, they were central to it, not least under Theodore Roosevelt, who was president from 1901 to 1909. By 1914, America was the world's third largest naval power after Britain and Germany. A geographically informed political consciousness became more significant, and wide-ranging ambitions developed accordingly. Atlas and map production and use increased, and geography was democratised.

A vigorous Republican reformer, Roosevelt held office as a successful assistant secretary of the Navy in 1897–8 and served in Cuba in 1898, before being first governor of New York that year and then vice-president in 1901. McKinley's assassination led to Roosevelt becoming president that year, and he proved an active protagonist of a stronger America: reform at home and strength abroad. Seeking to regulate big business, he regulated trusts, creating the Department of Commerce and Labor, and pursuing what he termed 'a square deal for every man'. Roosevelt sought to throw out the corrupt from government, and helped push through the Pure Food and Drug Act and the Federal Inspection Act, both of 1906. These represented a new version of the relationship between regulation, in this case the Food and Drug Administration, and capitalism, one that in practice benefited bigger businesses. At the same time, greater federal regulation, which included the Federal Reserve established in 1913, increased the size and power of government, a process that was to be even clearer with Prohibition (the production, import and sale of alcohol) when it was introduced as a national measure in 1920. Progressives inherently turned to the state as a way to fulfil what they saw as democratic ideals.

Roosevelt also created National Parks, National Forests, bird reserves and game preserves, placing about 230 million acres under public protection. Roosevelt's environmental concerns remain a hallmark of federal policies today. To this and other ends, Roosevelt made extensive use of executive orders. A key figure in moulding the modern United States, Roosevelt, one of the most colourful, mercurial and unorthodox presidents in American history, defined the Progressive Era.

Rail Encounters Problems

Reform, however, affected the profitability of rail. In the 1900s, the fiscal environment in America moved against rail companies, with the federal and some state (including

New York) governments placing legal restrictions on institutional holdings, in part in order to pursue 'trust busting', while from 1907, despite wage and price inflation, rail companies found rate increases banned. This led to low profits and dividends, which caused limited creditworthiness and investment, and pressure on solvency, not least in the 1910s when industrial stocks and war finance provided other investment opportunities.

Already strong, America was the prime beneficiary from World War I (1914–18), a conflict that centred in Europe and hit its economies hard. The European powers, especially Britain, sold many of their foreign investments in order to finance the war effort, increasing American control of the domestic economy. The disruption of European trade and the diversion of manufacturing to war production encouraged the growth of manufacturing elsewhere, and America, which did not enter the war until 1917, benefited most of all. The British war effort rapidly became heavily dependent on American financial and industrial resources. American forces on the Western Front played a role in the German defeat in 1918 and the prospect of far more American troops arriving was crucial in signalling a sense of shifting advantage towards the Allies. The war also saw a major fall in immigration into America which helped create opportunities in the Northern industrial cities for Blacks from the South, many of whom moved north.

After the war, Congress refused to let America join the League of Nations as the particularly arrogant President Woodrow Wilson had planned, and therefore did not act as guarantor of the post-war international situation, a fatal weakness for the latter. Furthermore, although the Danish West Indian Isles (St Croix, St John and St. Thomas) had been purchased by America in 1917, no attempt was made to gain territories as a result of the war. In contrast, Australia, Belgium, Britain, France, Japan, New Zealand and South Africa all gained control over parts of the German and/or Turkish empires, as mandated territories under League of Nations supervision, in a great colonial hand-out. For example, this controversially left Japan with the Caroline, Mariana and Marshall Islands, challenging the American position in the Western Pacific.

However, the terms of the world economy were set by America, which became not only the world's largest industrial power, as it had already clearly been by the late nineteenth century, but also the principal trader and banker. Already, from the 1890s, the rapid development of selling stocks had encouraged an emphasis on finance with company mergers not only providing operational economies of scale but also offering the opportunity to expand the stock market by encouraging speculation and thus creating large firms with little cash but dependent on stock. This strengthened pressure to make profits. The world war brought in more profit and capital that helped lead to the boom of the 1920s. Optimism was particularly pronounced in newly developed sites such as the port of Mobile. New York replaced London as the world's financial centre.

America was the desired destination for most immigrants, with the proportion of the foreign-born population reaching a peak in the 1910 census at just below 15 per cent. A large number did not match conventional nativist assumptions about Americans, being Catholics or Jews, and coming from Southern and Eastern Europe. Xenophobic critics associated the immigrants with ignorance, machine politics and disease, all arguments earlier used against the Irish. Immigrants also provided plentiful cheap labour for the expanding economy, notably the industrial sector.

American industrial growth satisfied domestic demand, not only in well-established sectors, but also in the growing consumer markets for cars and 'white goods', such as refrigerators and radios. Technological and organisational advances were seen aplenty, with the flight of the Wright brothers at Kitty Hawk in 1903 and the first commercial radio station being established in Pittsburgh in 1920; there would be over 583 by 1934. With Hollywood the leading film producer in the world, spreading potent images of American society and material culture, from women smoking in public to Mickey Mouse, weekly cinema ticket sales were over 100 million by 1933. American film production began in New York in the 1890s, but California took over due to its climate, landscape and the extent to which Los Angeles was a non-union city. In the 1920s, Hollywood produced close to 90 per cent of American films. Consumerism was encouraged by the availability of credit.

The spreading use of electricity helped economic growth, as well as underlining the need for energy, and the rise of plastic as a product affected several branches of manufacturing. New plant and scientific management techniques, notably Fordist mass production, Taylorist efficiency, and an emphasis on functionality, helped raise American productivity, which increased profitability and consumer income, and, therefore, the domestic market. This increase helped ensure high volume use and the economies of scale, with the resulting prosperity and profit. In 1907, Henry Ford had almost $5 million in sales and there were 13 million cars on the roads by 1923. They created a market for a range of industries and services. While capitalists thrived, the public acquired such labour-saving machines as vacuum cleaners, irons, washing machines and electric cookers, with electricity offering a more general improvement in living standards as well as ease. At the same time, the effects of scientific management and mass production on the workforce were often highly disruptive and very harsh.

The hard work that economic expansion entailed can be seen from the growth of the production of oil, with for example the Louisiana industry beginning in the 1900s and the Arkansas oil industry in the 1920s. This entailed new developments, such as drilling at sea in the Gulf of Mexico, as well as a hard world of fires, blowouts, poor living quarters and extensive pollution. So also with the conditions of most workers. In *Lochner v New York* (1905), the Supreme Court voided a state law restricting the hours of male workers on the grounds that it infringed contractual freedom, but three years later, in *Miller v Oregon*, it upheld a state law restricting women laundry workers to a ten-hour day. Women were seen as a particular category of workers deserving legal protection, although they did not gain the vote in all states until 1920. The Suffrage Procession and Pageant in Washington in 1913 was a major demonstration of support, but there were divisions within the movement over race.

That, however, only went so far. The strike of women workers in the New York clothes industry in 1909 (and another in Lawrence, Massachusetts in 1912) resulted in a 52–hour working week and paid time off, but most working women did not benefit, not least because the majority were domestic workers and middle-class women reformers generally did not focus on them nor indeed on the Black workers (male and female) who moved into the Northern cities from the 1910s. Middle-class women increasingly moved into white-collar work, while, in the pre-war Progressive Era, aided by a more sympathetic government under Roosevelt, they took greater charge of two important aspects of their lives, food and philanthropy, and passed the first food and domestic hygiene laws, founded the American Red Cross in 1881, and improved the lives of families, while empowering themselves at the municipal level. During World War I, women redirected their charitable activities towards more organised, broader action for the health of their communities. Expanded employment opportunities for married women were linked to a fall in the average number of children. Black women, however, were mostly in the 1920s still in domestic service.

Alongside the bleak circumstances of African Americans in the South, where many were share-croppers, their urban circumstances were very difficult. In the 1900s and 1910s, African Americans died from typhoid and dysentery, leading causes of death, at roughly twice the rate Whites did, in part because water mains were inadequate in poor areas. The situation was to be much better by 1940, by when typhoid was largely eradicated and water systems more accessible. In the South, the use of arsenic-based poisons to kill the boll weevils that attacked cotton harmed tenant farmers, most of whom were Black. The brutal treatment of African Americans in the South continued, with new as well as established discriminatory legislation, as in Georgia where Black voters were disfranchised in 1908. There was also periodic White mob violence, notably in lynchings and in full-scale riots, as in Atlanta in 1906. This violence, which encompassed many as perpetrators and observers, did not tend to encounter police restraint or judicial punishment, and it reaffirmed racial segregation.

Jazz

The combination of syncopation, improvisation, ragtime and the blues was to be crucial to jazz, which developed in New Orleans, drawing on local music-making, for example by the talented cornetist Buddy Bolden, as well as the national popularity of ragtime by 1910. Jelly Roll Morton, who was presented as the 'inventor of jazz', released the *Jelly Roll Blues* in 1915. New Orleans in that period was a hardworking city focused on the docks, but one also devoted to pleasure. From 1897–1917, there was a legal red light district in the city, called Storyville.

At the same time, for many, suburbia became the American condition, this suburbia characterised by low-density home ownership and a related car culture. This was possible due to inexpensive land and cheap and convenient transport, with the real price of cars and fuel low from 1910. Suburbanisation and car culture took forward the rejection of the past that had been seen strongly outside the South since the Civil War.

Yet World War I put a brake on the liberal progressivism seen in American society and political culture in the early years of the century, a progressivism that had been defeated in the 1912 election when espoused by Roosevelt who had then backed compulsory social insurance. The war was followed by a conservative reaction that reflected hostility to socialism and immigration, and concern about the example of the Russian Revolution. Paranoia was seen in films such as *The Face at Your Window* (1920). As a consequence, the 1920s saw an emphasis on a non-interventionist role by the state, although such a bland remark does not do justice to the depths and consequences of social tension in 1919–22, which included a very heavy level of often-violent labour conflict that had wider political and ethnic resonances. These included high levels of race violence between Blacks and Whites in 1917–21, including a major race riot in Chicago in 1919 over housing pressures and access to a public beach, and widespread concern about anarchism and radicalism that focused on immigrants and led to repressive government action. Indeed, the army devised War Plan White for military action in the event of a left-wing insurrection.

Warren Harding (1921–3), Calvin Coolidge (1923–9) and Herbert Hoover (1929–33), successive Republican presidents, benefited from a reaction against change, immigration, and city life and mores that led to a stress on supposed White and Protestant values. In contrast, the 1928 Democratic candidate Al Smith was Catholic, anti-Prohibition and a New Yorker, and he did well in other East Coast cities, notably in Boston, Massachusetts. In Hawai'i a Republican White elite of WASPs (White Anglo-Saxon Protestants) were able to outbid the indigenous and Asian majority who became Democrats.

Matching the Republican values of the 1920s, there was an emphasis on an early America that was under the British Crown. This situation was given visual form in the 1920s in John D. Rockefeller's sponsorship of Colonial Williamsburg and in the comparable emphasis in the South on an historical tourism focused on the settings of White life and history. In the 1950s, this combination recurred.

One aspect of the reaction was that against what was seen as the accent and parlance of immigration and commonplace New York and, instead, towards a standard American pronunciation, although that had to wrestle with strong regional variations. The emphasis moved towards pronunciation from the Midwest, which was held to be purer.

This reaction contributed directly to Prohibition (1920–33), the banning of alcohol, which was a focus of the culture wars of the age, and that both criminalised what had hitherto been seen as normal and provided a major source of opportunity for organised crime. New York City, seen as the capital of 'wet' America, helped focus the energy of Prohibition, and there were many arrests there, 10,000 in 1921 alone. Prohibition, however, was also a last gasp of Progressivism, prior to its transformation into the New Deal, and, in that light, was a reminder that the reformist change impulse can overlap with what is seen as reactionary. The Anti-Saloon League and the Women's Christian Temperance Union offered a defence of the conditions of workers and families, both concerns of the progressives. Prohibition tied directly into women's suffrage and into anti-Catholicism. The religious groups that were strong proponents of Prohibition were the Baptists, Methodists, and Congregationalist polities that had strong traditions of women's suffrage in church governance. These were also the groups that heavily emphasised sobriety as a key component of the virtuous Christian life. Women's suffrage would allow them to 'steal a march' on the Catholics and Lutherans who were more hierarchical in governance or cast votes by family with the father determining choices. These two denominations had dramatically increased in size over the nineteenth century with the steady influx of Italian, Irish, Polish, German and Scandinavian immigrants. Women's suffrage was seen as a measure against the Catholics. Al Smith, the Democratic Party's candidate for president in 1928, was the New York-born son of an Irish American and an Italian American, and the first Catholic to be nominated by a major party. A keen 'wet', he opposed Prohibition as Governor of New York in 1919–20 and 1923–8.

The Gangs

Like other major cities, Chicago had a long history of criminal activities such as gambling, extortion and prostitution, which tainted urban politics and particularly affected some of the ethnic groups. In the 1920s, during the turf wars between organised bootlegging gangs taking advantage of Prohibition, the term 'Public Enemy' was coined by the Chicago Crime Commission, established in 1919 by concerned businessmen. The proximity of the various gangs helps explain why Chicago's so-called beer wars raged violently for several years. Al Capone's criminal syndicate was dominant in the South Side, but the boundaries of gang territories were contested and changed constantly.

Prohibition was also linked to a Christian fundamentalism, wary of modernism, which included opposition to the teaching of evolution, a thesis seen by its critics as anti-religious. In 1925, this led to the 'Monkey Trial' in Dayton, Tennessee, in which, in a test case, John Scopes, a local teacher, was tried for his teaching. He was convicted, although the conviction was overturned on a technicality. The anti-evolution law remained on the state statute book, which offended many, as, for others, did the extent to which religious instruction was prohibited in publicly funded schools in many states.

Social Experimentation and the City, 1922

In his novel *The Beautiful and Damned*, F. Scott Fitzgerald presented social change in New York through a focus on a disruptive socialising, with fashion, cost and respectability as ways to attempt to create and order the relevant settings:

> . . . the little troubled men who are pictured in the comics as the consumer' or 'the Public.' They have made sure that the place has three qualifications: it is cheap; it imitates with a sort of shoddy and mechanical wistfulness the glittering antics of the great cafés in the theatre district; and . . . it is a place where you can 'take a nice girl' . . . There on Sunday nights gather the credulous, sentimental, underpaid, overworked people with hyphenated occupations: book-keepers, ticket-sellers, office-managers, salesmen, and, most of all, clerks – clerks of the express, of the mail, of the grocery, of the brokerage, of the bank.

The presentation of a nation-state in which new Whites were accepted provided they conformed to the standards of the old Whites was seen as necessary not only in response to immigration, but also as a result of the apparent challenge from far-left politics inspired by the Russian Revolution. By treating left-wing solutions as un-American, however, not only foreign models but also the once powerful American Progressive tradition were marginalised. This anti-radical conceptualisation of America remained potent until the late 1960s.

The reaction against change also led to a powerful revival of the racist, anti-Black Ku Klux Klan in 1921–6, with a national organisation and 25 million members by 1925, and opposition to Asians, Catholics and Jews as well as Blacks. The KKK was active not only in the South but also in the Midwest, especially Indiana and Ohio, as well as in Colorado and Oregon. Lynchings were common. Opposition to trade unionism was an aspect of Republican ascendancy, and reflected a conflation of revolutionaries with moderate trade unionism. There was opposition to closed shops and centralised bargaining, and, instead, employers supported work councils that were not under union domination.

It would be a mistake, however, to run together the three presidents and the three presidencies. There were major contrasts that tend to be underrated due to the contrast with the New Deal. Hoover was a more serious leader than Harding and also understood the plight of poverty, but he was not as progressive as Roosevelt was to be.

Although the connection was not a directly causal one, there was also a determination to control the 'informal' American empire in Central America and the West Indies. Prefiguring current difficulties, however, this proved much harder than had been anticipated. Popular guerrilla movements in Haiti and the Dominican Republic in the 1920s proved able to limit the degree of control enjoyed by occupying American Marine forces, who found that ambushes restricted their freedom of manoeuvre. American bombing was no substitute, particularly in the face of guerrilla dominance of rural areas at night. Although the Americans were not defeated in battle, and in 1922 the guerrillas in the Dominican Republic conditionally surrendered, the Marines sent to Nicaragua in 1928–33 failed to defeat a rebel peasant army, while the withdrawal from Haiti, which America occupied from 1915 to 1934, owed much to a sense of the intractability of the conflict.

Without any post-war equivalent to the economic growth that would be seen in East Asia after World War II, American economic expansion was not matched elsewhere. As a result, America became the major international lender in the 1920s. Yet America's economic strength and protectionism lessened its ability to take imports, and thus enable other countries to finance their borrowing from America: a major challenge to fiscal stability. Furthermore, the restrictions on immigration by the Emergency Quota Act of 1921 and the Immigration Act of 1924 helped restrict the global benefit from American growth. The system imposed in 1924 allocated places according to a quota based on national origins, limiting the numbers from Southern and Eastern Europe, and, even more, Asia. This system was not replaced until 1965 and had earlier been relaxed, notably with the Displaced Persons Act of 1948, although the Immigration and Nationality Act of 1952 was to reaffirm the 1924 system.

The overheating American economy, with consumption not matching production, collapsed as a result of a bursting speculative boom in share prices in New York in October 1929, the Wall Street Crash. This bursting of an asset price bubble became far more serious as the inexperienced central bank cut the money supply, a mistake that was not to be repeated in 1987, or subsequently in the 2000s. The tightening of the financial reins, including the calling in of overseas loans, caused financial crisis elsewhere. At the same time, the 1930 Smoot-Hawley Act put up American tariffs and depressed demand for imports.

Other states followed suit, leading to a worldwide protectionism that dramatically cut world trade, and therefore the American economic system. As export industries were hit, with Hawai'i affected by low sugar prices in 1929–33, unemployment rose substantially, to nearly 24 per cent in 1932, by which time manufacturing was at only 40 per cent of capacity. Alongside the initial consequences for spending, as the consumer patterns of the 1920s were abandoned and personal asset values fell, it was the continued hit to expenditure in the 1930s and the absence of buoyant sectors to stimulate recovery that contributed greatly to the Depression. In Boston, the value of products produced fell from $604 million in 1929 to $413 million in 1939, with the industrial labour force earning 37 per cent less and losing 25 per cent of its jobs.

Alongside these specifics, there was a more general transformation. Environmental change is commonly presented in terms of dams and other major works of construction, but was far more wide-ranging in its nature and consequences. These included the impacts, notably on surface pollution and sub-surface hydraulics, of large-scale oil extraction, and those of changes in wheat varieties. The hard red spring wheats (and later winter wheats) increased yields and also helped spread grain cultivation to the Great Plains and the Pacific coast. This meant that grassland was under pressure. The agrarian environmental degradation of Oklahoma depicted in *Grapes of Wrath* (1939) was to provide a metaphor for the human chaos of the 1930s as agricultural prices fell dramatically and forced many farmers off the land. Dust blew from the Pacific to the Atlantic, entire portions of the Midwest were buried in dust, and the poverty and despair of the people, captured in photography by Dorothea Lange, led to a great migration, mainly westwards.

A different form of environmental pressure arose from the boll weevil beetle that feeds on cotton and migrated from Mexico, attacking Southern production hard from the 1910s, thus challenging the South's role as a low-paying producer of raw materials, such as timber, for Northern factories. This crisis further limited Southern liquidity, and therefore demand and investment, and encouraged Southern migration northwards, notably of African Americans, for their standard of living in the South was dire.

The Grand Depression fused financial collapse, environmental disaster, industrial slumps and unemployment. People were hit very hard as businesses collapsed, industries shut down and farmers were reduced to ruin by the drop in agricultural prices.

10

New Deal and War, 1933–45

The Slump and the subsequent Depression caused a marked fall in confidence in the old market economy. From 1930, despair led to higher levels of protest and violence. It also helped put paid to the *laissez-faire* state and to end self-help in social welfare. Instead, there was greater federal economic intervention. The welfare and economic reforms known as the New Deal, introduced under the Democrat Franklin Delano Roosevelt, a New York politician, after he became president in 1933, satisfied the powerful political need to be seen to be doing something, and, in gaining the initiative, to set a tempo for change that resisted deflation and kept non-governmental populist options, such as those offered by Huey Long, the governor of Louisiana, at bay. There were intimations of more violent opposition. In 1934, a House of Representatives subcommittee investigated charges of an attempted coup against Roosevelt, one with financial and military support. Yet, none of this opposition gained traction. Roosevelt established a coalition of the South, the Unions, Catholics, Jews, Northern city political machines, and small business, and, alongside the policies and packaging of the New Deal, this gave him dramatic success in the 1936 presidential election.

The New Deal was a political event designed by self-styled reformers who were seeking not only to deal with crisis, but also to create a new political order that would represent a marked progressivist rejection of the previous, pro-business conservatism. Indeed, this New Deal order lasted, being given an internationalist flavour in the world crisis of the early 1940s until it became Cold War Liberalism and endured until its crisis at the close of the 1960s.

With his emphasis on the president as moral leader and public educator, not (unlike later Lyndon Johnson) law maker, Roosevelt's legislative role was in fact smaller than later believed, as much was due to Congress. Nevertheless, Roosevelt backed public works, and work creation schemes, such as the Civilian Conservation Corps and the Works Progress Administration (from 1939, Work Projects Administration), developed to fight unemployment. This was the principal aspect of the New Deal and was both federally administered and non-means-tested. These well-publicised work schemes led to an extensive development of infrastructure, especially roads, and helped create a sense that a corner had been turned. The National Recovery Administration, established in 1933, was designed to improve working conditions and affirm union representation, although it was declared unconstitutional in 1935, and in 1934 had proved ineffectual in the context of a general textile strike in the South, a strike in which workers were unable to improve working practices. The extent of Native American poverty led in 1934 to the Wheeler-Howard Act, referred to as the Indian New Deal, which encouraged both a move to regard tribes as acceptable political entities and, in addition, to end land privatisation.

Partly as a result of pump-priming measures, the federal debt rose from $22.5 billion in 1933 to $40.5 in 1939, although, rather than relying on reflationary deficit financing, Roosevelt favoured balanced budgets and put up taxes on the rich, a policy that greatly contrasts with that of recent decades. Having introduced the Federal Emergency Relief Administration in 1933 that provided direct federal relief to the unemployed, a measure not under local control, the new government replaced it in 1935 with the Social Security Act. Alongside the Banking Act, the National Labor Relations Act, the Works Progress Administration, all measures of 1935 that created a national infrastructure, and the Rural Electrification Act of 1936, this was a measure termed the Second New Deal. It brought to fruition Progressivist ideas, as did the National Industrial Recovery Act of 1933.

With the federal government not involved in the administration of direct relief, this was not the state socialism decried by some alarmist critics and in effect unwelcome to the Supreme Court. There was a race and gender dimension as Social Security did not cover agriculture and domestic service and therefore hit African American and poor female workers particularly hard. Public work programmes had to make their employees available to farmers at harvest time. This was also an aspect of the way in which relief became work relief that was designed to reduce unemployment.

A combination of the conservative nature of American public opinion, hostility to interference with property rights, and growing political opposition from 1937 that had an impact in the 1938 Congressional elections, prevented Roosevelt from doing more. To a degree, he became a 'lame-duck president'; he was uncertain whether to run for a third term and this pushed him closer to isolationism than he wanted. The economy did not recover in the late 1930s as had been hoped.

It was only in World War II that the major moves towards a stronger, more expansive and more expensive American state were made. Unemployment remained high in the 1930s, indeed until World War II, but GNP per capita recovered, rising from $615 in 1933 to $954 in 1940, and those in work became considerably better off, increasing domestic demand. Moreover, there were improvements in output, in part due to the productivity advantages stemming from electrification, mechanisation and better roads.

Roosevelt was rewarded with relatively easy re-elections in 1936 and, to a much lesser extent, 1940. He benefited from a coalition between Southern Democrats (however uneasy) and big-city Northern counterparts. If, in part, this was a yoking of contrasting traditions, that was typical of the coalitions that made up American politics, particularly when ideological conformity was of limited importance. Instead, politics owed much to coalitions between interests that, to a great extent, were grounded in particular geographical areas and wielded power through dominance of state and local governments. The scale of the country and the nature of its politics and government were such that implementation of the New Deal rested largely on local and state bodies which were subject to local attitudes, interests and power. The civic nationalism of the New Deal, an aspect of a national consciousness also seen with the spread of radio and cinema, was one that had to work with federalism. The car was also important in breaking down regionalism as it led to far greater interregional migration throughout the century.

The regionalism of politics has ebbed since the 1960s, as ideological coherence has become more important, with the Republicans becoming more clearly conservative. Phrased differently, politics has since become national rather than confederal, a process that has created serious strains for many established party machines. In the 1930s, in contrast, the Democrats were the party of the Solid South, resentful of defeat in the Civil War of 1861–5 at the hands of the Republican North, and also brooding on the subsequent rule of the South from 1865 to 1877 by federal troops, outsiders and Blacks in the Reconstruction era. The Democrats thus stood for states' rights as the guardian of the (White) Southern way of life; at the same time they were also the party of Northern outsiders in the shape of trade unionists and immigrants, particularly Catholics and Jews. The Republicans were the WASP party of the former Northern states, and were particularly the party of business and the affluent. They were very weak in the South, and indeed it was only in 2004 that Louisiana elected a Republican senator for the first time since Reconstruction.

Far from revolutionary, the New Deal revealed how democracy could deliver both results and change. Government was shown to be responsive, and this encouraged confidence in the current situation and optimism about the future, to a greater degree than in some other democracies. But there was misery and poverty, as depicted in John Steinbeck's *In Dubious Battle* (1936) and *The Grapes of Wrath* (1939).

The Misery of Life

'... one water tap for 'bout two hundred people ... They got a block of shacks thirty five of 'em in a row, an' fifteen deep. An' they got ten crappers for the whole shebang.'

John Steinbeck, *The Grapes of Wrath* (1939)

From 1935, the Farm Security Administration helped poor farmers, many of who had been driven from their land due to drought, and farm foreclosures and repossessions by the banks. Droughts caused resulting dust storms in large part due to the ploughing up of the prairie grassland.

The 1938 report on *Economic Conditions of the South* produced by the National Emergency Council noted, 'The richest state in the South ranks lower in per capita income than the poorest state outside the region.' Racist local government, notably in the South, prevented much New Deal relief from reaching African Americans. There was also a general problem of a shortage of investment, in part because, as a consequence of the National Banking Act of 1863, the national capital market was centred in the Northeast, where transaction costs were therefore lower. Indeed, Southern capital as a result moved north.

Yet, in the 1930s, there was not in America either political or social breakdown, but rather a widespread public mood that included much opportunity for democracy and democratisation, an opportunity presented in numerous films. Thus, many national archetypes relate to those willing and able freely to strive for their betterment, notably the frontiersman, the homesteader and the determined youngster. A pragmatist, Roosevelt both created new institutions and sought to work with existing ones, notably the states. He also proved good at selecting effective colleagues. Some measures, such as the Fair Labor Standards Act (1938), and new institutions, like the Rural Electrification Administration, helped address particularly striking instances of rural disadvantage. The latter helped in an economic integration that proved especially valuable in the South.

This did not really extend, however, to much of an identification with what were really subject peoples, notably in Alaska and Hawai'i and, to a degree, Blacks. So, also, with cultural images, as for example Hawai'i with the film *Waikiki Wedding* (1937), a comedy with Bing Crosby offering popular songs such as *Blue Hawaii* and *Sweet Leilani*, while a volcano provided somewhat different action. Waikiki developed in the 1920s as a tourist resort. Plantation cultivation of pineapples and the naval base at Pearl Harbor were also important.

A benign account of revolution avoided can lead to an underplaying of the violence and radicalism of these years, the violence a matter of the suppression of radicalism as much as of its expression. On a pattern seen from the previous century, strikes frequently involved violence on both sides, while general strikes, such as that in San Francisco in 1934, led to political speculations, both radical and paranoid. The disruption after World War I provided a background to a new crisis that was better addressed by positive government action.

Roosevelt, Address on the Declaration of War with Japan
'The Government will put its trust in the stamina of the American people ... Assembly lines are now in operation ... the United States can accept no result save victory ... We have learned that our ocean-girt hemisphere is not immune from severe attack.'

During World War II, which America entered in 1941, American industry developed rapidly in one of the most dramatic economic leaps of the century. The Americans mobilised their resources far more speedily and extensively than they had done in World War I. The *Philadelphia Inquirer* on 13 February 1942 depicted a resolute Uncle Sam above a map of the country full of economic effort focused on the needs of war. The country's overall productive capacity increased by about 50 per cent between 1939 and 1944, a major shift that was of lasting importance to the American economy, and that indicated the close relationship between international and domestic circumstances.

The dynamic of American resource build-up relied on lightly regulated capitalism, not coercion. Having had cool relations with much of business during the 1930s, Roosevelt now turned to the business success to create a war machine. The War Resources Board was established in 1939, in order to ready industry for a war footing, and the Office of Production Management under William Knudsen, head of the leading car manufacturer General Motors, followed in 1941. The attitudes and techniques of the production line were focused on war. The absence of a need to defend industrial capacity from attack was important. Moreover, the American emphasis on a mechanised and high-tech military entailed (by relative standards) a stress on machines, not manpower, in the military. As a consequence, a larger percentage of the national labour force worked in manufacturing than it did in Germany or Japan.

$186 billion worth of munitions were produced, as well as an infrastructure to move them. By 1943–4, the USA was producing about 40 per cent of the world's total output of munitions. In 1944, the USA produced 89 million tons of steel, about half of the world's total production. Most of the 42 million tons of shipping built by the Allies during the war were constructed by the Americans. Many were Liberty Ships, built often in as little as ten days, using prefabricated components on production lines. The organisational ability to manage large-scale projects, and to introduce new production processes, was important. For example, all-welded ships replaced riveting, speeding up production.

The flexibility of American society directly helped: by 1944, 11.5 per cent of the workers in the shipbuilding industry were women. The participation of women in high-wage jobs rose, as did that of married women in the labour force. Rosie the Riveter, the shipbuilding poster-girl of World War II, was the model of a very different domesticity. The pursuit of corporate, competitive and individual advantage brought great benefits for the national economy. For companies, corporate profits rose markedly, helping fund investment in production. Workers benefited from a rise in real wages, which ensured both labour mobility and good labour relations. Greater prosperity provided a growing tax base for rising federal expenditure that, in turn, led to economic expansion. Major changes in the geography of America's people and economy flowed from the development of war production, particularly of aircraft and ships. The population of Washington, Oregon and, in particular, California, where many of the plants were located, rose greatly, while the Alaska Highway helped integrate into the state an area that, in the Aleutians, was under Japanese attack.

By the end of the war, eight million people had moved permanently to different states. Some of the internal migrants were Black: about 700,000 Black civilians left the South, especially for California. The opportunities that war industrialisation, labour shortages and democratic attitudes provided for Black workers helped their conditions. However, much segregation remained, and racial tension led to serious outbreaks of violence, particularly in Detroit in 1943. Race riots during the war, notably in 1943, including the anti-Mexican Zoot Suit Riots in Los Angeles, reflected in large part White discrimination in employment and housing despite wartime needs and geographical mobility. There were Black protests against this situation, notably the March on Washington planned for 1941. In response, and leading to the cancellation of the march, and further established in 1941 as a result of pressure from African-American politicians, the President's Committee on Fair Employment Practice was designed to ban employment discrimination for employers with defence contracts, labour unions, and civilian agencies of the federal government.

Military service helped break down gender and colour barriers. Just as in World War I, women became indispensable, and not just as typists or riveters. There were ambulance drivers, Red Cross volunteers, telephone operators (who were crucial in battle) and code breakers, a task that required highly skilled mathematical knowledge and was gruelling work. The army also desegrated for African American and Native American soldiers. Even though incomplete, this opened the era of the Civil Rights movement. Military service was also to democratise education after World War II with the 'G.I. Bill' of 1944, the Servicemen's Readjustment Act which provided benefits for veterans. They were treated much better than their counterparts after World War I, and within a decade of the war nearly eight million veterans were to receive education under the Act.

In the spring of 1942, in a context of alarm over Japanese expansionism, over 100,000 Japanese and American citizens of Japanese ancestry were moved to desolate War Relocation Authority camps where they were held prisoner. Nevertheless, there was nothing like the coercion or tension involved in the German or Soviet war economies. Much smaller numbers of German Americans and Italian Americans were also sent to camps, but German Americans, a large group, provided many of those who fought in the war.

America benefited from its already sophisticated economic infrastructure and recent experience of government intervention, and surmounted the domestic divisions of the 1930s to create a productivity-oriented political consensus that brought great international strength. The resources, commitments and role of the federal government all grew greatly, and taxes and government expenditure both rose substantially. Government spending totalled $317 billion, and nearly 90 per cent of this was on the war.

As president during the war, Roosevelt experienced no equivalent to the uncertainty that had faced Abraham Lincoln in Congressional elections of 1862 and the presidential election of 1864. In part, this was because of the course of the campaigning. In the American Civil War, there was a clear relationship between Robert E. Lee's successes and Union war-weariness.

Roosevelt confronted no such problems. Although America's direct participation in the war did go very badly in the early months, notably with Pearl Harbor and the fall of the Philippines and Wake Island to Japanese invasion, the charge of poor preparation and planning was not brought home on the government, as, in part, it should have been. There were accusations of neglect in the aftermath of Pearl Harbor, accusations that led to controversy, to government enquiry, and to Congressional hearings, notably the Roberts Commission and the Congressional inquiry of 1945–6. However, it was the commanders on the spot who took the criticism. Attempts to argue that the president had been culpable failed to gain traction.

Later failures were short-term, for example the German victory over American units in their first major clash, in the battle of the Kasserine Pass in Tunisia in February 1943, and also the initial success of the German surprise attack at the expense of the defending Americans in the Battle of the Bulge in December 1944. In each case, the Americans recovered and were victorious. Moreover, controversies, such as over the risky conduct of the navy in the battle of Leyte Gulf of 23–26 October 1944 – dividing its strength in the face of Japanese attack – or over the need for the very costly attack on the Japanese-held island of Iwo Jima in

February and March 1945, were neither particularly prominent at the time, nor brought home on the government. Indeed, the over-complicated Japanese attempt in the battle of Leyte Gulf to attack the American landing fleet was thwarted with the loss of four carriers, three battleships and ten cruisers. Moreover, Iwo Jima was captured. Earlier, the lack of preparedness at Pearl Harbor was covered by the shock of the Japanese surprise attack, and the devastating nature of this surprise attack encouraged a rallying round the government, which was further aided by Hitler's declaration of war on America.

Pearl Harbor had destroyed the logic and force of the isolationists' critique of Roosevelt. More specifically, the direct attack on the United States undermined the isolationists' argument that Roosevelt was in fact propping up the moribund British empire by offering assistance against Germany. Indeed, isolationism was the last major instance of anti-British sentiment in American public culture (a sentiment shared by Roosevelt), although it amounted to much more than that. The cultural and political sources and manifestations of isolationism were very varied and drew on both left- and right-wing views, for example liberal concern that war would hit domestic reform, as well as xenophobia. The Japanese preference for operational rather than strategic thinking was shown by the treatment of Pearl Harbor solely as a military target, and the failure to appreciate the political consequences of the attack for the isolationist cause within America.

Within five months, the conflict in the Pacific had been stabilised at the battle of the Coral Sea (7–8 May 1942) and, on 4 June, the American navy achieved a major and obvious victory at Midway. Thereafter large-scale Japanese offensives in the Pacific ceased and the flow of the war was clearly in America's direction. Thus, the Congressional elections in November 1942 took place against a more benign background than if they had been held earlier in the year. Indeed, the Americans had landed on

Guadalcanal in the Solomon Islands on 7 August and, although that proved a difficult campaign, their navy defeated the Japanese off the island that November.

In the November 1942 Congressional elections, criticism of Roosevelt focused on the New Deal and on domestic issues, notably taxes, high prices, rationing and the efficiency of war agencies. In particular, the Republicans benefited from opposition in the Farming Belt to the regulation of farm prices under the Stabilization Act of 1942. Indeed, throughout the war, the bulk of the political critique of Roosevelt was directed at domestic policies, and a coalition of Republicans and conservative Democrats dismantled aspects of the New Deal during the war. The 1942 elections led to a marked shift in Senate representation, but, despite the strengthened Republican position (from 28 to 37 Senators), the Democrats retained the majority. The Republicans also gained 44 seats in the House of Representatives, and, if the Democrats also retained the majority there, Roosevelt no longer had one. Indeed, this result represented a loss of his margin for domestic reform. In turn, the Democrats tried, and failed, to use the issue of isolationism against the Republicans.

In contrast, Roosevelt had faced little criticism over foreign policy during the 1942 campaign. Wendell Willkie, the unsuccessful Republican presidential candidate in 1940, who was an opponent of isolationism, travelled the world representing Roosevelt in the Middle East, the Soviet Union and China.

By the time of the presidential election in November 1944, the question was really how soon the war would end. The Americans had conquered the islands of Saipan, Tinian and Guam earlier in the year, bringing Japan within bombing distance, and, in October, invaded the island of Leyte in the Philippines, defeating the Japanese navy in the battle of Leyte Gulf. As a further instance of the folly of the Pearl Harbor assault, the Americans benefited in 1944 from deploying battleships sunk in that attack: although the *Arizona* had exploded, several battleships had gone down in the mud in what was a relatively shallow anchorage and could therefore be salvaged. In Europe, France and Belgium had been speedily liberated by Anglo-American forces from June, and, although the Germans had mounted strong resistance on their borders, notably to the Americans in the Huertgen Forest, it was clear that they had lost. The British failure at Arnhem in September 1944 did not challenge this impression of inevitability, any more than the German counter-attack in the Battle of the Bulge was to do (after the election) in December.

Roosevelt won the 1944 election, held on 7 November. If the results were less satisfactory than in 1940, or indeed 1932 and 1936, there was no comparison with Churchill's defeat the following year. Indiana, Ohio, Wisconsin, Iowa, the Dakotas, Nebraska, Kansas, Colorado, Wyoming, Vermont and Maine went Republican in 1944, compared to Indiana, Ohio, Iowa, the Dakotas, Nebraska, Kansas, Colorado, Maine and Vermont in 1940. Thus, the Republicans carried two more states, Wisconsin and Wyoming. The Midwest was the centre of isolationism. Regarded as too left-wing by many Republicans, Wilkie was not selected as the Republican presidential candidate in 1944. He also refused to endorse the candidate, Thomas Dewey, governor of New York. Dewey gained 22 million votes, compared to 25 million for Roosevelt (a lower number than in 1940): the figures in the electoral college were 99 to 432. Norman Thomas (Socialist), Claude Watson (National Prohibition) and Edward Teichert (Socialist Labor) had a combined vote of 200,152, indicating that there had been no move towards fringe parties. As an indication of the extent to which the military was a citizen army, 2,7 million ballots were cast by the military. The Democrats also retained control of both Houses of Congress.

In the 1944 campaign, Dewey focused on domestic issues, not least on the argument that a younger generation was needed in government. There was criticism of Roosevelt for standing for a fourth term. Dewey presented himself as vaguely internationalist, thus nullifying foreign policy as a big issue. The approaching end of the war enabled the Republicans to argue that, since the Americans were nearly across the stream, the argument about not changing horses in midstream was not valid. This argument was far less successful than the Labour critique of Churchill's Conservatives in 1945.

Dewey was less ideological than focused on competence. He had made his name, as district attorney for New York from 1937, as a crime-buster, becoming governor in 1942, and was not comfortable centring his political attack on foreign policy. Indeed, after the 1948 presidential election, in which Dewey, the favourite, was surprisingly defeated by Harry Truman (the incumbent president since April 1945 when Roosevelt died in office as a result of a cerebral haemorrhage), Dewey was to be criticised in Republican ranks for failing to attack Truman over foreign policy.

The 1944 election had been most notable for the unexpected selection of Truman, a relative unknown at the national level, as vice-president. This was not a selection that was directly related to foreign policy issues, although the decision to replace Henry Wallace, a New Dealer and the current vice-president, was in part a function of his reputation as someone who was too Liberal, even Socialistic and potentially sympathetic to Communism, which had foreign policy implications. This decision also reflected the Democratic consensus that, while Roosevelt remained personally popular, the electorate had moved to the right during the war. Truman was known within the Senate as a keen and sharp member of the Armed Service Committee; so his selection was in part based on defence considerations.

The shift away from isolationism was shown by the bipartisan commitment to a new international order. The House of Representatives adopted a measure introduced by J. W. Fulbright, supporting 'the creation of appropriate international machinery with power adequate to establish and to maintain a just and lasting peace' and American participation 'through its constitutional process'. A similar resolution passed the Senate by 85 votes to 5, and, on 28 July 1945, the Senate ratified the United Nations Charter by 89 to 2 votes. There was to be no repetition of America's failure to join the League of Nations after World War I. Fulbright later launched the Fulbright Program in order to create Americanophiles across the world and disseminate American ideas.

Nevertheless, a sense that the Democrats had not been put under sufficient pressure over foreign policy in the 1944 campaign played a role in the development of McCarthyism, which in part was, like isolationism, a product of the Midwest. By the end of the war, there were intimations of a linkage by some Republican critics of the strong opposition to the New Deal (lambasted by the hostile as Socialism) with a foreign policy allegedly overly favourable to the Soviet Union. For critics, Roosevelt could thus serve as a link between a much-decried domestic policy and a new focus of foreign policy concern: in place of isolationist criticism of interventionism came hostility to an alliance with Communism. This critique looked towards the subsequent argument that Roosevelt had allowed the Soviet Union too great a role in Eastern Europe, and that the Democrats 'lost China' by failing to support the Nationalists (Kuomintang) against the Communists during the 1946–9 civil war. The latter argument was to be highly significant to the development of an influential strand of Republican thought.

Popular support for the war was also encouraged by government effort. Norman Rockwell was one of the many artists enlisted to help by producing posters that were deployed to assist the military and to persuade all Americans to help the war effort; while Frank Capra produced the *Why We Fight* series of public education films. Posters and photography were used for recruitment, to boost production, to motivate, and to assist rationing and the conservation of resources, for example oil; and they linked the Home Front to the front line.

America played a key role in the defeat of Germany and by far the leading part in that of Japan. When the war closed, American troops were on the Elbe in central Germany and American bombers ruled the skies over Japan. The dropping of two atomic bombs on Japan in August 1945 was not only decisive in leading to its surrender but also a demonstration of America's unique technological capability and its ability to apply scientific advances. About $2 billion was spent in rapidly creating a large nuclear industry. The electro-magnets needed for isotope separation were particularly expensive, and required 13,500 tons of silver. Roosevelt's successor, Truman, issued a statement shortly after the first atomic bomb was dropped on Hiroshima, in which he declared, 'Hardly less marvelous has been the capacity of industry to design, and of labour to operate, the machines and methods to do things never done before, so that the brain child of many minds came forth in physical shape and performed as it was supposed to do'.

A broader sense of achievement, one very typical of American public culture, was presented in the *Historical Atlas of the United States* (1944) by Clifford and Elizabeth Lord:

> 'The startlingly rapid growth and development of the United States . . . the spread of our crop areas, the development of manufacturing regions, the westward advance of population . . . the spread of reform.'

Crisis for Rail

The expansion of the late nineteenth century had proved difficult to sustain in the face of an upsurge in anti-trust pressure and federal intervention from the 1900s. The latter began with railway charges, but extended to labour conditions. In 1916, the Adamson Act, the first federal law regulating the hours of workers in private companies, was passed in order to avoid a nationwide strike. It established an eight-hour day for interstate railway workers with overtime for more work. In 1917, the Supreme Court upheld the constitutionality of the Act.

In December 1917, under the Army Appropriations Act of 1916, the railways were nationalised as a wartime measure, and placed under the United States Railroad Administration, which retained control until March 1920. The railways were organised into three divisions – East, West and South – while duplicate passenger services were reduced, priority given to freight, and standardised locomotives ordered. After the return to peacetime conditions, a higher degree of control of railways still remained in the shape of the Interstate Commerce Commission. Government and law had moved from serving the interests of railways to regulating them by the Transportation Act of 1920. This was more generally important because they were key businesses. A higher cut in wages paid to maintenance and repair workers provoked the Great Railroad Strike of 1922, a nationwide strike launched by many (but not all) of the railway labour organisations, in total about 400,000 railway workers. In response, the companies hired strike-breakers, in the shape of replacement workers, who were protected by private guards. Opening fire on strikers led to deaths, and there was also violence and sabotage by strikers. US Marshals and National Guard units helped the companies who rejected compromise and were backed by the courts, leading to the end of the strike.

At the same time, there were the other classic biases of American society. For example, African-American railway workers were poorly treated, given the low-paying jobs, excluded from unions, and expected to behave with servility. In the 1920s, while White stewards working in Pullman cars had sleeping berths, African-American dining-car men were expected to sleep on dining-car tables. Like the porters, they at least were partly visible, unlike the African Americans who put in hard work in building and maintaining the system.

The period saw the bringing to fruition of earlier plans. Thus, once finished in 1919, a rail link to the east was important to San Diego's development into a major port. The significance of freight movements ensured that rail companies generally did well in the 1910s and 1920s, only to be hit hard by the Depression of the 1930s. At the same time, there was expansion to meet particular opportunities, for example the expansion of the major rail lines in north-west Texas in response to that of oil discoveries. In America, the 1918 flu epidemic spread along rail routes. Very differently, the Depression of the 1930s hit railway companies not only with reduced business, but also because of the cost of credit. In America, as a result of the highly leveraged nature of most companies and much long-term debt, by 1938 about a third of all railway mileage was in bankruptcy. Already, in 1915, the Missouri Pacific had declared bankruptcy, and it did so again in 1933, entering into a trusteeship that lasted until 1956. The larger companies had more access to outside finance and financially sound companies continued maintenance whereas those in difficulty saw their system decline. This encouraged the consolidation of the industry with larger companies taking over the smaller.

At the same time, the train was important to the American image, with a long one going westwards in 'Portrait of America 1939', a double-page illustration in the 'America's Future' issue of *Life Magazine*, that of 5 June.

The mileage of American railways that were owned (not all were operated) fell from 249,052 in 1930 to 234,398 in 1940, a fall considerably greater (5 per cent) than in the

1920s (1 per cent). At the same time, there was flexibility, with the encouragement of Las Vegas as a marriage destination including having a licence bureau in the train station. Somewhat differently, there were many brothels at the major rail junction of Ogden.

11

A New American World? 1945–68

At the end of World War II in 1945 America was the dominant economy in the world to an even greater extent than at its start. Of the other victors, the Soviet economy had been devastated, while Britain had large debts. The new economic order was established by the Americans and reflected the goals they were seeking on a global scale. The international free trade and capital markets that had characterised the global economy of the 1900s were slowly re-established in the non-Communist world. The availability of American credit and investment was crucial to this process as, among the major powers, only America enjoyed real liquidity in 1945. The dollar's role as the global reserve currency in a fixed exchange-rate system ensured that much international trade, foreign-exchange liquidity and financial assets were denominated in dollars.

Under the Bretton Woods Agreement of 1944, American-supported monetary agencies, the World Bank and the International Monetary Fund (both of which had American headquarters), were established in order to play an active role in strengthening the global financial system. The Americans did not want a return to the beggar-my-neighbour devaluation of the 1930s. Free trade was also actively supported as part of a liberal economic order, and this was furthered as America backed decolonisation by the European empires, and the creation of independent capitalist states, which were seen as likely to look to America for leadership. The General Agreement on Tariffs and Trade (GATT), signed in 1947, began a major cut in tariffs that slowly re-established free trade and helped trade to boom.

From 1945 to 1973, there was what would subsequently be termed the Long Boom. This period of rapid economic development was one in which the American model played a key role in the West. With the economy producing consumer durables in large quantities, and much of the population able to afford them, America became a society of mass affluence, which helped to make it more generally attractive, not least as positive images of American life were spread by Hollywood and on the television, and channelled by advertising, which became a major industry. Food was inexpensive and plentiful, as was housing. The movement of individual American savers into the stock market through national companies such as Merrill Lynch proved important both to Wall Street and to the capitalism of middle America. In 1955, Robert McNamara, then general manager at Ford Motor Company, informed graduates at the University of Alabama: 'The test of your generation will not be how well you stood up under adversity, but how well you endured prosperity.'

Rail to Air

The adventure and romance of American train travel was captured by Ian Fleming in *Live and Let Die* (1954) with a description of 'The Silver Phantom' service from New York to St Petersburg, Florida, a train also known as the Silver Meteor. It had begun life in 1939 as the first diesel-powered streamliner to Florida and was operated by Amtrak from New York to Miami, with the west coast Florida, Silver Phantom, section lost in 1968:

> It lay, a quarter of a mile of silver carriages . . . up front, the auxiliary generators of the 4000 horse-power twin Diesel electric units . . . the usual

American train-smell of old cigar-smoke . . . The crack train thundered on . . . streaked past . . . the steady gallop of the wheels . . . pounding out the miles.

The romance of trains was also to the fore in Alfred Hitchcock's highly successful film *North by Northwest* (1959), with a romantic journey on the *20th Century Limited* express which ran from New York to Chicago from 1902 to 1967, a train that had had streamlined train sets from 1938.

Long-range passenger services, however, were greatly hit by aircraft competition, contributing to a crisis in the rail passenger system in America, where it ceased to be viable across much of the country. In 1952, an American Airlines advertisement contrasted a trainbound Don who 'made the trip – too late again' and his younger colleague John who 'made the sale – he took the plane.' The development of interstate bus companies, such as Greyhound, operating on interstate and regional highways, also proved important.

The crisis of rail at the national level was seen in the cutting back on the maintenance of track and equipment, which led to a slowing down of services.

Prosperity was widely diffused, such that in 1960 most families owned a house (with internal toilet, running water and indoor plumbing), car, television, fridge, telephone, and washing machine. 1950 was the first year the average household owned a car, and that encouraged the popularity of drive-in cinemas, of which there were 4,000 in 1958, fast food, much served to the car-window, and road-trips for holidays and weekends. At the same time, cinemas in the South were segregated until 1964, as were many state parks. Popular television programmes such as *I*

Love Lucy and *Yogi Bear* depicted consumer goods. In a period of particular global wealth in America, consumption there encouraged economic growth, and that encouraged the growth of the middle class. This was regarded as akin to Jefferson's idyll of democratic yeoman-farmers, one that was politically as well as economically beneficial. Suburbanisation both encouraged and expressed this process. In the 1950s and 1960s, 83 per cent of growth took place in the suburbs where the population increased from 36 to 74 million, becoming larger in category than city or rural dwellers; by 1990 it was greater than the latter two combined. The process continued thereafter, with the development of the categorisation of suburbs and ex-urbs, although that helped to provide a new geography for social division, indeed exclusion. Nevertheless, economic growth brought an improvement also for Blacks, with the gap in life expectancy with Whites falling from 15 years in 1900 to seven in 1960.

1945 to 1973 was also a period that was to be looked back on as the formative one for modern American society and culture, with contrasting accounts of what was best about, and for, America. This remains the case today, not least as culture wars are presented in terms of competing images derived from particular views of the 1950s and the 1960s. A society that is at once conservative and progressive lives in the past as much as in the future.

Furthermore, the period 1945 to 1973 was a formative one in that there was no return to a peacetime of non-intervention and small government comparable to that which had followed World War I. Under the Democrat Harry Truman (r. 1945–53), who came from Missouri, the New Deal settlement was consolidated, but Truman's hope for universal healthcare was not brought to fruition. Had it occurred, a Republican victory in 1948 might have encouraged a move to a smaller federal government, not least due to the need to cut back on wartime expenditure, but any such trend was to be cut short by the costs of confrontation with Communist powers.

Within America, there were also new developments, many reflecting the extent to which the traditional South had less of an impact under Truman than had been the case under Roosevelt. Desegregation in the military was important given its size and social significance. In addition, in 1947, the Supreme Court ruled that the First Amendment separation of church and state also applied to state governments that supported religious instruction and public prayers in schools. This was unwelcome to many, and, in opposition, encouraged the articulation of Creationism.

Instead of pursuing post-war isolation, America – replacing Britain and France as leading powers, both in Europe and in their former empires – played the key role in the confrontation with Communism known as the Cold War. World War II was followed by American external commitment in the shape of membership of the United Nations (which was based in New York) and its Security Council, as well as the occupation of Japan and parts of Germany and Austria, and the placing of the former Japanese territories in the Western Pacific under American trusteeship. There was an American interventionism designed and presented as co-operative in interest and intent, and as serving global concerns. With the Marshall Plan, America was heavily and expensively committed to rebuilding Europe, while it also worked to rebuild and refashion East Asia, succeeding in Japan and South Korea.

There was also demobilisation in the late 1940s as the 'peace dividend' was taken. Nevertheless, driven by concern about Soviet control of Eastern Europe, in 1949 America was a founder member of the North Atlantic Treaty Organization (NATO), creating a security framework for Western Europe – a clear contrast with the failure to support the League of Nations after World War I. Furthermore, the American discovery that the Soviets had developed an atomic bomb of their own helped fuel early Cold War paranoia in policymaking and domestic politics, along with military spending and international alliance-building in the areas they referred to as 'Third World' and elsewhere.

Furthermore, the military situation changed as a result of the invasion of South Korea by Communist North Korea in 1950. In the resulting Korean War (1950–3), America played the leading role in the United Nations coalition that came to the help of South Korea, driving back the North Koreans and then resisting a large-scale intervention by (Communist) China. The Americans suffered 33,741 battle deaths and 2,827 non-battle deaths. The war also led to a major increase in military expenditure, as a percentage of total government expenditure, from 30.4 per cent in 1950 to 65.7 in 1954. A military-industrial complex, in President Eisenhower's view, came to play a greater role in the economy and governmental structure. Conscription was revived, and the size of the armed forces greatly expanded, with the army being increased to 3.5 million men. This helped to give the 1950s their particular character.

The Korean War also greatly increased American sensitivity to developments and threats in East Asia, leading to an extension of the containment policy towards the Communist powers, the maintenance of American bases in Japan and a military presence in South Korea, and a growing commitment to the Nationalist Chinese in Taiwan. From 1950, substantial American forces were also stationed in Western Europe, and they remained there until the end of the Cold War. Behind the front line, America encouraged political, economic and cultural measures to limit support for Communism. This extended to attitudes and policies in the United States, not least the presentation of trade union activists as Communists.

America also pressed on with the development of advanced weaponry. It first tested a hydrogen bomb in 1952, destroying the Pacific island of Elugelab. Two years later, John Foster Dulles, the secretary of state, outlined a willingness to launch massive nuclear retaliation against any Soviet attack. In response to NATO's vulnerability, Eisenhower pushed the use of the atom bomb as a weapon of first resort, and, indeed, in 1953, he threatened its use in order to bring the Korean War to an end. The B-52 heavy bombers entered service in 1955 and upgraded American delivery capability.

James Bond

'This must be the fattest atomic-bomb target on the whole face of the globe.'

Ian Fleming's *Live and Let Die* (1954) on New York.

In *Goldfinger* (1959), Bond is collected in Miami in a 'gleaming Chrysler Imperial . . . The interior of the car was deliciously cool . . . carried along on the gracious stream of speed and comfort and rich small-talk.' President Kennedy was a great fan of the novels and had Fleming to stay with him in the White House, while Fleming's short stories appeared in Hugh Hefner's *Playboy*, then an iconic publication and one that with the appearance of the film *Goldfinger* in 1964 proclaimed Bond the hero of the age. It was the fastest-grossing film yet made in America. United Artists provided the key finance for the films.

In the Bond films, America was repeatedly the intended target of attack. Bond stopped Dr No from 'toppling' a crucial American missile test (1962), prevented Goldfinger from making the Fort Knox gold reserves radioactive (1964), thwarted Largo's attempt to blow up Miami (*Thunderball*, 1965), and Blofeld's to destroy Washington (the villain rejects Kansas – 'the world might not notice' – *Diamonds Are Forever*, 1971), as well as Zorin's plan for the devastation of Silicon Valley (*A View To A Kill*, 1985).

However, the Soviet launch in 1957 of Sputnik I, the first satellite, into orbit, triggered a fear of Soviet rocket attack. This led America to step up its program for the development of long-range ballistic missiles, and in 1958 the first American one was fired. From the outset, the space race was linked to military dominance. Nuclear war appeared possible, and this helped produce a shadow over the widespread prosperity of 1950s America, particularly after the Soviets acquired a rocket capacity.

The National Security State also developed as a result of the Cold War. The CIA was created under the National Security Act of 1947. Anti-Communism, which reached its spectacular apogee in the claims made by Senator Joseph McCarthy, but, in practice, was far more wide-ranging, helped define public culture at both governmental and popular levels, and was an important contribution to the conservative ethos of the 1950s. The Republican Eisenhower presidency of 1953–61 was a reflection of this ethos, with the Democrats attacked, particularly by the Republican vice-presidential candidate, Richard Nixon, as soft on Communism. Eisenhower's re-election in 1956, with a margin of nine million votes, was a product of widespread satisfaction with the economic boom and social conservatism of these years. This conservatism included an upsurge in religiosity as church membership and attendance rose, popular culture reflected religious factors, and Eisenhower encouraged the ostentatious commitment of the addition of 'under God' to the Pledge of Allegiance and 'In God We Trust' on the currency. He also sought to keep inflation down and to ensure the economic growth necessary for stability at home and strength abroad. Meanwhile, the legacy of the Depression was such that Eisenhower did not dismantle the New Deal. Instead, he increased the minimum wage, expanded social security, and created a Department of Health, Education and Welfare.

The Eisenhower years were to be the background to modern America. In many respects, the new social and political currents of the 1960s were to be a reaction to this conservatism, but, at the same time, much of the politics of the early 1960s represented a bringing to fruition of the liberal conservatism and anti-Communist international activism of the 1950s, while many of the shifts of the 1950s had a lasting impact, not least with growing suburbanisation and car culture. The latter had a pronounced regional dimension in opening up the South to outside influences, a process that traditional politicians could not control. It is instructive that massive expansion of the highway system in the South was contemporaneous with the movement towards the federal imposition of Civil Rights. The Supreme Court's 1954 unanimous decision that segregation in public schools must be ended accorded with Eisenhower's anxiety that the issue, if not settled, might lead to discontent exploited by the Soviet Union. Alongside action by the federal government, there were challenges to discrimination by Blacks, notably a bus boycott in Montgomery, Alabama in 1955.

The 1950s saw a major shift in the pattern of American geography, which had never itself been fixed. In the late nineteenth century, the country had been dominated economically by a portion of the Eastern seaboard – essentially from Baltimore to Boston, and the abutting area west to Chicago, Milwaukee and St Louis. Aside from financial and corporate dominance, this was also the region of key manufacturing activity and of much of the population. Given the modest range of federal government activities, the remainder of America was essentially self-governing, through largely autonomous states, but, nevertheless, there was a feeling in the South and the West that they were dominated, economically, financially and politically, by the East. This lay behind much of the populism of the period and was the background to the trust-busting of the early twentieth century. However, the dominance of national life by the powerful zone remained a factor, and, despite the significance of Texan oil, it was there that much of the industrial growth of the first four decades occurred, not least in the automobile industry.

Wartime industrial activity in the West shifted the balance of economic activity as part of a greater focus on the Pacific littoral that included the movement of many troops through West Coast ports to fight Japan. The shift might have occurred anyway, but the instrumental role of the war is important to this change. The war was followed by large-scale internal migration. In part, this was local, with suburban expansion reflecting the spreading use of cars, as well as decentralisation in employment, and, increasingly, leisure, education and other service activities. Suburbanisation was further encouraged because it was the product of movement not only from the inner cities but also from rural heartlands. The shift from the land, indeed, was a major theme in mid-twentieth-century American history. About 5.5 million farm people left the land in the South in the 1950s, so that it increasingly became urban.

There were also important changes in the relationship between regions. With electrification encouraging agricultural modernisation and the movement of industry away from the cities, the South and the West became far more important in economic and demographic terms during the 'baby boom', a period of rapid population growth. If California's growth attracted most attention, there were also spectacular developments in the 'New South', for example the growing centres of Atlanta, Dallas and Houston, as well as in other parts of the West, such as Seattle. In 1938, Roosevelt had referred to the South as 'The Nation's No. 1 economic problem'. Wage rates remained relatively low in the South until federal expenditure became important, both during the war and after, and also thereafter, as with the space programme. There was also a degree of national integration as a result of retirement of Northerners in the warmer South. The average family income by region in 1949 was over $15,000 in the Far West and Mid-Atlantic, $12,000-$15,000 in the Great Lakes, Rocky Mountains, New England and Great Plains in that order, $11,600 in the Southwest and $8,900 in the Southeast.

At the same time, as everywhere throughout history, there was wealth and poverty in all regions and cities, poverty bricked in by restrictive covenants on house purchase and leasing until the Fair Housing Act of 1968, discriminatory mortgage policies, and roadbuilding that walled in difference. Thus, Manhattan displayed extraordinary opulence, but also slums with rats, rubbish, drug addiction, and high disease and crime rates.

Criminal Gangs

'The Hugheses, the McLaughlins, they were all eliminated, and I was a participant in just about all of them.'

'Cadillac Frank' Salemme, testifying to Congress in 2003 on the early 1960s' Irish gang wars in Boston

Although the population center of the country moved westwards in the 1950s, it was still in 1960, as in 1950, in southern Illinois. In part this reflected the continued demographic weight of the Northeast. In 1960, the national population density was 50.5 people per square mile, but Massachusetts, Rhode Island, Connecticut and New Jersey had over 500 people per square mile. Due to Alaska and Hawaii becoming states in 1958 and 1959 respectively, which, in part, reflected their Cold War strategic role and the movement there of veterans, the geographical center of the country moved north and west – from northern Kansas in 1958 to western South Dakota in 1960 – but, with 0.4 people per square mile, Alaska had little impact on national population trends. Idaho, Montana, Nevada, New Mexico, Wyoming and the Dakotas all also had under ten people per square mile in 1960. In demographic terms, the westward impact of the rise of California was lessened by that of Florida's growing importance. Florida, Nevada and Alaska were the states with over 75 per cent population increase in 1950–60, followed by Arizona with 50–75 per cent, and California, Colorado, Connecticut, Maryland, New Jersey, New Mexico and Utah with 25–50 per cent.

In part, statehood for Alaska and Hawaii was an aspect not only of the National Security State but also of the control of 'native populations'. The federal government transferred to the state government 1.8 million acres seized from the Hawai'ian kingdom. Yet, statehood for Hawai'i also served as another form of Civil Rights for it ensured a state in which 'Anglos' – WASPs or indeed those of European descent – were in a minority. The Alaska Native Claims Settlement Act of 1971 was a response to attempts to transform the environment notably with the development of oil production. Similarly, on the mainland, after the war there were moves to hand over Native American programmes to states, but that policy was ended in the early 1970s.

Culturally, a shift to the South and, far more, the West, challenged the influence of the East, and particularly of New York. The migration of Southerners ensured that country music became national as jazz earlier had done. Moreover, there was a growing assertion on the part of regional centres. The most dramatic in the 1950s was the Beat movement, which focused on San Francisco. Popular music frequently still retains a regional flavour. Alongside regional assertion, there was a move in the national focus of cultural activity, with a diminished emphasis on New York. This move had already happened with cinema, but television remained more New York-oriented. However, in the 1950s, major New York baseball teams moved to California, while in 1972, the highly popular NBC *Tonight Show* moved from there to Burbank in the Los Angeles conurbation. Popular prime-time television shows included *Bonanza* (1959–73) and *The Beverly Hillbillies* (1962–71), both with Western settings.

Space is defined by human activity. In the 1950s, this involved the overcoming of the constraints of distance, most significantly with the extensive Interstate Highway System pushed forward by the Eisenhower administration, in part in order to help speed military response to any major war, and also with the development of civil aviation. The Interstate highway system approved by Congress in 1956 saw the federal government provide 90 per cent of the cost of the relevant highways, allowing state revenues to be spent on secondary roads. In many cities, such as Chicago and New Orleans, the new highways wrecked or isolated established poor neighbourhoods, often Black.

There was also a powerful use of the new transport system to spread national brands. This was obvious to travellers, as local restaurants and hotels were replaced by chains selling homogenous products. McDonald's (founded in 1940) and Kentucky Fried Chicken, which had its first franchise in 1952, both ballooned along highways, as did Wendy's, founded in 1969. Companies seeking to create national markets for their products, and thus further economies of scale, were aided by television advertising. Television, cinema, popular music, and sports teams playing for national audiences, all contributed to if not a homogenisation, at least to a growing awareness of what became national trends. This, ironically, was to provide a stronger adversarial basis for politics. In part, this was because whereas many who thought in terms of the local and the regional were able to accept the more insistent national as part of the trend, others felt challenged. A shifting emphasis towards national issues and, indeed, politicians, one that was encouraged by the growth of the federal government, also emphasised a focus on the pursuit of views and policies at the national level. This was to link political contention to culture wars.

Integration in the national capital market was significant, especially in the South. This encouraged the flow of capital southwards, and a reduced cost of borrowing in the South for companies large enough to have easy access to the national capital market with their relative disadvantage ending in the 1960s. There was significant industrial expansion in the South in the 1950s and 1960s.

If much politics, nevertheless, revolved around local issues of control, with the opportunities and problems they posed for financial benefit and expenditure, there were also major issues of policy. The Civil Rights issue of the 1960s was, in part, a matter of states' rights. Indeed, this linked the issue to that of slavery in the Civil War, helping provide both sides with a sense of historical positioning and therefore legitimacy. The rejectionist Southern position was, in the end, overcome in the 1960s because the Democratic coalition of Southern populism and Northern city politics that had long underlain the Party collapsed.

This coalition was first put under pressure under President John F. Kennedy (r. 1961–3). Yet, he was less willing to support legislative action and support judicial and other administrative action than might have been suggested by his language of hope, notably his use of the concept of 'The New Frontier' and his ability to draw on ideas of Hollywood heroism. Indeed, the reality of Kennedy, who came from a world of corrupt Boston politics, was less polished than the image of a young philosopher hero-president. The commitment to manned space flight reflected the latter, but also the Cold War, which was greatly escalated under Kennedy. This escalation was a product of his innate conservatism and the narrowness of his presidential victory in 1960: by 34.2 to 34.1 million. This narrowness made his re-election in 1964 appear likely to be no pushover. Northern Liberals and Black activists both justifiably felt a considerable measure of disappointment in Kennedy's conduct, although, in June 1963, he used federal troops to desegregate the University of Alabama, successfully outmanoeuvring the state governor, George Wallace. Kennedy went on to introduce a Civil Rights Bill, but his assassination in Dallas on 22 November 1963 led to a hiatus.

A Sense of Potency, 1961

'Man holds in his mortal hands the power to abolish all forms of human poverty and all forms of human life.'

Kennedy, inaugural speech as president

The Warren Commission concluded that the assassination was the work of a single individual, but the number of conspiracy theories that circulated (and continue to circulate) testified not only to the strength of paranoia but also to a sense that the barrier to an alternative world, in which violence played a major role, had been surmounted. This was partly a matter of the bridging of the division between international conflict and domestic politics, most obviously with reports that the Cuban government or anti-Castro Cuban exiles, disillusioned by a lack of support in 1961, had been responsible. There were also reports suggesting that domestic politics were themselves more complex, with Kennedy the victim either of organised crime, or, in contrast, of sections of the military or intelligence world who wanted a tougher anti-Communist stance. In practice, aside from the absence of conclusive proof for any of these interpretations, it is far harder to organise conspiracies than to allege their existence, but the murder began a decade in which assassinations or attempted assassinations (Malcolm X, 1965; Martin Luther King and Robert Kennedy, both in 1968; George Wallace, 1972) played a role in politics. Partly as a result, it became easier to think in terms of conspiracies. The assassinations certainly indicated the consequence of one aspect of the broader context of politics, the prevalence of guns and (linked but different) the widespread readiness to use them.

Kennedy was succeeded by his vice-president, Lyndon Johnson, who, in 1964, convincingly won the presidential election, defeating Barry Goldwater by 43.1 to 27.2 million votes, the largest margin, and highest percentage, hitherto won by a president. He also won the largest majority in Congress since that of Roosevelt in 1936. Johnson's subsequent reputation has been far more mixed than that of Kennedy. In part, this is due to his role in building up American participation in the unsuccessful Vietnam War, a conflict that lasted longer and had far less success than that in Korea; and in part because, in hindsight, his looks and personality proved unattractive in a television age that, instead, gave posthumous plaudits to Kennedy.

Yet, in domestic politics, Johnson was willing, and able, to engage with profound inequalities that Kennedy had largely only proved willing to talk about. This reflected the legacy of his particular Texas Southern populism, one that was far less geared to ethnic exclusion than that represented by Southern segregationism, let alone the Ku Klux Klan. Indeed, one of his election advertisements in 1964 associated the Klan with Barry Goldwater, the Republican candidate.

Johnson, who came from a middle-class background, instead tapped into powerful iconic language with his talk of frontiers and society, affirming a possibility of national greatness and being willing and able to link this to government action. The notion of social betterment through legislation bore testimony to Johnson's early start as a protégé of Roosevelt and an agent of the New Deal, and also to his long experience in Congress: in the House of Representatives from 1937 to 1948 and in the Senate from 1948 to 1960, from 1955 as majority leader. Another election advertisement in 1964 attacked Goldwater for threatening the Social Security system, adding 'President Johnson is working to strengthen Social Security'. At the same time, he was not seen as a challenge to big business, much of which had a corporatist character, and indeed Henry Ford II endorsed his candidacy.

As a supporter of the New Deal, Johnson looked back to Progressivism, declaring 'unconditional war on poverty' in his first State of the Union address in 1964. His 'Great Society' program entailed a marked rise in expensive social programmes. As a result of this, and of the Vietnam War, public debt per capita rose from $1,585 in 1960 to $1,811 in 1970; the 1950 figure had, as a result of World War II, been $1,697, but there had been a fall in the 1950s. Furthermore, the balance of payments deficit put pressure on the dollar, leading to a crisis of confidence in its value.

More than legislative fiat was involved in the 'Great Society' program. Johnson was also committed to betterment, and understood social mobility to mean the improvement of the entire population, not the enhancement of only part of it. Thus, he looked back to his experience as a teacher and also to the wider progress, and social problems, of his Texan homeland. Johnson declared of Blacks in 1965, 'Their cause must be our cause, too . . . And we shall overcome.' Desegregation, which Johnson had earlier also supported in the Senate, was moreover seen as a way to improve America's international reputation at a time of global competition with Communism, as well as to end a potential route for Communist subversion. The early to mid-1960s were subsequently to be praised by Bill Clinton, Democratic president from 1993 to 2001, as a time of hope, and indeed they helped shape him, although Clinton felt it necessary to announce 'the era of big government is over'.

Dreaming the Future, 1963

In his 'I have a dream' speech, delivered on the steps of the Lincoln Memorial in Washington in front of a crowd of about 210,000, King declared that, despite the Emancipation Proclamation of 1863,

> 'One hundred years later, the life of the Negro is still sadly crippled by the manacles of segregation and the chains of discrimination . . . We cannot be

> satisfied as long as the Negro's basic mobility is from a smaller ghetto to a larger one . . . in spite of the difficulties and frustrations of the moment I still have a dream. It is a dream deeply rooted in the American dream . . . I have a dream that one day even the state of Mississippi, a desert state sweltering with the heat of injustice and oppression, will be transformed into an oasis of freedom and justice.'
>
> Martin Luther King

Johnson isolated the Southern segregationists in Congress, ensuring that they no longer possessed the voting numbers to use the blocking device of filibustering. The weakness of the segregationists owed much to the degree to which the moderate Republicans in Congress were unwilling to ally with them in order to thwart the Democratic leadership. Under Nixon, the Republicans were later to begin an alliance with the South that was to help give them considerable electoral power, but that policy first required the dismantling of *de jure* Southern segregation achieved under Johnson, as opposed to the *de facto* practices that were common in the Northern cities, where particular school districts were White or Black. The Civil Rights Act, passed in 1964 with Johnson's eager support and thanks to Republican Congressional backing, banned employment discrimination on the basis of race, religion and sex, decreed an automatic end to the funding of discriminatory federal programs, and beefed up the federal administration in order to fulfil these goals. An Equal Employment Opportunity Commission was created, and the Justice Department was authorised to be proactive in order to help the desegregation of schools.

To segregationists, what they termed federal oppression was a resumption of the unwanted Reconstruction of the 1860s and 1870s. In light of the brutality of the Chinese Cultural Revolution of these years, the oppression was negligible. Officially established in 1908 as the Bureau of Investigation, the FBI (Federal Bureau of Investigation, its name from 1935) in the 1950s under Edgar Hoover, director from 1924 to 1972, acted against both the Ku Klux Klan and leading members of the Civil Rights movement.

A top-down legislative account of desegregation does less than justice to the pressure for change arising from Black direct action, which had played an important role from the mid-1950s. Direct action took the form of demonstrations in the North, but, more dangerously for segregationists, of attempts, many of them successful, to breach and discredit segregation in Southern strong-points, such as Birmingham, Alabama. There was considerable resistance. Revisiting Alabama in 2005, Condoleezza Rice, the first Black secretary of state, declared, 'I remember a place called Bombingham, where I witnessed the denial of democracy in America and where Blacks were terrorised by rebel yells and nightriders', the first a reference to a Birmingham racist bombing of 1963 that killed four Black girls. The willingness of local and state bodies, such as the Birmingham police in May 1963, violently to suppress attempts to protest about segregation, and to do so in the full view of the national media, now more immediate and potent due to television news, ensured pressure for federal intervention, which in fact was one of the main goals of the anti-segregationist activism. Indeed, Federal Marshals were dispatched to the South, while National Guardsmen were federalised in order to end state control over them. Protests involving buses and also involving facilities at bus terminals, mounted by 'freedom riders', were particularly effective in encouraging federal intervention as the regulation of interstate travel was a federal matter.

The range of discrimination and the determination for reform were such that success in one sphere was followed by pressure in others. Demands for an end to methods used to prevent Blacks from voting led to demonstrations and a violent response, most clearly in Selma in March 1965, and also to the passing that year of a Voting Rights Act that allowed many African Americans to register to vote, thus helping change the nature of the Democratic party in the South.

Violent episodes in the South might suggest that the issue was a sectional one, but there was also to be significant opposition to school and workplace desegregation, and harsh policing, outside the South. Although the reasons were in part different, there were also large-scale riots in Black neighbourhoods in cities outside the South, particularly in Los Angeles in 1965, Detroit and Newark in 1967, and Washington in 1968, but also in Atlanta, Chicago, Cleveland, Tampa and many other cities. These riots indicated that a sense of lack of opportunity, and indeed an alienation that could, at times, be pointlessly destructive, was not only an issue in the South, but affected Black neighbourhoods more generally. Ironically, the major riots in Watts (Los Angeles) in 1965 occurred within a week of Johnson signing the Civil Rights Act of that year. Although 1968 saw the first Black-owned McDonald's franchise, most Blacks in the urban ghettos were stuck in poor housing, and their areas were generally shortchanged in terms of metropolitan and state expenditure on infrastructure, as well as on new industrial and retail investment. Many of the riots reflected a particular sense of police oppression of Blacks. The situation had not greatly changed by the time of the Los Angeles riots in 1992, touched off by the acquittal by an all-White jury of police officers who had brutally beaten Rodney King, a recalcitrant speeding motorist. The riots of 1965–8 produced potent images of the underside of the American Dream, prefiguring the very different Hurricane Katrina in 2005, and were exploited by Soviet apologists to argue that America was a fundamentally oppressive society riven by conflict. There were also suggestions by radicals that the rioters were in some way part of the same struggle as the Viet Cong. This was a seriously flawed analysis. So also is any attempt to remove the more general rise in crime rates in the 1960s from a political context.

The political impact of the riots was to undermine Great Society liberalism, to ease the reconciliation of the Republicans with the South, and to weaken gravely the Democrat 'big tent' approach. At the local level, the riots encouraged White flight from inner cities into suburbia, and also made it harder to maintain social and political cohesion in Black neighbourhoods. Radicals such as Malcolm X, a spokesman for the separatist Black Nation of Islam, Stokely Carmichael and H. Rap Brown of the Student Nonviolent Coordinating Committee, Floyd McKissick of the Congress of Racial Equality, and Huey Newton, who co-founded the Black Panther Party in 1966, rejected the hitherto dominant influence of leaders – many, such as Martin Luther King, driven by Gospel values, who favoured gradualism, rather than separatism, and were keen to ally with White liberals. The Black Power movement, with its interest in separatism and willingness to turn to violence, was not generally representative of the Black population, most of whom continued to support integration, and if it helped drive forward a divisive assertiveness and empowerment, Black nationalism proved to have only limited traction.

More than federal action and Black activism were involved in the changing position of Blacks. The degree to which the South was integrating with the national economy, which was dominated by Northern markets, manufacturing and finance, was also important. It created a sense of opportunity, particularly in such 'New South' centers as Atlanta, but of opportunity on terms. National employers were far less prone to adopt segregationist practices than local or regional counterparts. Another significant factor was the 1965 Immigration Act which was to affect the percentage of both White and Black people in America.

Sex discrimination in employment was prohibited in 1964, but change took time, and the headline stories of feminism did not cover the situation. Nevertheless, leading feminists such as Betty Friedan played a key role in the national debate. While for

White women, the women's movement meant emancipation from patriarchy, for Black women the women's movement was inseparable from the Civil Rights movement. This was also a period in which *Playboy* rose from its monthly circulation of a million by 1959 to seven million in the early 1970s. The magazine supported Civil Rights, but its emphasis on female sexuality was designed to serve male voyeurs.

Another aspect of national convergence was provided by mechanisation, which became more insistent across the economy, for example with the diffusion of agricultural machinery, especially tractors, and, later, the mechanical cotton harvester, commercial production of which began in 1948 and rapidly increased. Encouraged by low fuel and credit costs, and by the mass production of machinery, this adoption of said machinery became more attractive from the 1950s, notably in the South, which had hitherto focused on hand-labour with the backbreaking stooping and drudgery it involved. As a result, the migration of workers from the region was encouraged, while the South saw a shift from agricultural poverty to low-skill industrial work. The South's percentage of manufacturing employment rose from 16.3 in 1899 to 27.5 in 1972. In turn, whereas cotton production in 1930 produced nearly half the South's agricultural income, by 1970 it was less than a fifth, soybeans and livestock becoming more profitable and important.

The migration of African Americans from the South was an important backdrop to the history of the century. In Northern cities, they became voters and consumers who were important to Democratic politicians as well as entrepreneurs. In 1974, in Detroit, Coleman Young was the first African-American mayor in a major Northern city. This was an aspect of the creation of the 'New South', a change that also affected the 'New North'.

Mechanised equipment, notably tractors, the number of which in the South increased fivefold between 1940 and 1960, helped across America to ensure a major decline in the amount of cropland used to feed horses and mules, from a peak of about 93 million acres (79 million for farm animals) in 1915 to 65 million (63 million for farm animals) in 1930 and only five million in 1960. So also with the decreased use of pasture, of which about 80 million acres had been used for farm horses and mules in 1910; by 1960 most of this was used for cattle. These were fundamental changes.

Somewhat differently, the Americans had landed on the Moon in 1969, a goal announced to Congress by Kennedy in May 1961 in the hope of beating the Soviet Union. The Saturn project provided powerful rockets able to carry the astronauts beyond Earth's orbit. The triumphalism in 1969, however, was short-lived. The crisis in American power, prestige and self-confidence was gathering pace. What had been a widespread self-confidence had become an incessant and divisive contention.

12

Years of Crisis, 1968–80

While the context of American politics was weakened by inflationary policies, the 1960s are often remembered in terms of the froth of pop festivals, especially at Woodstock in 1969, and the counter culture. In fact, the politician who emerged victorious from them in 1968 was Richard Nixon. This would have seemed surprising in 1960 when Eisenhower's two-term vice-president, Nixon, had been the Republican choice for president, but had been defeated by Kennedy in part as a result of fraudulent electoral practices in Illinois and Texas. In marked contrast to Al Gore in 2000 who turned to the courts, and even more to Donald Trump from 2020, Nixon did not challenge the result in the courts as he said the country was too divided: the election had indeed been very divisive. In 1962, his attempt to stage a comeback was thwarted when he was heavily defeated for the governorship of California. This seemed the end, an angry Nixon telling newsmen, 'You won't have Nixon to kick around any more.'

In 1964, the Republican choice for president was Barry Goldwater, a vocal hawk and opponent of the 1964 Civil Rights Act, who famously declared that 'extremism in the defense of liberty is no vice'. Goldwater was backed by Nixon and his principal opponents within the party were the more liberal Nelson Rockefeller, governor of New York from 1959 to 1973, and William Scranton, both representatives of the Northeastern wing of the party. In a clear sign of the way in which Republican politics was going, the progressive Rockefeller, who was a supporter of desegregation, was booed off the stage.

Nixon's return reflected both Goldwater's failure to sustain his position after his defeat in 1964, and the growing weakness of the Northeastern wing. The moderate Republican movement had lost traction. Rockefeller was unsuccessful again in 1968, as was George Romney, another moderate, and Ronald Reagan, since 1966 the conservative-sounding (but socially liberal) governor of California. Instead, Nixon easily won the nomination, in part because he told Southern Republicans unhappy with integration that he sympathised with their views, and in large part because he was more of a coalition candidate: less liberal than Rockefeller and less conservative than Reagan.

The Democrats were weakened by association with the Vietnam War, which led Johnson to pull out from standing for re-election and also hit his vice-president, the eventual Democratic nominee, Hubert Humphrey. The Democratic coalition fractured over both the Vietnam War, which was increasingly met by popular disquiet and an active protest movement, and over integration. The Baby Boomers were coming of age in a new, democratised and divided society. Opposition to the war tended to be strongest among liberals, and they also backed welfare and integration to an extent that the pro-war camp was increasingly unwilling to countenance. By 1968, the war was clearly going badly, while the use of conscription, in part a result of the growing numbers going to university and thus not eligible for the draft, ensured that the war was a personal issue, not least for the articulate and demanding middle class. The volatility of the political atmosphere also owed something to the new-found assertiveness and radicalism of large sections of the young. Their illegal drug culture demonstrated this breakdown, and in the army was linked to a crisis in morale. There was also a major change in attitudes to marriage, with pre-marital sex increasing and divorces more than doubling in the decade from the mid-1960s. The Stonewall Riots in New York on 28 June to 3 July 1969 were a key element in the birth of the gay rights movement.

The Real Sexual Revolution, 1969

'As the Negro was the invisible man, so women are the invisible people in America today . . . The real sexual revolution is the emergence of women from passivity.'

Betty Friedan, speech at conference
for repeal of abortion laws

The Democrats were also hit in 1968 by the ending, through an assassin's bullet, of the liberal hope for president, Robert Kennedy, and by the leaching of support in the South (but also in Northern cities) to the segregationist third-party candidate, George Wallace, the governor of Alabama, who was to carry Georgia, Alabama, Mississippi, Louisiana and Arkansas in the presidential election. Wallace's populism hit hard at the Democratic coalition and was given added political direction by his opposition to the anti-war movement and to the counter-culture. He brought together important strands on the American right, not least an ardent patriotism, including firm support for the war. His running mate, Curtis LeMay, was a bellicose former Air Force general, and critical demonstrators chanted 'Bombs Away. With Curtis LeMay'.

Nixon was elected in 1968 with 43.4% of the votes (31.8 million), compared to 42.7% for Humphrey (31.2) and 13.5% for Wallace (9.9). Outside the Northeast, Humphrey only carried Washington State, Hawai'i, Texas, Minnesota, Michigan and West Virginia. The election reflected the increased conservatism of the South, although, in part, that arose from there being a Southern candidate in the shape of Wallace, who repeated the success of the pro-segregationist States Rights Party in the election of 1948.

Nixon was less rigid in office than might have been anticipated. Aside from abandoning South Vietnam and ending the draft, he was responsible for a reconciliation with China, including a visit to Beijing, that was a striking contrast to the long legacy of Republicans accusing Democrats and the State Department of 'selling out' (Nationalist) China, which after 1949 only controlled Taiwan. This reconciliation, which was made possible by the rift between China and the Soviet Union, proved of enormous geopolitical and strategic value to the United States. Furthermore, although Nixon was keen to win over the South, there was no prospect of any resumption of segregation.

In fiscal policy, he had to cope with inflation, which had gathered pace from 1965, fuelled by a major loosening of the money supply by the Federal Reserve. The Consumer Price Index rose from 2.9 per cent in 1967 to 5.9 per cent in 1970. In response, Nixon, authorised by Congress, which in 1970 had given the president authority to impose wage and price controls, struggled to maintain continuity. The reality was a fiscal policy of some confusion, with Nixon imposing, in August 1971, the wages and prices controls he had promised, in 1969, that he would never turn to. This was the first time such controls had been imposed in peacetime. Phase One froze wages and prices for 90 days, followed by a Phase Two, from November 1971 to January 1973, that set standard rates for labour contracts and price increases, to be administered by the Pay Board and the Price Commission respectively. In 1971, Nixon also imposed a 10 per cent surtax on imports in a desperate attempt to tackle the deficit. Rising prices and unemployment contributed greatly to a sense of uncertainty. Hitting savings, inflation rose to 12 per cent by 1974, having been only a quarter of that in 1967, while unemployment rose to 6 per cent in 1973. America as an industrial society was confronting major difficulties, and this was the beginning of the post-industrial society with the service and information revolution.

Pressure on the fixed value of the dollar had led West Germany, which was exporting heavily to America, to allow the Deutschmark to float upwards against the dollar in May 1971. That August, in the face of the massive foreign holdings of dollars that arose from a negative balance of trade, and the obligation, if required, to redeem them in gold, Nixon suspended the convertibility of dollars into gold, the key element that had anchored fixed exchange rates. In turn, the Smithsonian Agreement reached that winter created a new system of fixed rates, with the dollar devalued against the Deutschmark, the yen, the Swiss franc and gold; but the agreement collapsed in 1973, in part because of a loosening of price and wage controls after Phase Two of the American wage and price controls came to an end. As a result of a flight from the dollar, America devalued it by ten per cent in February 1973, but West European governments now preferred to float their currencies against the dollar, and the Smithsonian Agreement collapsed.

Despite the problems of government, Nixon was helped politically by his ability to define his constituency in terms of a 'silent majority', a term he used in 1970, which summed up the idea that the consensus was naturally conservative. In the Hard Hat Riot that year in New York, building workers attacked protesting anti-war students. The riot helped embolden Nixon to use this term.

In practice, however, Congressional activism on social issues revealed that there was a path between left-wing radicalism and Nixon's definition of appropriate stability. This activism extended to environmental policy with the Occupational Safety and Health Act (1970) and the National Air Quality Control Act (1971). This activism was matched by the Supreme Court, most prominently in the *Roe v. Wade* decision of 1973, which established abortion as a right by constructing the constitutional right to privacy to cover abortion.

Nixon, however, a cynic, had little time for activism, in particular if it challenged his constituency. He saw big business as a key interest, and had scant time for environmentalism. In 1970,

Walter Hickel was sacked as interior secretary after he had alienated oil interests by his concern about pollution. In 1971, Nixon responded to opposition from the motor industry and stopped regulations that would have required the installation of air bags in cars, an expensive way to save lives.

Nixon's position was eased by serious divisions within the Democratic Party as it struggled to respond to the more radical agenda of the late 1960s, and to make its liberalism more broadly popular. This policy challenged support from blue-collar constituencies, particularly in the Northern cities, support that was already qualified by the association of the party with racial integration. Indeed this had hit the Democrats badly in the 1966 mid-term elections. The resulting tension was seen during the Democratic National Convention in August 1968, when the police force of Chicago, a corrupt Democratic fiefdom under Mayor Richard Daley, set about radical demonstrators with alacrity, although none were killed. In 1972, the Democrats chose a liberal candidate as their presidential candidate, George McGovern, a noted critic of the Vietnam War, who defeated Humphrey for the nomination. Nixon, however, easily beat McGovern, with one of the largest margins of the period: 47.1 million to 29.1 million votes. McGovern only carried Massachusetts and the District of Columbia. Although Black voters still gave them firm support, the Democrats had lost much of their middle-class constituency, and McGovern was seen as too radical by most voters. He changed the system of Democratic primaries, increasing female and minority representation, and making the party more of a radical and less of a coalition-building force.

Before being shot, badly wounded and withdrawing from the race, George Wallace again acted as a spoiler, in another hurrah for third-party politics. Wallace represented a separate Southern populism that, however, was to be replaced by a determination to become powerful within the major political parties.

Nixon's political dominance did not assuage his paranoia, and indeed these were years of radical opposition to the state, most prominently with the terrorism of the left-wing Weathermen movement and also with widespread anti-war protest, which revived markedly in 1969. Most of the demonstrations were peaceful, but the government focused on what they saw as subversion.

Convinced that he and the government were the target of conspiracies, Nixon displayed some of the phobias earlier seen with J. Edgar Hoover, but translated them to the particular circumstances of the radical fringe of the period and the challenge from the anti-Vietnam movement. This involved Nixon in encouraging a systematic campaign of illegality including telephone tapping and break-ins. The break-in in June 1972 at the headquarters of the Democratic National Committee, in the Watergate Building in Washington, was the act that brought the edifice down. Ironically, discovering their plans, as part of an illicit campaign to weaken the Democrats, was unnecessary as Nixon was in a strong position to win the 1972 election.

The long aftermath of the discovery of the break-in overshadowed the second term. Nixon was forced in August 1974 to resign for his conspiracy to obstruct justice, thus avoiding impeachment on three counts including violation of the constitution. As his vice-president, Spiro Agnew, a bitter critic of radicals, had also had to go for tax evasion in 1973, the new president was Gerald Ford, a more moderate Republican Congressman who had replaced Agnew.

The Watergate scandal led not only to the fall of Nixon, but also to a crisis of confidence in national leadership, one that left a powerful legacy in terms of the role of conspiracy theories in fiction and on the screen. Nixon's paranoid response to opposition, and his obsessive concern about security, were in truth more a personality problem than a sign of breakdown in the American political system, but that was unclear to many contemporaries, who were affected not only by the clear moral failure of the president, a man who mistook lawlessness for leadership, but also by the developing sense of collapse over the Vietnam mission. Nixon's visit to China in 1972 transformed the international situation, ensuring that America felt less vulnerable at the geopolitical level. This was a background, although not the only one, to the end of the Vietnam War, with the Americans pulling out the following year and letting their former allies collapse in 1975. This is a war that deeply divided and shamed America. By the early twenty-first century, Vietnam veterans were a highly vocal group, while there are more Americans who claim to be these veterans than the number who served there.

If Watergate, a term that for long did not require explanation, overshadowed Nixon's second term, for most Americans it was recorded in a growing sense of economic crisis, notably by the rising price of oil in response to a Saudi-led embargo, which resulted in a 39 per cent increase in retail fuel prices between September 1973 and May 1974. Given the increase in annual per capita oil consumption from four barrels in 1920 to 26 in 1970 and the general assumption that cheap energy would be plentiful, this hit hard. Statistics meant wrecked aspirations for many individuals, and also challenged a more widespread confidence in American governance.

Rail Changes

The fall in railway mileage was sharpest in areas of significant early activity, notably New England, so that, whereas the total owned mileage in America fell 26 per cent in 1930–78, that in Massachusetts fell 57 per cent, to only 857 miles. There was a parallel in the decline of trolleybuses and other urban light systems. Thus, Cleveland's trolleybus system saw its usage by 1996 only just above 10 per cent of its 1946 peak. In part this was a product of urban decline in central Cleveland, but this was also more generally part of the decline of urban systems under competition from cars. To a degree, this decline was an aspect of a cultural and social move away from the public space of mass transit. There was also, however, a functional response to the remoulding of the cityscape as central city destinations declined and were replaced by suburb-to-suburb journeys: office parks and new industrial capacity tended to be in suburban locations and these were frequently linked to major roads, as, indeed, were shopping malls.

Rail was of particularly minor importance in travel or commuting into Southern cities, or, indeed, for travel to them: Phoenix's passenger train service ended in 1996.

As an example of public ownership and union workforce, Amtrak was repeatedly hit by Republican criticism, in part also because of opposition to its major role on the East Coast and the resulting geographical-political tension. Politics played a significant role in the assumptions that framed the debate about financial support.

Deregulation in the 1980s and 1990s helped the railways profit as freight carriers. The threat of an American freight train strike in late 2022 led to a wider realisation of the continuing economic significance of rail in the most car-obsessed country in the world. Food, energy, carmaker and retail groups urged Congress to intervene in the rail talks, noting that a freight shutdown could freeze almost a third of American cargo, pushing up inflation, hitting food and fuel supplies, and costing the economy an estimated $2 billion daily. About a quarter of American grain shipments are made by rail. Rail indeed remained particularly important for bulk goods for which there was no real time constraint, such as coal, iron ore and stone. There was a degree of going back to the original uses of rail, and this focus proved profitable.

Ford suffered from the economic consequences of the 1973 oil price hike and from the legacy of the Vietnam War. The full pardon he gave Nixon in September 1974 was also politically inopportune. It contributed greatly to the sense of national cynicism and disillusionment, hit Ford's approval rating, and helped the Democrats win the 1974 midterms. Ford had tried to draw a line under the recent past, also offering those who had evaded military service under the draft a form of leniency. Congress sought to respond to the economic crisis by turning to traditional remedies, increasing expenditure on job creation and welfare, only for much of the legislation to be vetoed by Ford, who was opposed to increasing the public debt.

Standing against Jimmy Carter, in 1976, Ford lost by 47.9% (39.2 million) to 49.9% (40.8 million) of the popular vote, in a vote against the graying of the American dream and also for the outsider. A combination of stagnation and inflation led to a widespread sense of malaise. This was accentuated by what was presented as a breakdown in the social fabric, as seen in particular with rising crime rates. Cities were the maelstrom of this crisis, and New York neared bankruptcy in 1975. In Cleveland, the centre became poor and increasingly a ghetto, and without a viable tax base, in the aftermath of rising crime rates, of the race-riots of the 1960s, and of a suburbanisation gathering pace in the 1970s, following a pattern seen with the car from the 1920s. The same was very true of other cities, including Detroit, Newark and Gary.

An anti-authoritarian theme, critical of government, was seen in many films, such as *All the President's Men* (1976), an account of Watergate. Authority, at all levels, was also presented as corrupt and dangerous in a range of films, from *Chinatown* (1974) to *Apocalypse Now* (1979). The vacuous quality of affluent society was a theme of *Shampoo* (1975), and a wider alienation was displayed in films such as *Taxi Driver* (1976).

Due to the onset of serious problems during the Ford presidency, Carter was the short-term beneficiary of this sense of malaise, but it then came to characterise his presidency. Carter's progressivism did not win him continuing support, and was unable to overcome important differences between sectional interests. Carter also seemed a less than competent director of the government. The oil crisis of 1979 contributed to a global economic downturn that helped America into recession in 1980. The humiliation of the failure to rescue the American hostages held captive by Iranian radicals in the American Embassy in Tehran, particularly the unsuccessful rescue mission of April 1980, was scarcely a second Vietnam; nevertheless, it combined with other factors to associate Carter with repeated failure. Just as politics under Nixon had shrunk, or, at least, appeared to shrink to the Watergate case, so for Carter and the hostages. On the heels of Vietnam, the trauma arising from the hostage crisis and the failed attempt at rescue fuelled a sense of decline and desire for rejuvenation that Reagan understood and exploited. The 1979 accident at the Three Mile Island nuclear power plant, in which half the core had melted, showed problems in governance, both business and political.

In part, this was cause and product of the failure of American liberalism, a liberalism that had always been more conditional than is appreciated, not least in terms of social attitudes and the ability to implement federal policies. This was seen in the reluctance to embrace social welfare, with 'welfare' associated by most Whites with help to poor Blacks, who needed it in large part due to discrimination in the labour market, while most state assistance went to the relatively well-off, as in the tax deductions for mortgage interest. This contrast served as one basis for the politics of the 1980s. So also did the weakness of the earlier conventional wisdoms, as well as their refraction into new or newly powerful movements, such as the tax revolt and the pro-choice movement on the right and the pressure from the left for feminism and disability rights. Alongside continuing serious difficulties in the conditions of African Americans, there were improvements, as also with Native Americans, who benefited from the 1972 Indian Education Act and the 1978 American Indian Religious Freedom Act. For both, poverty, high mortality rates and poor health provision remained problems, but there were also changes for the better, including the slow growth of a middle class.

If there was an awareness of problems, that was not new and there was no shortage of suggestions as to how they could be solved. A malaise arose from an international dimension – defeat in Vietnam, dependence on OPEC for energy resources, and national humiliation by Iran in the hostage crisis of 1979–81; and domestic counterparts. The latter focused on ineffectual national leaders and uncontrollable inflation. These factors set the stage for a conservative-nationalist leader promising to restore America's primacy.

13
Cold War Realities Reshaped, 1981–2000

Ronald Reagan was the beneficiary of Carter's unpopularity. His sunny optimism provided encouragement, while his preference for homely dictums over sophisticated analysis helped him with most electors and was perfect for a television coverage that focused on 'sound-bites' and did not match the content of Roosevelt's radio 'fireside chats'. To Reagan, and his influential supporters, government was the problem, as he declared in his inaugural address in 1981. To them, 'big government' was associated with liberal lobbies and causes, and the redistributive nature of government expenditure entailed an economically and morally damaging, and socially enervating, movement of money, via taxation, into welfare. Reagan benefited from the popularity of tax-cutting, which he presented as the way to push economic growth and thus raise tax revenues, enabling him to fund tax cuts and yet balance the budget and increase military expenditure. To critics this was voodoo economics, to supporters supply-side economics.

The change in income from dividends, interest and rent in the 1980s showed that in New York the financial benefits were concentrated in White, upper-middle-class areas, a pattern also seen in other cities. Much of the boom took the form of higher return on such assets rather than wages.

Reagan was also helped by the weakness of the Democratic coalition and by Republican success in making inroads into it. In 1980, he won 50.8 per cent (43.9 million) of the popular vote, compared to 41 per cent (35.5 million) for Carter, the largest margin since Nixon's victory over McGovern in 1972; and the Republicans also gained control of the Senate for the first time since 1952. Reagan's election was the culmination of the American West's assertion as a major region in its own right. His attack on 'big government' was a reflection of the libertarian tendencies of the West that characterise left and right in the region. Under Reagan, the Republican party became a coalition of the conservative South and the libertarian West.

Reagan was to prove both popular and divisive. He was a successful head of state, helping change the mood from 'can't do' to 'can do', and providing a strength of conviction that helped overcome the sense of emergency in 1979–80, but was a more questionable chief executive. He won re-election in 1984, defeating Walter Mondale by a very handsome majority: 58.8 per cent (54.3 million) to 40.5 per cent (37.5 million) of the popular vote. An ability to create 'Reagan Democrats', usually socially conservative, blue-collar workers, willing to break from their traditions and vote for Reagan, was important. This was a period of frenetic consumerism as the spread of malls, credit cards, Sunday shopping and television marketing fired demand. Many films of the period such as *Ghostbusters* and *Die Hard* were critical of government agents and the only ones treated as heroes were soldiers, especially Special Forces types. Journalists were no longer presented as heroic.

In foreign policy, Reagan benefited from a perception that Carter had not maintained national interests, and was associated with a marked intensification of the Cold War. Military expenditure was greatly increased, and there was an active engagement against radicalism in Latin America and pro-Soviet states in Africa. In combination with the crises in Soviet power and policy, this increase in expenditure and demonstration of resolve helped lead to the end of the Cold War, with the fall of the Berlin Wall in 1989 followed by the largely peaceful collapse of the Soviet Union in 1991.

Reagan seemed a particularly appropriate president for a country that was increasingly aware of the pull of its Pacific rim and the declining influence of Europe and the East Coast. Yet, California had a maverick character in American culture and politics, and Reagan's success was not that of a narrowly regional candidate. Instead, he benefited greatly from reaching out to wider constituencies. Reagan's policies proved particularly attractive in the expanding Sun Belt, but far less so in traditional industrial areas in the Northeast and Midwest. These suffered from international economic competition and rising unemployment, sharing disproportionately in a national unemployment rate that rose to 10 per cent in the early 1980s, although the fall of manufacturing employment in part reflected a growth in labour productivity.

A lack of regulation helped in the free movement of capital, trade, people, and economic and technical information to America. This contributed greatly to economic growth both in America and in the global economy, and also helped in the Cold War confrontation with the Soviet Union. Whereas the annual growth rate of real GNP had fallen from 3.5 in 1947–73 to 1.6 in 1973–82, it rose to 2.8 in 1982–90.

A lack of regulation was also seen with political misdemeanour: the 'Iran-Contra Affair' revealed in 1986 indicated that Reagan, like Nixon, was prepared to circumvent the law and to run covert activities and even agencies. Reagan was fortunate that the domestic political situation was more favourable than that which Nixon had encountered. There was also a sense that the prime victims of the somewhat complex scheme were foreign, unlike in the Watergate affair, although, in practice, the illicit financing of the Nicaraguan Contras was a direct defiance of Congressional authority.

Another legacy of the Reagan years was the imprisonment of an unprecedented number of citizens, as punishment was pushed more aggressively in response to public concern about crime rates that had risen markedly since the 1960s, and to the emphasis by conservatives on personal responsibility, rather than social problems, as the cause of criminality. In California, the 'three-strikes' law made imprisonment an automatic provision (and an attempt to revise it was defeated in a referendum in 2004). The marked rightward drift of the Supreme Court and the federal judiciary under Reagan contributed to this process, as did a rise in drug use, particularly a crack wave. The process continued under Reagan's successors. Between 1993 and 2003, the number of prisoners rose significantly to reach 482 for every 100,000 people, compared to 91 in France.

A World-View Suitable for Americans

From 1922 the maps of the American National Geographic Society, maps that were the staple for schools, newspapers and the government, employed the Van der Grinten projection which continued the Mercator projection's practice of exaggerating the size of the temperate latitudes. A large Soviet Union appeared menacing.

In turn, the Robinson projection, devised in 1963 but adopted in 1988, offered a flatter, squatter world that was more accurate in terms of area. America moved from being 68 per cent larger in the Van der Grinten projection than its accurate area to being 3 per cent smaller. Among the major states, this distorted America least.

Reagan was succeeded by his vice-president, George H. W. Bush, in 1988. Bush went into the campaign well behind his Democratic challenger, Michael Dukakis, but the East Coast liberalism of the Democratic Party proved of limited lasting popular appeal, not least after the Republicans had depicted it as soft on crime. Like Mondale in 1984, Dukakis had tracked to the left to help win the nomination, but then found it difficult to regain the centre. In 1988, Bush claimed that Dukakis was 'an out-of-the-mainstream liberal'. Bill Clinton was to be the response. Although, by background, a member of the East Coast elite, Bush had been careful to present himself as Texan by adoption. This re-identification was key to Bush's success, both in the Republican Party and in the country. Bush took 54 per cent (48.9 million votes) of the popular vote.

Bush, however, lacked Reagan's charisma and popularity. Furthermore, he was hit by the overhang of the vast Reagan deficit, the need to bail out the Savings and Loan institutions, for which the federal government was the guarantor, and an economic downturn that led him, in the face of falling government revenues, to raise taxes in 1990, despite having promised in his presidential campaign not to do so. The Savings and Loan bail-out was also responsible for the tax increase. Serious economic problems in the early 1990s, with a recession which reached a trough in March, indicated the reliance of the economic and financial systems on a sense of boom, and led to concern about American competitiveness.

Nevertheless, sweeping victory over Iraq in the First Gulf War in 1991 as part of Bush's attempts to forge an American-led New World Order in which 'rogue states' like Panama in 1989 and Iraq were beaten, led many commentators to conclude he would win re-election the following year. As a result, the Democratic field was weak. This provided an opportunity for Clinton, the young governor of Arkansas, a brash and bold populist who sought to recreate the Democratic coalition. Although personally agreeable to East Coast liberals, who provided much of his campaign finance, Clinton sought to move the Democrats from the liberal causes that he argued had helped ensure defeat in 1984 and 1988. Instead, in line with the Democratic Leadership Council, which had called for change, he favoured searching for the middle ground, and defining Democratic aspirations for Middle America. This was a matter of social image as much as policy. Bush was made to seem a 'Country Club' Republican and Clinton like a neighbour at the barbecue. Clinton also benefited from his youth. Bush's willingness to raise taxes, having declared 'Read my Lips: No New Taxes', was a major issue in sapping Republican support for his candidacy and Clinton won many suburban areas. Neglect of domestic affairs helped cost Bush the election. Clinton won 43 per cent (44.9 million) of the popular vote, compared to 38 per cent (39.1 million) for Bush, and 19 per cent (19.7 million) for the anti-government, multi-millionaire, third-party candidate, H. Ross Perot, who helped destroy the Reagan coalition. A fair amount of packaging was involved in Clinton's presentation, but it worked, and did so again when he beat Robert Dole, an experienced senator, in 1996.

Gated Communities

By the mid-1990s, about 2.5 million American families lived in such communities. The numbers have grown greatly since, including to eleven million households by 2009, not only in new developments, but also with retrofitting. The social dimension has also spread. Initially there were private streets and fenced compounds for the affluent, notably on the East Coast and in Hollywood, but, from the late 1960s, the practice spread, first to retirement developments, subsequently to resorts, and then to suburban tracts. Concern about 'others', whether criminal or not, is the key issue: gated communities were another aspect of rising gun-ownership in America, and, in practice, bear little relationship to actual crime rates. Moreover, gun ownership leads to a marked rise in suicide rates for men and women. The extent to which such security considerations have been mentioned in advertisements for house sales (and also for renting) in America is notable, and has become more prominent and normative with time. There has also been a rise in Homeowners Associations.

The Clinton years were a period of economic growth, a marked increase in the number of jobs and a major fall in poverty, in which America also benefited from a collapse in Soviet strength. Sound economic fundamentals and skilful economic management, particularly by Alan Greenspan, Chairman of the Federal Reserve Bank from 1987 to 2006, ensured sustained growth without inflationary pressures. Greenspan put the maintenance of economic growth as a central goal. He avoided an inflation target, as well as measures to further full employment, preferring a flexible and fluid approach to management. Soviet collapse, however, led to complacency about America's international position, while the stock market bubble of the late 1990s ended in a bust. The Dow Jones Industrial Average, which had risen past 1,000 in late 1982 and 2,000 in early 1987, rose to an average of 11,400 in December 1999.

The emphasis on the stock market led to a focus on the short term: the financing of company activities was increasingly by the stock market rather than, as before, by banks. Important business and financial interests were perceived in a context of optimism, hot money and hostility to regulation, and regulators found it difficult to resist pressures towards both financial speculation and commercial consolidation. Banks proved willing to lend at very optimistic valuations, while big companies, such as Wal-Mart, proved successful in hitting local competition and securing preferential tax rates, strengthening the growing homogeneity of the retail world.

The Clinton presidency struck many as wasted years, although, at least compared to those of his successor, they were a model of fiscal probity. In particular, the budget was balanced and progress was made in paying down the debt. Clinton, a charming but also lazy and self-indulgent figure, claimed the mantle of Roosevelt and, like him, was the target of conspiracy theorists, but lacked his steel, and did not win the support of Congress in pushing through reforms. Instead, he allowed the Republicans to make his personal life into a key issue, particularly in 1998–9 with the Monica Lewinsky case, thus taking culture wars into presidential sexual habits. Given the domestic and, even more, international problems that were to emerge on his successor's watch, the impression was one of wasted opportunities. The failure in 1994 to provide the universal health insurance Clinton had pressed hard for revealed the president's inability to manage the legislative process to achieve change comparable to that coaxed through by Johnson.

This failure also indicated the strong conservatism of the political system, the role of vested interests, and the unwillingness to accept fiscal changes that might benefit others. Clinton, indeed, was accused of trying to socialise American medicine. The poor, who were the uninsured, were widely regarded as lacking merit and self-reliance, and their dependence on governmental action (a target of conservative populism) was seen as demonstrating this. The fact that they were disproportionately Black added to the unpopularity of Clinton's attempt to engage with poverty, and this prepared the way for the Congressional elections of 1994. When the Republicans under Newt Gingrich gained control of the House of Representatives for the first time in forty years Gingrich attacked what he termed the 'liberal welfare state' and pressed for welfare reform and a balanced budget. The Contract for America proposed by the Republicans promised small government and an assault on cronyism, an instructive contrast with what was to happen in the mid-2000s.

The midterms in 1994 were a nadir for Clinton, and a testimony to Republican skill in exploiting their presentation of him as left-wing, not least as a result of his health-care reforms, his support for homosexuals in the military, and his interest in arms control. The Republicans, however, were then wrong-footed, being perceived as extreme, not least for pushing unfundable tax cuts and for intolerant moralising, while Clinton recovered the centrist ground he had cultivated in 1992, coming down harder on law and order, restricting welfare and cutting the federal payroll. In short, he adopted a moderate Republican agenda, at a time when the Republicans had ceased to be moderate, challenging Social Security and Medicare. Clinton also benefited from the apparent dullness of Robert Dole, his Republican challenger. Dole suffered from divisions within the opposition to Clinton, from the discrediting of the extreme critique of the president after the Oklahoma bombing of 1995 by right-wing extremists, and from Clinton's ability to package himself, particularly to women, as well as to focus on the issues of crime and education. In 1996, the percentages were 50 (47.4 million) for Clinton, 41 (39.2 million) for Dole, and 9 (8.17 million) for Ross Perot, who had behaved in an erratic fashion during the election. Clinton carried the Northeast, the Midwest bar Indiana, the Far West, and parts of the South.

Having failed to defeat Clinton at the polls, the Republicans were then unsuccessful in impeaching him for lying over the Monica Lewinsky case. As the focus shifted to this issue, the Republican-dominated House failed to maintain its earlier pressure against spending. Whereas spending growth had fallen in 1995 and 1996 as a result of Republican pressure for a balanced budget, it thereafter rose, as Clinton and the Republicans accepted each other's priorities for spending increases. Meanwhile, abroad Clinton devoted attention to attempts to stabilise violent regions, successfully so in the former Yugoslavia and unsuccessfully so in Somalia. China grew economically but was not seen as a geopolitical threat and relations with Russia were reasonably good.

14

Identity Crisis Renewed, 2001–23

Clinton's vice-president, Al Gore, won more votes (51 million) than his Republican opponent, George W. Bush (50.5 million), in 2000, and the latter's policy proposals did not enjoy marked popularity, but Bush benefited from a presentation of Gore as dull. After a contest over the contested Florida return, finally settled on partisan lines in the Supreme Court, Bush won more seats in the Electoral College. To outsiders, the 2000 presidential election seemed to indicate a corrupt system, with voters' wishes deliberately ignored and the Supreme Court settling the matter on partisan grounds, stopping the Florida recounts. Both those factors were indeed present, but the result did not lead to an attempt at violent overthrow comparable to the Capitol riot on 6 January 2021 in response to a presidential election result that was far more clear-cut.

Much else was involved in 2000. Despite the popularity of local propositions for fiscal measures and policy-making, American politics at the federal level is not politics by referendum, and, although the practice appeared to violate democratic principles, it was entirely compatible with the constitution for the candidate with the fewer votes to emerge victorious. Indeed this could have benefited John Kerry in 2004, while in Britain, in 1951 and in February 1974, a party with more votes had fewer seats than its principal opponent.

American elections also respond to other factors, not least a relationship between federal and state levels and agencies which led to a practice of difference seen in particular in the ways of recording votes. At the state level, the number of votes in the Electoral College and in the House of Representatives change in order to reflect demographic shifts, but there is no such change in the Senate. To foreigners, this presents the absurd spectacle of Wyoming having as many senators as California, but this is an aspect of a federalism deliberately designed to prevent the most populous states from so dominating the political process that the remainder do not need to be considered, whether at election times or between them. The role of the courts, both state and federal, in the 2000 election was also typical of the country that contests issues in judicial forums.

The choice of presidential candidates in 2000 was symptomatic of a trend in American politics. It was between two blue-blooded Americans, both male and each the son of prominent politicians: Gore's father had been a senator. Each had been educated at an Ivy League university, as had Bush senior and Clinton. This tendency was to recur in 2004 with the choice between Bush and Kerry, while a hereditary dimension in politics was suggested by the prominence of Hillary Clinton, the Democratic candidate in 2016.

The weakness of class-based politics at the national level made it possible for both political parties to be comfortable with leaders who came from similar backgrounds and that in a society in which in 2000 the wealthiest one per cent owned about 40 per cent of national individual wealth, compared to 30 per cent in 1900. In part, this can be seen as a willingness across the spectrum to recognise success, but, in some cases, success was more a matter of which beds politicians had been born in than subsequent achievement outside the field of politics. A similar trend can be seen in other aspects of society.

If this indicated an oligarchic character to society, with 'the limousine Liberal' replacing the Country-club Republican, while discrimination by university attended continued, it was also an oligarchy open to new members, talent and money, as seen with the impact of Internet plutocrats. Money, indeed, was a key characteristic of the system, with a large number of senators and governors, as well as of candidates for these posts, being millionaires or multi-millionaires. Nevertheless, alongside many indications of declining social mobility, the elite's composition changed. The role of WASP men in politics and society, while still important, is smaller than had been the case in the 1950s. George W. Bush's two successive secretaries of state were Black, the latter also a woman. At the local level, despite the over-representation of lawyers, the diversity of politics, in terms of the background of politicians, and indeed of individual politicians, was more apparent across the nation as a whole.

In 2004, in contrast to the 2000 result, Bush was not only to win, but also to win 3.5 million more votes than his opponent. Bush therefore secured a more convincing election, after a very divisive campaign that saw a marked rise in the numbers voting for both sides, with the total number voting rising from 105.4 million in 2000 to 119.8 million, 59.5 per cent of the electorate. Despite benefiting from a powerful anti-Bush vote, and from considerable disquiet over the economy and the Iraq War, Kerry found it impossible to win the affection of the electorate or to overcome the widespread antipathy to liberalism, or, rather, to how liberalism was presented. He reminded many of the defeatism of the Democrats of 1972. Kerry followed the strategy of bringing out the Democratic base, but this was matched by the Republicans, while the extent to which Kerry appeared more leftwing than Clinton led much of the centre to gravitate to Bush who pressed the case for 'compassionate conservatism'. He was also the commander-in-chief during a 'War on Terror' that had arisen from the devastating Islamic terrorist attacks on New York and Washington in 2001, and there was unease about changing the leader in such a frightening context.

The geographical contrast was marked, with Kerry winning Hawai'i, the three West Coast states, the Upper Midwest

(Minnesota, Wisconsin, Michigan and Illinois), and the Northeast of the country down to, and including, Pennsylvania, Maryland and Washington DC. Bush won everywhere else, sweeping the South and the hinterland West. A Texan, he took advantage of the major growth in the state's population, from 9.5 million in 1960 to 20.8 million in 2000. Thanks to the energising of his conservative base, Bush won 51 per cent of the vote, and Kerry 48 per cent. Nevertheless, the presidential decision hinged on the Ohio result where Bush's margin of victory was only 135,000. In the campaign there, he had benefited from the Democrats' focus on canvassing in their core areas rather than in the greatly expanding suburbia round Columbus. The Republicans also won seats in the Congressional elections, the first time in which a re-elected president had done so since Franklin Roosevelt. Again, there was a clear geographical shift. The Democrats won Senate seats from the Republicans in Colorado and Illinois, but the Republicans won five Southern senatorial seats from the Democrats (Florida, Georgia, Louisiana, North Carolina and South Carolina), as well as South Dakota. On a pattern that was to become more pronounced in the 2010s and 2020s, the Republicans elected to Congress were more conservative than their predecessors and, in particular, more hawkish on moral issues, such as abortion.

Bush was not inept as widely depicted, and clearly had a considerable measure of political shrewdness, not least in following Reagan and Clinton in melding with the common man, at least in presentational terms. He also used his presidential position with reasonable success in his first term to control the tempo of politics and to reward his supporters. It cannot be said, however, that Bush proved a wise or enlightened leader, and in some fields, particularly environmental stewardship and fiscal policy, he proved badly remiss. The tax cuts did not have the trickle-down effects their supporters predicted. The cuts in capital gains, dividend and income tax rates in 2003, led, instead, to a marked increase in the household wealth of the wealthy, although this was as part of a socially skewed situation that saw no increase in the federal minimum wage throughout the Bush years, while median household income also fell in the early 2000s. Combined with low interest rates, tax cuts helped consumer demand, and thus economic activity and employment, although the cuts increased the deficit.

Low interest rates that remained the case until 2022 discouraged restraint on the rise in government expenditure, which rose greatly, particularly but not only on defence, homeland security, transport and Medicare, the likely cost of which was greatly expanded by the major extension of the programme agreed in late 2003. This was the largest extension of entitlement to state benefits since Johnson's Great Society, although it was accompanied by the cutting of progressive social welfare schemes such as the Youth Opportunity Grant programme. From 1994 to 2005, domestic discretionary non-defence spending rose 70 per cent, with federal spending as a whole growing 30 per cent in Bush's first term. Despite their anti-government rhetoric, Bush and the Republican-dominated Congress were responsible for a major extension of the cost, personnel and role of government, for example spending far more on the Department of Education; and this process was greatly accentuated by events in the shape of Homeland Security and Hurricane Katrina.

Cities Devastated

New Orleans

In 2006, Hurricane Katrina dramatically cut the population, from 484,674 to 230,172. The poor, mostly Black, population of East New Orleans found their homes flooded and lacked insurance. Many moved away, in that they chose to settle where they were taken to emergency accommodation, largely in Dallas and Houston.

Detroit
Halved in population since its heyday as the Motor City, the city lost 7.5 per cent of its population in the 1990s, and 25 per cent in the 2000s, resulting in vacant properties prone to decay and arson.

Reagan vetoed the 1987 transport bill, but Bush did not veto a single spending bill although many envisaged expenditure that was much greater than he had requested. The Medicare Prescription Drug Improvement and Modernization Act of 2003, which came into effect in 2006, represented a massive expansion in entitlement. In accordance with Republican preferences, the benefit was administered through competing health plans managed by insurance companies. There was also unprecedented expenditure and borrowing at the state level. Furthermore, America became more troubled, with balance of payments deficits, deindustrialisation and high rates of imprisonment, homelessness, drug abuse and inner-urban decay.

Although the Iraq war helped him hold the Republican coalition together, as well as win the 2004 election, Bush also proved a maladroit war president, finding it difficult to understand issues and assess options other than through the prism of his own convictions and those of his close supporters, although, compared to Trump, he was an example of probity. Furthermore, while promising compassionate conservatism and, after his elections, to be a unifier, Bush proved a clearly partisan figure, and was perceived as such, with the contrast between Republican and Democratic approval greater than for previous presidents, which again prefigured later changes. In large part, this partisanship reflected the convictions of rectitude on his own part that stemmed from religious beliefs and the sense of politics as a battlefield where victory is the sole option. Determined to push America in a more conservative direction, Bush certainly did so.

Thus, opposition to bilingualism – education in English and Spanish – became more marked among Republicans from the 1980s, in part because, like so much else, it was discussed in terms of 'culture wars', being seen as an aspect of multiculturalism. As a result, the Bush government replaced the 1968 Bilingual Education Act by the No Child Left Behind Act of 2001 which backed English-only teaching.

At the same time, conservatism is not a one-fit philosophy or policy, and, although a conviction politician proud of his integrity, Bush was tolerant in some directions. This was particularly seen with his greater willingness than most of the Republican Party and later Trump to accept immigration and to embrace its consequences. In part, this was a matter of cheap labour, but Bush's vision of America as a set of values was also one that he was happy to expound for all Americans and indeed for all non-Americans.

The contours of national politics reflected the strength of both longer-term and local configurations, although the latter were, in turn, affected by national policy, as with the appointment of many conservative judges to lower courts. Nevertheless, local political configurations became more powerful as the incumbency factor became stronger. In part, this was a consequence of the rampant gerrymandering of electoral districts in order to ensure predictable, as well as favourable, results: affirmative action for politicians. This predictability encouraged candidates to woo activists, rather than the electors, and also accentuated the investment in politics seen with lobbying and related practices. Companies push lobbying hard to the benefit of politicians. The oligarchic tendency in American politics is a matter not only of the politics of lobbying, but also of the willingness of the wealthy to enter politics and to send their own money in order to help achieve victories.

Alongside the oligarchic tendency has to be set the democratic practice that sees large numbers of posts, including non-federal judgeships (nine out of ten judgeships) and sheriffs, filled by election. This process became more partisan in the 2000s as rules in some states restricting the partisan nature of electioneering were relaxed under pressure from populist partisanship. As a result of this electioneering, there is a marked contrast with the European pattern, ensuring that the bureaucratic politics of the latter is tempered in America by a character of populism. This, however, is not always conducive to professionalism, while populism is itself constrained by political manipulation; not that the two are necessarily separate processes, as the Trump presidency demonstrated. This presidency drew on a nativism that presented itself as the acme of Americanism.

A Voice from the Past

'You're sounding the warning bell just like what happened in that midnight run and just like with that original Tea Party back in 1773. I want to tell him [President Obama] "Nah, you know, we'll keep clinging to our constitution and our guns and religion and you can keep the change."'

Sarah Palin, 2008 Republican vice-presidential candidate, to a sympathetic Boston audience in 2010

Democracy also means the representation of special interests, as seen for example in the determination to achieve the most beneficial tax/benefit combination. This is true of election campaigns and of lobbying between elections, and encourages the bribing of the electorate with their own, or another part of the electorate's, or the future electorate's, money. This of course is a habitual aspect of politics, democratic or otherwise. In America, the popularity of bribing the electorate by borrowing against the future helped weaken fiscal restraint and undermine good government. The promise not to raise taxes became a key *leitmotif* of one strand of populism, and indeed helped Arnold Schwarzenegger to victory in California in 2003. Hostility to immigration is another aspect of populism.

The role of special interests is also displayed in the allocation of government funds, for example road finance or disaster relief, by both parties. The ready availability of relief in Florida after hurricanes during Bush's first term helped him greatly in the 2004 presidential election. Combined with the nature of political representation, the role of money and gerrymandering in electioneering, and the distribution of power between national and state authorities, this role suggests that America is truer to its eighteenth-century roots than might be anticipated. The ability to sustain oligarchy in democracy is far from unique, but its American character is distinctive.

The 2008 presidential election saw a convincing win for the Democrat Barack Obama with 53 per cent of the popular vote compared to 46 per cent for the Republican John McCain. Obama, the first African-American president, campaigning on the theme 'Washington must change', won nine states that had voted Republican in 2004 – Colorado, Florida, Indiana, Iowa, Nevada, New Mexico, North Carolina, Ohio and Virginia, as well as every region of the country except the South, notably the Deep South, becoming the first Democrat to win without Arkansas and Missouri. This was an instance of the major changes seen not only in the election but also in longer-term political trends. The majority of both Whites and the elderly voted for McCain.

As president, Obama had to respond to the global financial crisis as well as conflicts in Iraq and Afghanistan that reflected accelerating American interventionism during the War on Terror. The first led to the American Recovery and Reinvestment Act of 2009, a $787 billion economic stimulus package. The pressure on the debt limit, however, led to a risk of default, while government action could not replace the shift from long-term investment in industrial assets to shorter-term speculations resting on easy credit. Obama's failure to punish the leaders of the American banks and investment houses that caused the housing collapse and financial meltdown of 2008 underlined the extent to which the Democrats' relationship with Wall Street, 'Big Business' and technology firms was similar to the traditional Republican alignment with them. Yet, the consumer pressures that contributed to the meltdown, and notably the sub-prime mortgage debacle, reflected the widespread grip of suburb home ownership, a grip that was inherited from the desire for a freehold.

In both substantive and symbolic acts, Obama sought to offer more inclusive administrative and legislative programmes, including funding for embryonic stem cell research and measures to extend rights for women, notably the Lilly Ledbetter Fair Pay Act of 2009 and support for the Fair Labor Standards Act. Obama sought moderation and compromise, but not necessarily on social issues, which were the Republicans' main sticking point as they were more hawkish on abortion and gay marriage.

In the 2012 presidential election, Obama's margin (51.1 per cent – 47.2 per cent) over the uncharismatic Mitt Romney was closer, but he still won the key swing states with the exception of North Carolina. The Republican vote particularly increased in the Rockies, the Midwest and Appalachia, and, although the Democrat vote increased in the South, it remained a Republican stronghold.

The Opiate Scourge

The nature and lethality of addiction increased greatly from 1996, when the painkiller Oxycontin was launched, with drug overdoses becoming the leading cause of accidental death from 2008, passing road accidents, and over 400,000 people dying of opiate use by 2019. By then an opioid called fentanyl was the prime killer. Painkiller addiction proved lethal, and there was no real regulatory or social corrective, certainly none to match the strength of advertising for the opiates.

In 2016, the Democrat candidate, Hillary Clinton, was the first female presidential nominee of a major American political party. Facing the conspiracy theories engendered under her husband, she ran as a solid if uninspiring candidate and won more of the popular vote (66 to 63 million, 49% to 46%). However, the maverick, politically inexperienced Republican Donald Trump, with his aggressive 'Make America Great Again' campaign, did better than widely expected, and than Romney had done, notably in swing states: those in the 'Rust Belt' – Michigan, Ohio, Pennsylvania, Wisconsin – as well as Florida and Iowa. Angry and worried White workers were an important support to Trump in the 'Rust Belt', but he also won a higher percentage of the Black vote than Romney had done.

With Trump and some of his supporters, there were echoes of past tendencies that had not been dominant in the Republican party for several decades, notably nativism, especially in response to illegal Hispanic immigration, and a degree of isolationism. He benefited from being able to portray his Republican rivals as lacking new ideas and answers. Trump's policies proved particularly popular among White males, and particularly those who were lower-income, and notably so in rural areas and, to a lesser extent, suburbs; but not cities. Clinton referring to some of Trump's supporters as a 'basket of deplorables' was very unwise. In practice, far from being solely angry and worried White Midwestern workers attracted to an isolationist foreign policy, nearly half the electorate of 2016 voted against decades of Republican and Democratic policies of economic globalisation that had gutted the nation's small manufacturing centres, impoverishing their inhabitants, and policies of apparently endless military interventionism that had done nothing to advance the national interest while killing or crippling a large number of patriotic, marginalised young Americans.

Trump was a volatile president. He embraced a hard-edged hostility to global free-market capitalism, pressing for protectionism, tax cuts notably on business, deregulation, low interest rates, the retention of jobs in America, fracking as a way to produce more energy in America, and opposition to illegal immigration. This was a reflection of the views of many voters looking for an anti-globalist, non-interventionist alternative to the prevailing status quo – voters who were fed up with the established policies of the two parties, parties who in their view had become little more than corrupt, self-serving patronage machines. Trump had many drawbacks, but also represented 'revolutionary' change in 2016 away from the two, entrenched 'business-as-usual' parties. He was a populist nationalist tapping into the previously unrepresented views of half the nation. Indeed, ending 17 years of stagnation, median household income rose by 9 per cent between 2016 and 2019, and economic growth and full employment were combined with scant inflation. Yet, a series of concerns about aspects of his personality and conduct led to a failure to focus adequately on the extent to which he did not anyway fulfil his goal of making America great again and also lacked the relevant competence. The federal deficit increased, with foreign investors holding $6.2 trillion in American public debt by 2019. There was the longest American federal government shutdown so far, in part a product of the extent of a dysfunctional politics to which he greatly contributed. In the 2018 midterm elections, the Democrats won control of the House of Representatives, although attempts to impeach Trump failed.

In turn, in 2020, not only was Trump, who had shown an erratic response to the Covid-19 pandemic, the first sitting president to be defeated since George H. W. Bush in 1992, but the Republicans also lost ground in Congress. Alleging electoral fraud, Trump proved a very bad loser and also took an ambivalent role during the riot by his supporters at the Capitol on 6 January 2021, a violent attempt to thwart the certification of the result. In 2022, having weakened American democracy by his conduct in 2020–1, Trump announced that he would run again.

The victor in 2020 was Joe Biden with 81 million (51 per cent) to 74 million (47 per cent) for Trump, and 306 to 232 electoral votes. Biden regained Michigan, Pennsylvania and Wisconsin from the Republicans and also, crucially, gained Georgia and Arizona. Trump had the majority of voters among men, the married, Protestants, those over 50, and those who lived in rural areas, the Midwest and the South. Biden had the majority of women, the unmarried, Blacks, Latinos, Asians, Catholics, Jews, those under 50, first-time voters, those in the East and West, urban voters and (narrowly) suburban voters.

A background was the major changing distribution of the population both within regions and also notably movement from the 'Snow Belt' in the Midwest and Northeast to the 'Sun Belt.' A continuation in part of the move to the West Coast in the first half of the twentieth century, there had also been longstanding movement to parts of the South, notably Florida, North Carolina and Texas. These were aggregate destinations for more complex moves. Thus, eastern and coastal North Carolina had relatively little in-migration, while in Appalachia it was restricted to a few places, notably Asheville, which focused on retirement and education. In contrast, the cities of the Piedmont of North Carolina, such as Charlotte and Durham, had much in-migration, notably from the Northeast.

By the mid-2010s, the fastest-growing states, with the exception of Florida, were in the West, although no longer including California: Arizona, Colorado, Idaho, Nevada, Oregon, Utah and Washington. Phoenix and Houston, each products in part of modern technologies such as air conditioning, saw major growth as cities, with Chicago, in contrast, having heavy losses, as did Illinois as a whole. Many African Americans moved south, for example leaving Chicago, while Atlanta became much more populous. Economically hit Detroit saw its population fall from 1.8 million in the 1950s to 670,000 by the late 2010s, in part as it became a largely Black city, with Whites moving to the suburbs.

So also with Cleveland, Buffalo and Pittsburgh; whereas Columbus, Ohio has benefited from a booming and diverse economy. Democrat strongholds lost voters, many of whom moved to Republican areas.

As president, Biden, a mainstream Democrat born in 1942, who was close to the party's working-class image, struck many as lacking the health and energy for the job. Seeking to restore a civic religion of humane morality that Trump lacked, he liberalised some aspects of government policy, pursued economic stimulus through state expenditure, antitrust regulation, and a view of social justice, and benefited from economic growth in 2021. Expenditure included a $1 trillion infrastructure measure, $369 billion for clean energy programmes, and $280 billion to support semiconductor research and congestion. The 'America First' of Trump took a new form. In 2022, the situation was affected by global inflation and high food prices. Yet, the 2022 midterms, which Biden presented as a 'battle for the soul of the nation', saw the Republicans, weakened by poor pro-Trump candidates, perform below expectations, winning only a small majority in the House of Representatives and failing to win the Senate. Republican voters had claimed that the Democrats were throwing money behind the pro-Trump candidates in the primaries as they knew that they had far better chances against them than against non-Trump Republicans.

A Sign of Change, 2022

In 2021, the first Black senator elected from Georgia, Raphael Warnock, a Democrat, won re-election in 2022 against a weak Republican rival, also Black, and provided a powerful speech about change. Speaking about his mother:

> 'She grew up in the 1950s . . . picking someone else's cotton and someone else's tobacco. But tonight she

helped pick her youngest son to be a United States senator ... It is my honour to utter the four most powerful words ever spoken in a democracy, "The people have spoken" ... You can't lead the people unless you love the people. You can't love the people unless you know the people, and you can't know the people unless you walk among the people.'

These midterms suggest the extent to which much of the electorate was less doctrinaire than the divisiveness of culture wars might imply. Polls indicate a strong support for tolerance, especially among the young. In 2020, about twenty million people took part in civil-rights protests after the killing by a White policeman of the unarmed George Floyd in Minneapolis. Whereas, in 1993, a majority of Americans polled disapproved of interracial marriages, by 2020, 90 per cent approved, over 8 per cent of babies are mixed race, and one in three couples meeting online are mixed race.

There is also a widely diffused patriotism and religious faith that contrast with the situation in Europe. Moreover, some religious partisanship has been reconceptualised in terms of politics. Contention over judicial appointments saw the two linked. The combination of pre-marital sexual licence with the popularity of marriage and parenthood indicates that the values of both the 1960s and the 1950s remain important. There was a combination of the 'Baby Boomer' values with the *Leave it to Beaver* ones of the 1950s. The latter, a television situation comedy of 1957–63, had the perfect suburban housewife vacuuming her perfectly manicured living room in a lace apron and pearls and perfect hairdo, with the perfect bread-winning husband, while their rascal son, Beaver, gets into all kinds of trouble that is discussed around a dinner table that carries elegant china and plentiful food. This was an American image depicting a superboom very different from the crises of the later 1960s that created rust belts and social tensions.

To some critics, division, indeed diversity, has become excessive and a threat to social cohesion and political interest. These arguments in particular are applied against liberal individualism and against large-scale Hispanic immigration. Each, indeed, challenges any attempt at direction. Liberal individualism leads many conservatives to a sense of cultural and social crisis that is in part a reflection of their response to changing social values and currents. From 2019, non-Hispanic White children have been a minority, while the share of each age group identifying as of two or more races is of growing significance as they enter the voting cohort. In practice, many of the fears expressed in the 1960s and 2010s have not materialised. Drug use remains a serious problem, but, although it has helped cause major social difficulties in inner cities, with savage consequences for many, it has not led to the general breakdown that was feared. In suburban areas, drug use is a cause of individual and family problems, rather than general societal crisis, and the same is true of violence. Ironically, suburban anxieties are more easily expressed by transposing them onto the inner cities. Yet, looked at differently, the high death rate from opioid use has indeed created what should be seen as a societal crisis. It is a serious issue in rural areas as well, although different drugs are used: meth instead of heroin.

The marked rise in pre-marital sex in the 1960s did not lead to the end of marriage but to its postponement, with many young people having relatively stable relationships in the meanwhile, and not the promiscuity depicted by critics. The major increase in divorces in the late 1960s and early 1970s, creating a situation that has persisted, has not led to the breakdown of the family, as was feared, but instead to an unprecedented rate of remarriage. Furthermore, many of these 'problem indices' improved in the early 2000s, with abortion, crime, divorce and teenage pregnancy rates all falling.

This does not mean the end of culture wars, but rather that the charge that liberalism and 1960s values led to social breakdown can be rejected. Instead, American society has reshaped, with a differing mix of conformism and individualism to that in the 1950s. Generational issues played a major role in the reshaping, as issues were reformulated or new ones framed. The power of the Baby Boomers and their liberal expectations reached out in many directions, creating new expectations. For example, new approaches to generational issues, such as the menopause, hair loss and weight gain, influenced medical practice and drug companies. Yet, from the 2010s there was a reaction against the Baby Boomers. They were talked about not in terms of their real power, but of the disastrous consequences of their influence.

This reshaping interacted with that of changes in the world of work. The make-up of the work force changed dramatically after 1950. Today, the percentages are 3 agricultural, 16 manufacturing, and the balance service-oriented. This change from a manufacturing to an overwhelmingly service society is as great as it was in the latter part of the nineteenth century, when America was transformed from a predominantly ruralist agrarian society to an increasingly urban manufacturing society, albeit with important regional variations. In 2019, 86 per cent of Americans lived in metro areas and produced 91 per cent of national income.

As America has developed greatly since 1960, most particularly with the rising relative importance of the South and the West, this reshaping of society also has a geographical aspect. If the Northeast has changed, so also have the South and the West. Outsiders perceive the latter in terms of homogeneous communities, and sometimes starkly so. I was assured in 2005 by one resident of Alabama, who was not locally born, that the state's politics were run by 'Bapto-Fascists', but the Southern Baptists themselves have diverse views on social and political topics, while Alabama, like other Southern states, contains a variety that, while it is in aggregate different in tone to Connecticut or Massachusetts, is also far from homogenous in particulars.

Indeed, alongside the emphasis on uniformity as a consequence of national consumerism and other factors, there are important elements encouraging variety. The hegemony of the television networks has fractured as new technology and media have allowed more ways to communicate and thus define identity. America played a key role, being the major site for the new information technology. In 1998, based in Los Angeles, the Internet Corporation for Assigned Names and Numbers was established to manage the Internet, assigning the unique indicators essential for the address system. Also in 1998, nearly half of the 130 million people in the world with Internet access were Americans. By 2006, about 70 per cent of Americans had mobile phones. America increasingly saw itself as a knowledge society. Culture, economics and politics were presented as dynamic, with 'messaging' a major form of interaction, work and opinion-formation. Whereas in 1970 it cost $150,000 to send a trillion bits of data between Boston and Los Angeles, the cost in 2000 was twelve cents.

In 2012, after a major rise in earnings that drew on the global popularity of the iPod (digital music player, 2001), touch-screen iPhone (2007) and iPad portable tablet (2010), Apple had the highest valuation on the American stock market, at over $630 billion, over 1.2 per cent of the global equity market. Launched in 2004, Facebook had 900 million users by the spring of 2012 by which time Google's Android operating system ran on over half the phones sold globally. Twitter, Instagram and Tiktok took further the American role.

Yet, at the same time, the very themes of conformism have been greatly attenuated. This is not so much a consequence of 1960s values, but, rather, a broader process of economic opportunity, social individualism, and an assertiveness that is not only a matter of youth and women but, instead, of all social groups and of most individuals. Assertiveness can of course be an aspect of conformism; for example rejecting one's looks through diet, exercise, plastic surgery or hair transplants, in order to share in social suppositions about appeal. Nevertheless, however much we are influenced by advertising and other factors, the relationship between difference and choice has shifted towards the latter. This is an aspect of the restlessness that is part of the essence of the American experience. This restlessness helps explain the energy of Americans, which clearly has such positive and negative manifestations. The sources of this restlessness are cultural and environmental, the former in part an aspect of the extent to which America is an immigrant society whose people, directly or through their forebears, chose to come to America. Furthermore, the presence of so much physical and material abundance (magnified by popular accounts and images) stirred the imagination and presented Americans with the idea of improvement and upward social mobility. Unity within so much diversity is to be found in a rough allegiance to the idea of America as a place where liberty and freedom (variously conceived) prevail, and provide opportunity. Technology corresponded to this unity within diversity. The spread of information technology that had been so important to productivity growth since 1995, and has been significant culturally in creating common experiences and new languages, both contributes to similarities and yet also provides a way in which to express different views.

As far as immigration is concerned, integrationists have to hope that immigrants will identify with what are presented as American values; they cannot be coerced into doing so, and this has led pessimists to fear a re-shaping of America as a result of its porous frontiers, external and internal. Yet, the re-shaping of the country is scarcely new, and the very drive to settle in America reflects the potent attraction of its opportunities and the appeal of its sense of possibility. That offers a powerful antidote to the reality of a prominent sector of American society that is mired in crime and drugs. Talking to Americans, it is clear that many identify the latter with inner cities and Blacks, but that scarcely describes the reality of a far more widespread drug-taking, nor indeed of criminality that is as much about Whitewater, Enron, WorldCom and Tyco, as of the violent criminals that haunt much of the collective psyche. Indeed, polls indicated considerable distrust of the leadership of large companies. In addition, structural factors such as serious conflicts of interest led to disquiet about the probity of important tranches of business and public life. Just as the political history of this period can, at least in part, be discussed in terms of violence and of cultures of fear, so the economic history can, in part, be considered in terms of crime and fraud. As with violence, this is a matter both of top-down activities, such as fraudulent accounting, and also of independent action by the many, for example the piracy and downloading of videos and DVDs.

Other countries have similar and sometimes worse problems. However bad American crime figures may be, they are good compared to Brazil or South Africa. Although there is popular apocalyptic fiction predicting environmental crisis, such as Kim Robinson's *Forty Signs of Rain* (2004) and *Fifty Degrees Below* (2005), in which Washington DC faces the flooding consequences of melting icecaps, in fact pollution and environmental degradation are worse in China and India. American geographical sectionalism is less acute than that of Canada. Yet, to take this course is scarcely to find much positive support for the aspiration that is America, and there is no consolation, at least in so far as comparisons with other major states are concerned, when the exceptionalism in sight is that of per capita energy consumption or widespread obesity. Australia also offers can-do optimism and the sense of a young country, and without some of the less desirable features of American society including high levels of personal violence and cultural combativeness. If, in America, the material standard of life is much higher than in 1960, this is, more generally, true of the developed world. However, the rise in the material standard of life has been particularly marked in America when compared to Western Europe.

Alongside problems, America's per capita income remains higher than that of Japan, and far higher than those of China or India, which helps account for its attraction as a destination of immigration. The national dimension and trends, political and otherwise, remained composed of regional ones, and, due to America's federal structure, more so than elsewhere. Thus, the Republican versus Democrat struggle has played out alongside that of images of states, with rapidly growing Texas contrasted with a dystopian California of high property prices and taxes, fiscal pressure and political tokenism.

The global image of America today is less favourable than was the case in the 1990s. In part, this is due to a widespread failure to appreciate the limitations of rival states/models, notably China; in part to the legacy and revival of the anti-Western and anti-capitalist ideas of the Cold War, particularly from the 1960s; and in part to specific angers with the War on Terror, American consumerism, and the Trump presidency and its image. None of these adequately note the extent to which there is still much fascination with America, as well as a requirement for its support, while it remains the favoured destination for immigration.

An exciting story, an uplifting ambition, and, as the Ukraine crisis of 2022 abundantly demonstrated, more of a friend to liberty around the world than other major states, America captures the exhilaration and disappointment of freedom once it is translated into a political system. But the world, and not just the Americans, has been very lucky that America, and not Nazi Germany, nor the Soviet Union, was the leading power of the last eight decades. President Zelensky of Ukraine in his speech to Congress in December 2022 echoed Churchill in 1946 in his warning about a divided world and the expectations that the United States would defend freedom wherever it is threatened.

This serves as a reminder that the Cold War of 1946–89 was simply two generations' experience with the hope that the United States would play an international role never played before by anyone else. That this book can be sold in America without censorship is a reminder of the truly liberal character of its political culture. Whether, for the future, America can provide its own citizens, or indeed others, with a sense of freedom that encompasses necessary and desirable degrees of economic growth and environmental protection, social justice and national security, is for you to consider.

15

Into the Future

All histories are uncertain and incomplete, with the pressure of the present and the prospect of the future shaping not only our views of the past but also our understanding of the present and anticipations of the future. For America, there are issues that are global in their nature however much they may hit home at the level of the particular in and within each country and community. These include environmental change, population growth, global state confrontations and, as Covid showed, disease.

The climate has played a major role in dystopian events in recent years, particularly so in terms of drought and fire. Both have been especially prominent in the most environmentally marginal area, the Southwest. In particular, rainfall was repeatedly poor from 2000, ensuring that groundwater levels fell, as did those in reservoirs such as Lake Mead. Global warming in America was most apparent in Alaska and western Colorado: average snowpack continued its long-time decline, river temperatures have risen, quarrels between states over water rights became more harsh, notably over water from the Colorado river, and wildfires became more common, with California and Colorado hitting records for them in 2020. Between 1895 and 2018, Santa Clara County, California saw its temperature rise by 2°C, twice the global average, while between 2011 and 2019, drought in California killed nearly 150 million trees, and in 2020 the temperature in Death Valley rose to 54.4°C (130°F). In the period 1900 to 2016, two-thirds of the counties in Minnesota saw the average mid-winter temperatures rise by over 2°C. Many millennials and members of Generation Z have been especially scathing about the irresponsible policies of their elders, in particular about the environment.

Engineering and the Environment

The coastline of Louisiana was greatly affected by the combination, with the more general process of global warming, of specific human activity in the shape of the channelling of the flow of the Mississippi, to deal with floods, such as a major one on the German Coast (named after German settlers) of the Mississippi in 1927. This channelling resulted in more of the river-borne silt being deposited deeper into the Gulf of Mexico. The net effect was that the shoreline receded, while former offshore islands became sandbanks, which was significant both economically and for natural life, as the mudflats were where many animals seeded, for example providing a major source of oysters.

There are also the events of the particular country. For America, there is the concern, especially prominent in recent years, about social and political division, governmental dysfunctionality and fiscal imbalances. Each indeed is serious, although the perspectives of history might suggest that America has not exactly had an earlier history free of serious division. Indeed, with all states, there may be a mismatch between expectations of unity, the stuff, variously, of national identity, culture and myth, and of constitutional norms, and the reality of divisions, with the last particularly marked in participatory democracies.

This extends to religion, which is becoming more diverse and less denominational in America. While the percentage of White Protestants identifying as evangelical rose from 53 in 2009 to 56 in 2019, that of White evangelicals in the population as a whole fell from 20 to 16 and those who described themselves as Christians from 77 to 65. Among the latter, Catholics became more important. The American Methodist Church divided in 2021 over issues of sexuality.

Amidst the rush of change, there are striking continuities. Many are those of physical geography, from the mighty imperatives of terrain and climate to the detailed configurations that provide the weft of local life. It may be that the distribution of slope features and surface waters now ensures that particular fields sprout houses rather than crops, as farmers find developers offer the best price, but there is still the pattern of influence. Other continuities arise from social patterns. Alongside the pressures for both change and homogeneity, it is easy to turn from the highroads and find byways where there is still a strong sense of place and one that is specific and distinctive in character. The causes and consequences vary, and it is often a mix of race and religion, topography and livelihood, climate and distance, but these particularities are important and numerous. That is the most important conclusion, the traveller's conclusion. Look and listen, and America and Americans refract through the prism into kaleidoscopes of contrast. These can be compartmentalised and analysed – blue and red states, liberals and conservatives, metro and retro, 1960s and 1950s values, and so on – but these are, all too often, attempts to categorise and classify varieties in order to make them simpler and more explicable than is the case.

These varieties have been ably captured by novelists keen to offer a realistic account of particular states of mind, such as Larry McMurtry's accounts of Texas, particularly of rural and small-town Texas, as in *Moving On* (1970) and *The Desert Rose* (1983). Crime writers offer the same sense of place, as in the distinctive Los Angeles setting of James Ellroy's works. At the same time, different writers capture the same setting in very varied ways.

Yet, percentages and averages can also direct attention away from major problems, and these were highlighted by Hurricane Katrina. The latter led to a massive outing for anger, much of it of course from comfortably off commentators, and it is understandable in the wake of a crisis brought vividly home by the media, indeed magnified by it with exaggerated tales of disorder and casualties, that the theme of victimhood and national division was pushed hard.

Black novelist Alice Walker saw racism at play. Her novels, such as *The Third Life of Grange Copeland* (1971) and *The Color Purple* (1982), reflect her perception of the savage impact on Black men of the legacy of segregation and slavery. Copeland, an anti-hero, refuses to rescue a pregnant White woman from drowning, and the impact of the abuse of Blacks is a major theme in *The Color Purple*, which received a Pulitzer Prize, the first for a Black woman. The impressive growth of the Black middle class, the largest in the world, from the 1970s tended to receive less attention.

Katrina suggested that poor Blacks would suffer disproportionately from any crisis, and especially so if there is economic chaos. In addition, the general level of indebtedness is such that many of the affluent and moderately off, whatever their colour, also suffer from any major economic downturn.

Meanwhile, the understanding of poverty involves vexed issues, particularly that of race. Any Black–White dichotomy, not least with the misleading use of the oft-reiterated motif of slavery (which certainly does not describe current relations), is complicated, if not invalidated, by the extent to which diversity and variety do not correspond to such a stark divide. For example, the statistics of inequality need to make sufficient reference to Hispanics, a rapidly growing section of the population. Recent immigration ensures that they are often poor, although many, particularly in subsequent generations, display considerable social mobility, while the development of Spanglish is an important aspect of the engagement of all Hispanics with the dominant culture. Nevertheless, in 2003, only 57 per cent of Hispanics were high-school graduates, and in 2004 only 48 per cent owned their homes. The Hispanic narrative is not one of slavery nor of oppression within America. In part, this is because, although conditions in the latter are often harsh for Hispanics, for example for transient farm workers, they are better than the ever-present reality of conditions in the lands they left and others continue to seek to leave. This contrast is not present for African Americans, as their African experience is centuries old and eclipsed by that of slavery. As a consequence, the theme of division seen in some Black rhetoric, and in part of the Black experience, cannot be so readily applied as a model for other non-White Americans.

This can be seen further if religious belief and practice are considered. There are separatist Black religious traditions, and they have a variety of manifestations, although none threatens integration or social harmony to the extent that Islam does in Europe, and most religious Blacks are Christian. To restrict attention to Christianity, there is a major sense of separation (but not segregation) in religion, with Black churches frequently having largely, or exclusively, Black congregations and particular types of religious practice. Yet any emphasis on dichotomy is complicated by the extent to which there is a common Christian creed, and that many churches have both Black and White congregants. Furthermore, the extent to which Hispanics focus on the Catholic Church helps to restrict the theme of ethnic difference within American Christianity, although there are obvious differences in Catholic practice between churches in, say, Boston, where Catholics of Irish descent remain important, and southern Arizona, where Hispanics are more numerous.

If America then is so diverse, it is not easy to contrast it with other diverse societies, although America is heading towards being the largest wealthy state where no one ethnic or religious group will be in the majority, which contrasts starkly with China. One important basis for comparison arises from the extent to which diversity is accepted in America. In part, this is a circumscribed diversity, although diversity might be a new manifestation of conformity. This can be seen in the forms of diversity mandates and quotas, and the rise and actions of Diversity, Equity, and Inclusion officers.

Diversity is clearly strong when grounded in constitutional rights, and, conversely, less so when a matter of social preference that lacks such support. There are indeed powerful pressures against diversity and for conformity. These are not simply a matter of pressures in long-established communities, but also in the new frontiers of advancing suburbia where new communities are being established and moulded. In this context, indeed, there can seem to be scant support for diversity, not least if it is defined and stigmatised as liberalism.

Such stigmatism is understandable in terms of mainstream conservative values, because the latter are conformist, rather than libertarian. The extent to which the last have been pushed since the 1960s is part of the dialectical dynamic of American culture: libertarian individualism and conformist conservatism feed off each other, requiring their perception of the other in order to provide an apparent need for rhetoric and action. This is amply demonstrated in the literature produced by those who like to see themselves on one of the sides, but less so in individual and family lives in which the emphasis frequently (but far from invariably) is rather on compromise and, in place of consensus, on the shifting bases of acceptance.

Given the role of success, suburbia and the family in the collective psyche (success leads to the suburbs, where families are created and sustained), problems for any or all of them are particularly threatening. The high rates of mental strain indicated by surveys reflect in part a degree of prosperity as well as a striving for better relationships, but also the sense of failure seen in substance abuse, eating disorders and difficult relationships.

At the same time, the situation naturally was more complicated than the critical construction in terms of conservative conformism and liberal, or libertarian, individualism. There is also a liberal conformism in some spheres, one, moreover, that can be stridently asserted, not least in the language of the politically correct, and this conformism can be the antithesis of libertarianism. In accordance with American political culture, conservative conformism largely acts by means of trying to shift constitutional parameters, rather than to overturn the constitution. As such, any drive for conformity has to address the strong, and legally well-grounded, sense of institutional distinction and autonomy seen in such spheres as the judicial system, universities, the military, and state and local government. This makes the issue of appointments in these spheres so important.

Furthermore, liberalism and conservatism are only monoliths to uninformed outsiders. The strains that presidential policies placed upon Republican loyalties during the presidencies of George Bush, father and son, amply demonstrated the diversity of the right, not least over the role of government, the extent of public borrowing, the place of social conformism, and the desirability of an interventionist foreign policy. Far from lessening, these tensions have grown. The Republican party has certainly not become a homogenous force (some politicians, such as Mayor Bloomberg of New York, indeed being known as RINOS – Republicans in Name Only), and this is linked to the growing crisis in policy and personnel that affected it from the mid-2000s. Very different constituencies include the business establishment and the religious right – fiscal versus social conservatives, as well as the neo-conservatives who focus on a proactive foreign policy.

Awareness of these and other variations poses problems not only for discussion of the present but also for the presentation of the past. The latter was of growing importance given greater political interest from the 1990s in the depiction of American history. That in turn changes. Thus, whereas in the 1990s, American conservatives looked back to the 1950s, now they have a greater nostalgia for the 1980s and Reagan. In contrast, liberals look back to the 1960s and the left to the late 1960s and early 1970s.

The depiction of the past shares with accounts of the present issues about content, vocabulary and moralisation. The last in part relates to questions of what is the cost and who bears that cost. Thus, the various benefits of mass migration, or 'social justice', or 'affirmative action', or 'police', or 'women's rights', or gay marriage, or vaccine mandates, or green energy, may be clear to some and contested by others. Some/many of the latter tend to have a conviction that the democracy is a sham, that there are vast bureaucracies only mildly affected by the democratic process, with the 'army' of bureaucrats allegedly animated by interests, beliefs, and sensibilities formed in elite zip codes, schools and universities, and disdainful of the beliefs, sensibilities and democratic will of more middle-brow fellow countrymen. This sense that governing elites, in politics, culture and business, are unworthy of their power because they no longer know and understand, nor wish to know and understand, the people they lead and govern, was articulated and exploited by Trump in 2016, but may be employed from another political perspective in the future.

The extent to which currency inflows are in large part a matter of sustaining consumption – as, since 2000, foreigners, notably the Chinese central bank, have invested in bonds, particularly Treasury bonds, rather than, as previously, in American companies – is a matter of particular concern as this means a lack of underpinning for long-term economic growth. Furthermore, American corporate investment in future productivity is greater than in Europe, but less than in East Asia. This is a particular problem, as it is linked to a lack of comparative advantage, which, combined with the size of the domestic economy, means that there is a shortage of exports to help service the foreign debt.

The foreign debt is the product of the heavy borrowing that comes with a loose monetary policy, such that by the mid-2000s there were over 1.3 billion credit cards in America (and the design of wallets, and therefore of jackets, had to respond to the large number of credit and charge cards owned by individuals). This looseness of monetary policy, and the willingness to borrow, led to the marked rise in home ownership, and therefore house values, that has benefited all ethnic groups. This rise, however, further encouraged borrowing, pushing up personal debt. Indeed, personal and governmental indebtedness interacted in a disturbing synergy, carried forward by the heady drug of low interest rates and the ability to borrow.

As another aspect of the absence of monoliths in American public life, there is no institutional body to provide discipline in the cause of coherence, as the Communist Party seeks to do in China. Indeed, the Democrats and the Republicans still lack the disciplinary centralisation of political parties across much of the Free World. This approach can be taken further by referring to business, capital and labour, each of which resists direction and unification. Within the political parties, the lure of conformity to dominant themes, particularly the ideas held by activists, can be matched by a search for moderate support, although this was conspicuously not the case with Donald Trump.

Trump and Biden were the elderly rivals in the 2020 presidential campaign, and in late 2023 again led their parties' campaigns – Trump while facing four criminal indictments. Yet, younger generations are very engaged in politics, and mean to gain control of the nation's future. What that might mean for the future is unclear, but it was ever thus.

Index